A WORLD WITHOUT BOUNDARIES

A WORLD WITHOUT BOUNDARIES

A story of human atrocities, despair, migration, and interconnections

Ge Xiong

Two Harbors Press, Minneapolis, MN

Copyright © 2015 by Ge Xiong

TWOHARBORS
www.twoharborspress.com

Two Harbors Press
322 First Avenue N, 5th floor
Minneapolis, MN 55401
612.455.2293
www.TwoHarborsPress.com

All rights reserved. No part of this publication may be reproduced, stored in a retrieval system, or transmitted, in any form or by any means, electronic, mechanical, photocopying, recording, or otherwise, without the prior written permission of the author.

ISBN-13: 978-1-63413-482-8
LCCN: 2015905659

Distributed by Itasca Books

Cover Design by Alan Pranke
Typeset by Colleen Rollins

Printed in the United States of America

For my parents and Youa's parents, who have sacrificed everything in their lives for us.

To my children, Blia, Saleng, Dan, Chue Yee, Sandy, and Sarah, who are my greatest pride.

And to my grandchildren, who will become great Americans.

To all the people who have done good things for the world.

CONTENTS

Preface ix
Introduction 1

PART I: HOW IT GOT STARTED

Chapter 1: The World of Nature, the World of Men 11
Chapter 2: A Natural Way of Life Engulfed by Fire 35
Chapter 3: The Airplane Rice and the Singing Box 52
Chapter 4: A Move That Changed My View of the World 78
Chapter 5: Fleeing the Human Killing Storm 100

PART II: THE RAGING FIRE

Chapter 6: Facing the Worst Fears 123
Chapter 7: A Social/Political Culture of Despair 138
Chapter 8: Good-bye, Sam Thong 172
Chapter 9: Long Chieng, the Legendary Hmong City 190
Chapter 10: Hmong Students Striving for Success 205

PART III: THE AFTERMATH

Chapter 11: Becoming a Teacher 231
Chapter 12: Youa's Story: "Saving the Sun" 247
Chapter 13: The Cease-Fire and the False Peace 272
Chapter 14: At the Mercy of the Tiger 292
Chapter 15: Sheep without a Field 322

Epilogue *344*
Acknowledgments *351*
About the Author *353*
Index *354*

PREFACE

My grandmother had told me stories about what caused my great-great-grandparents to abandon their homes and migrate out of China, carrying only what they could on their backs. Her stories, which she had heard from her parents and passed on to me through an oral tradition, sounded like myths and legends.

Despite the atrocities my ancestors had faced, they always believed human cruelty only came as natural storms that affected certain territories and times, and they still could find peace somewhere over the vast horizons. They believed the vast natural world had places for everyone to live in peace. My grandmother had once said, "If the spirits of a mountain don't like you, you move to one where the spirits like you and protect you."

Constant migration in search for places to live in peace with both men and spirits had become a way of life, without a permanent field to raise sheep, as the Hmong frequently quote an old saying: "*Qiv luag toj yug yaj, qiv lug tais rau ntxhai*," meaning "Borrow field to raise sheep, borrow bowls to put foods." This old saying reflects a life frequently displaced by the atrocities of the dominant cultures and by lack of sustainable farmlands. It has become a way of life deeply rooted in our culture. Yet, times had passed and, as they had moved past many horizons, the place of peace had not been found.

My parents had repeated the same pattern of lifestyle and endured the same constant migration our ancestors had for centuries in the world my ancestors believed was created by nature without boundaries. The complexities in the world of men had begun to emerge and challenge the simplicity of their natural world. The expansion of colonialism, the wars, and the opium trade expanded their connections with the outside world. Then they had begun to realize what happened in other parts of the world and all the elements of men that had begun to affect them.

The post-colonial era had emerged with even greater complexities and had greatly affected our way of life. The migration, the human atrocities, the war, the way of life sustained and displaced by the slash-and-burn tradition, and the interface of cultures, genders, and ethnicities had intertwined as parts of our lives, complex and confusing like a dream in a world that is real. The events of horror and their recurrences, which we had witnessed in our consciousness and inherited through verbal tradition, had become profoundly embedded in our memories as powerless living souls.

For over three decades, because of language barriers, I have kept silent my story of the horrific war and experiences I and thousands of Hmong in an impoverished, war-torn country had faced. Learning English as a fifth language at the age of twenty-six was not a part of my natural development. I arrived in the United States as a refugee without a word of English, and for years I had struggled to learn the language to be able to express anything worth expressing to the people who needed to know more about me. This has been among the most challenging barriers for me to overcome.

After thirty years of learning English and struggling

PREFACE

to internalize the grammatical rules and nuances of the language, and earning a degree in Educational Policy and Community Study, I still have not come close to an ability to speak English smoothly. Searching for word choices that don't flow naturally from my mind to my mouth and my tongue's unwillingness to cooperate are among the difficulties and formidable boundaries that have confined me in the long years of my struggle.

For a non-native English speaker, when starting a sentence, everything seems to be going fine until the right preposition word (in, on, up, down, of, with, for, at, to, off, about, or across) is needed to complete what needs to be said. An expression of experience in one culture cannot be expressed and understood the same in another.

I have also repeatedly raised the question of whether my story and experience as a Hmong matter to the world. I am just a Hmong and a former refugee who faced the horrific experience in the war in Indochina, popularly known as the Vietnam War.

Discouraged by these dreadful thoughts and questions, the decision to write this book has been a fierce battle within me. After some profound debates within and much consideration, I realize that I cannot fault people who don't know me if I have not educated them about who I am. Hence, I have the responsibility to educate the people with whom I meet every day in my neighborhood, at my community shopping centers, and on the roads and highways that I travel. I am responsible for reaching across boundaries and telling my story, while reading and listening to others' stories, in hope that we, as humans, gain a mutual understanding of our differences and commonalities.

I believe, in a world of increasing racial and cultural interconnections, it is in our mutual interest and is our responsibility to educate and to learn about and from each other. As Hmong Americans, it is our responsibility to learn about the African Americans, Asian Americans, European Americans, Jewish Americans, Hispanic Americans, Arab Americans, and Native Americans as much as we want them to know about us.

Each of us (regardless of religious or ethnic background and gender) has been a victim of biases, prejudices, hatred, bigotry, and discriminations. There are countless instances of systemic discrimination that cause unimaginable suffering to millions.

Despite the fact that we frequently resent unfair treatments by others, we do have our own bigotry, which we don't like to admit. These human problems cause conflicts and mistreatment of each other throughout the human world. Therefore, this is not just a Hmong tale of the past, but a factual story reflecting our human society today and a voice calling for equal treatment of all people regardless of race, ethnicity, and culture.

From my childhood to my young adulthood, I traveled on countless migration trails, trudging on steep hills of northern Laos as I tried to flee atrocities and death. Every day there are wars and conflicts across the globe triggered by greed, hate, intolerance, and separatism as deadly motives for destructions, some for which we are currently paying heavy prices. Each conflict and war sends no fewer than hundreds or thousands of refugees, mostly women and children, on the trail of migration, enduring losses and fleeing for their lives. I see myself with them.

For a snapshot view of the global refugee popula-

PREFACE

tion, according to the United Nations High Commissioner for Refugees (UNHCR) 2011 report, the 2010 Global Trends reported that there were 43.7 million people displaced from their homes in 2010 alone. Among them, 15.4 million were refugees (10.55 million under UNHCR's care and 4.82 million registered with the UN Relief and Works Agency for Palestine Refugees), 27.5 million were people displaced within the borders of their home countries by conflicts, and of nearly 850,000 asylum seekers, nearly one fifth were in South Africa alone (UNHCR Report, June 20, 2011).

I believe—despite that we are separated (even some have wished to be separated) by the man-made sexual, ethnic, national, political, social, economic, and religious boundaries—problems and destructions have no boundaries. They send pain and suffering like shockwaves to all.

On the flipside of the coin, human love and care have crossed boundaries of human divides to heal wounds, soothe pains, comfort griefs and improve conditions. Humans, over the centuries, have been able to overcome the communication barriers among ethnicities, nationalities, and cultures. This human communication breakthrough has increased our mutual understanding and support.

I give thanks to a small number of writers, scholars, and historians who have authored their well-articulated books and journals, each worthy of its own pertinent account of Hmong history and culture. Their books contribute valuable insights that help practitioners understand Hmong traditional and cultural values, thereby assisting in providing culturally sensitive services.

In contrast to other books, this book describes my

personal experiences not only as a Hmong, but as an eyewitness who was among thousands of souls trudging in the jungles and on the hills, crossing valleys and rivers, crowding in temporary shelters and tight spaces, wailing for their dead without a simple ceremony for their human dignity, and confined in refugee camps, looking outside through spaces between barbed wires like animals in captivity. This is not just a story of what happened to the Hmong, but a story of human suffering across human society and throughout human history which will persist until all humans work together to resolve it.

Although, viewed from the surface, war refugees may seem to endure the same suffering, there are complex disparities between genders and among ethnicities and social castes. Thus the suffering among groups varies greatly. All of these are intertwined in the complexities of our experiences as war refugees, which we endured along our rough trails of migration. I only describe these experiences in a language that I was not born with and in the expressions of limited word choices, largely and awkwardly interfered with my native tongue.

My migration journey encompassing a half circle around the world and passing checkpoints and ports told me the world is divided by national boundaries crisscrossing the globe like cuts and wounds that will never heal. Within them, there are boundaries like cuts and wounds which we have witnessed with our very own eyes, and we have been profoundly affected by their toxins.

The division of political factions in Laos—worsened by factious leaders intoxicated with power indulgence and unwillingness to compromise and find solutions—

had resulted in devastating armed conflicts, losses of lives, and tormenting effects. These are examples of power hunger and narrow reasoning for personal and national pride of a few that served as deadly motives to trigger wars that killed thousands of innocents.

Despite the painful experiences by which my family and I have been endlessly haunted in our sleep, there are some strong aspects of humanity by which we have been inspired to become better persons. There are people, through the spirit of humanity, who are trying to bind us together as humans across ethnicities, genders, socioeconomic divides, and national boundaries.

There were instances in which I was personally affected by this aspect of human dignity. I still vividly remember when I felt flooded with love like an approaching heavenly light shining on my soul as I came out of the gate in O'Hare Airport in Chicago and met two complete strangers with whom I did not share a common language. But, they warmly welcomed my family and me into their warm hands and community.

I could only guess their thinking when Jan Wiseman and Molly (then Wiseman) Clemons were standing in front of the gate in the middle of January 1979 with the first things they had prepared for our arrival—heavy winter coats for Youa, Blia, Saleng, and me. The temperature in Bangkok, Thailand, was 80 degrees, but I did not remember the temperature that night in O'Hare. I did remember, however, that it snowed as we traveled all the way to our new home in Shabbona, Illinois. It was one of the worst snowstorms in Illinois in years.

The Calvary Lutheran Church in Lee County, Illinois, and members of the congregation provided joint support for our family. The two-bedroom apartment was completely furnished, including food in the refrigerator—more than what most parents provided for their grown-up and move-away children.

For the next twelve months, our kindhearted friends in the congregation took turns and took time out of the middle of their busy days to drive us to and from Kishwaukee Community College where we attended English as a Second Language classes and where I sat like any other who had never been in school. They extended their hands across oceans, continents, and boundaries to touch souls that were affected by human atrocities and destructions. The world would be a better place for humankind if each of us would, on our small part, try to understand the human suffering from the victims' point of view and prevent any causes of pain and suffering to others.

Molly Clemons is an extraordinary human being and a loving godmother to our family. She sends Christmas cards to us every year during the glittering holiday seasons to remind us that we are still in her heart. What we have learned about being a human and anything we have as the best in our hearts as benevolent members of this great nation, we owe to her.

INTRODUCTION

As a people surviving through centuries without a written language, the Hmong have been listening to verbal stories about their roots of origin like myths and legends, suggesting they might have come from places other than China. In search for the truth of their roots, the Hmong are in a historical reconstruction mode. Hmong and non-Hmong scholars alike have done research and formed opinions on where the Hmong, who have a unique culture and language for centuries, might have originated. The reconstruction of centuries-old trails of evidence that could form a consensus about their roots has been harder than making brick and mortar monuments.

Some scholars have speculated that the Hmong might have originated in Mesopotamia and migrated to Siberia and then Mongolia before migrating to China (Quincy, 1988, 1995).[1] Others hinted the Hmong were from Mongolia. Chinese historians have recorded that as early as 3000 BC the Hmong lived in southern China, where the vast majority of Hmong remain today. Based upon observation, Chinese historians have described tribal groups in southern China who had linguistic characteristics and lifestyles similar to those of the Hmong today.

There have been numerous research studies con-

---

1. Quincy, Keith. *Hmong: History of People*, Eastern Washington University Press, 1988.

ducted on the subject, but none has provided documentation of historical events, cultural artifacts, brick and mortar monuments, or linguistic traits and connections that serve as evidence to determine that the Hmong originated from a place other than China.

Recently, Gary Yia Lee, an anthropologist and researcher, has collected documents of claims and used numerous origin identification approaches, including a genetic approach, to examine the Hmong's origin. Dr. Lee proposed that, "in view of accessible evidence, including DNA testing and the Chinese deep impact on Hmong life for a long period, the Hmong might have originated from their current location in Southern China where they have been called Miao" (Lee, 2007).[2] Although they have been calling themselves Hmong for centuries, the Hmong in China are not taking issue with the term Miao, by which their dominant neighbors have called them. Knowing about themselves based on myths and legends through an oral tradition, the Hmong have misconceptions about their own origins, which have led to misinformation being given to non-Hmong observers.

Clustered communities of Hmong, formerly (or currently to some) known as Miao in China and Vietnam and Meo in Laos and Thailand, are found as an ethnic tribe in many parts of Asia, including China, Vietnam, Laos, Thailand, and Myanmar (formerly Burma). Recently, the term "Hmong" became recognized as the proper ethnic identity of the formerly known "Miao" or "Meo," consisting of several different regional groups: White Hmong, Blue Hmong, Green Hmong, and Striped

---

2. Lee, Gary Y. "Diaspora and Predicament of Origins: Interrogating Hmong Postcolonial History and Identity," *Hmong Studies Journal*, Vol. 8, 16 Feb. 2007:22.

INTRODUCTION

Hmong, distinguishable by dialects and traditional costumes.

The Hmong call themselves "Hmong" in White Hmong dialect and "Mong" in Blue Hmong dialect. It has never been any argument or contention within the Hmong community whether the White Hmong ("Hmong") and Blue Hmong ("Mong") are two different ethnicities. However, when the Hmong writing system became available in the mid-1950s, the term "Hmong" started to be used to represent Hmong ethnic identity (both Hmong and Mong) in written communication and literature. Consequently, arguments start to rise, contending that the term "Hmong" does not represent the Mong and that "the public does not know the differences between the two groups. Therefore, the Mong are lumped into the Hmong" (Thao and Yang, 2004).[3] The term "Hmong," spelled either "Hmong" or "Mong," is not merely a term by which the Hmong prefer to be known as an alternative to other derogatory terms by which they have been called by the dominant societies, but one by which they have, for unknown reasons, known themselves.

Despite recent arguments about whether the two groups are the same, I use the term "Hmong" throughout this book to describe all the Hmong who have walked across mountains, hills, valleys, and rivers together—enduring the same suffering regardless of superficial differences. The book includes the people in Phoukoum and Phou So as I call them "Hmong" in my dialect and they call themselves and me "Mong" in

---

3. Thao, Paoze and Yang, Chimeng. "The Mong and The Hmong," *Mong Journal* (MJ), Vol. 1, June 2004:1.

their dialect. The following details are aimed at shedding some light on the aforementioned confusion and what the Hmong, regardless of local differences, share in common. Speaking as a Hmong, while we have much to tell the world about ourselves, we have more to learn about ourselves.

Throughout the centuries, the Hmong had been faced with constant migrations, artifact destructions, adaptation, and abandonment of cultural heritage by force, fear, choice, or necessity. The recent grave digging in the Hmong refugee camps in Thailand is an example of destruction that contributes to our loss of historical trails and affirms our verbal tales of tragic historical events.

According to verbal tales passed on from generation to generation, there had been countless artifact destructions and grave desecrations throughout the trails of Hmong migrations. Many Hmong elders had shared stories about decorating graves to make them resemble those of their Chinese counterparts to prevent the remains of their deceased relatives from being dug up or destroyed. We have learned these events and circumstances from oral tradition as being cultural changing factors.

What we know for certain is the Hmong in Laos migrated southward from southern China toward Indochina to escape oppression and search for freedom and farmlands. Geographical separation, local ethnic associations, linguistic acquisitions, and education have been factors for changes in cultural and linguistic characteristics and ways of life. The Hmong are not immune to the power of these changing agents.

The influences of educational institutions and policies will have far-reaching effects on linguistic heritages, as we have witnessed within our lifetime. Ethnic identities will no longer be determined by linguistic or artifact characteristics, but only a willingness to maintain an association as a way to celebrate cultural heritages or as a tool to measure social justices.

The loss of cultural and linguistic heritages because of educational and economic gains or social associations may be an uncontrollable phenomenon in today's global society. The details and arguments of this dilemma may need to be addressed on their own.

These changes will continue at an even greater pace as racial and ethnic interactions increase in our modern society, though the pace may vary depending upon the force of influences of the dominant establishments and the closeness of relationships with others in each locality. Those who have converted to Christianity in the last half century, as a concrete example, have moved farther away from the cultural and traditional core.

Before and after their migration to Laos, the Hmong faced a series of conflicts, which resulted in massacres, deaths, starvation, suffering, and destructions. There have been stories told by elder members of the Hmong community about constant conflicts with the Chinese, even during funeral services.

To this day, most funeral ceremonies still feature acts of combat against Chinese attacks as part of the ritual. During burials of the dead, the Hmong still conduct acts of Chinese seizure of the clothing of the deceased before being buried. These widely practiced ceremonial features represent actual historical experiences, although their purposes are unknown. These practices may vary from group to group, depending on their circumstantial experiences during the course of migration.

After an uprising, called War of the Insane, against the French's unfair taxation from July 1919 to March 1921, some of the Hmong became allied with the French. Through this alliance, the Hmong played a crucial role in hiding the French from the Japanese during World War II. The relations ended after the French pulled out of Indochina. The Hmong gained citizenship and local administrative positions in Laos, especially in Xieng Khouang province, through this historical relationship.

In 1960, the United States approached then Lt. Col. Vang Pao, the only Hmong who had reached that rank as an officer in the Royal Lao Army, on an agreement that made the Hmong an ally of the United States. In this alliance, the Hmong took on the following roles: 1) rescuing American pilots shot down along the Vietnam-Laos border; and 2) preventing North Vietnam from using Laos as an ammunition depot and delivery route to support its war against South Vietnam and the US. The Hmong became the primary force in the fight against the Communist Pathet Lao and the North Vietnamese in the intensified war, holding the gate against the Communists' expansion in northern Laos for fifteen years.

The United States' secret war in Laos, in which the Hmong were involved, was part of its Vietnam War strategy and was kept secret because Laos had declared its neutrality in the Geneva Accord, signed in 1962, stating that it would be free from foreign military involvement. Therefore, the Hmong were left to fight the Communist Pathet Lao and more than 50,000 North Vietnamese forces without the full ground support of the United States. The Hmong suffered massive casualties that accounted to over 10 percent of their entire population.

INTRODUCTION

South Vietnam fell in 1975 and the United States pulled out, taking only Gen. Vang Pao's family and the families of his senior officers and American workers to Thailand. The rest of the Hmong were left behind to face the holocaust of the Communists' persecution as retribution for their action of supporting the United States during the war.

During their escapes from persecution, some Hmong were robbed of their assets and belongings by opportunists and crooks. Many more faced the Communists' ambushes as they fled to Thailand. Those who could not afford to flee gathered remnants of American ammunition to form resistance and continued fighting from mountainous jungles. They falsely believed their American friends would return to help them.

The Communist government used any means to eliminate the Hmong, including chemical attacks. Crop burning and destruction were also used to eliminate the Hmong or force them to surrender. These methods of cruelty, which were aimed at causing starvation, killed more children than adults.

Between 1975 and 1990, an unaccounted number of Hmong, far more than those lost during the war, had died of starvation or been killed through massacres. Their bones littered the valleys and hills of Laos, while hundreds more drowned trying to swim across the Mekong River.

The Hmong who eventually surrendered to the Communist government were joined by a larger or equal number of Hmong who had originally joined the Communists. As the war had drawn them to join the different political factions, fighting each other, and its aftermath slowly brought them together, a subtle sense of distant feeling toward each other remains. While those who had joined the Communists early in the conflict took part in high-ranking government positions, those who joined the United States fight against the Communists became powerless and low-profile citizens. They remained on the watched list for their activities. They had lost their farmlands. Many had become dependent on support from relatives living abroad. Many of their leaders who surrendered were killed in reeducation camps or arrested and executed on charges of conspiring and rebelling against the new regime.

From 1975 to 1990, more than 120,000 Hmong refugees who fled Laos were resettled in the United States, France, Australia, French Guyana, Canada, Argentina, and Germany. More than 100,000 Hmong refugees arrived in the US between 1975 and 1990. Currently, the Hmong population in the United States has grown to more than 270,000, with large concentrations in California, Minnesota, Wisconsin, North Carolina, Michigan, Colorado, Georgia, Alaska, Oklahoma, Oregon, Washington, Arkansas, Kansas, Missouri, South Carolina, Florida, Massachusetts, Pennsylvania, Rhode Island, and Texas. The remaining numbers are distributed in small concentrations in all other states, where they are less known to their neighbors.

Despite the Hmong being an ethnic nationality from Laos, they prefer to be identified by their Hmong ethnicity rather than Laotian, because they are concerned that their identity as an ethnicity with a unique language and culture will be lost.

PART ONE
HOW IT GOT STARTED

CHAPTER 1

THE WORLD OF NATURE, THE WORLD OF MEN

As their small community met with the French and the Japanese during the colonial era, the Namnya residents had come to a vague understanding that the world of nature without boundaries, which they had previously perceived, had a different reality—the world of men. They realized how vulnerable they were, and that something more complex and dangerous had begun to emerge.

Although Namnya no longer existed as a village on the map of Laos, it was the place where my world began.

In 1953, if one would look down from a plane flying at 15,000 feet above the dirt-barren village, it would look like an old, forgotten blanket lost in the middle of a rainforest jungle. There were no more than a half dozen houses, two with wooden-shingle roofs and the rest with thatched-grass roofs. Like a bird nest on a cliff, the village was built on a small plateau at a drop end of the mountain ridge, which seemed as if it was the only flat spot on the steep mountainside surrounded by steep hills and purple karsts.

Looking east from the village, there was a spectacular view of green and blue mountaintops peeking up one behind another and extending far into the horizon where the earth and the sky met.

Only two footpaths led to the outside world. One path led from the western corner of the top of the village toward Hamkheu (Humkher) and other villages, including Phou Duu—a well-known village during colonial times where many prominent leaders of the Moua clan lived. Following a narrow, coarse grass ridge with steep slopes on both sides, the path was rough and made by years of human walking and animal trotting. The ridge was so narrow that on a windy day we would fear being blown off the path and down onto the steep mountainsides below. The path split near the top of the ridge.

The left path cut across the mountain slope, leading to Hamkheu, where my grandmother and my mother's half-brothers lived. The right fork continued on the ridge, leading up to the mountaintop toward Phou San, one of Laos's highest mountains where people from all the villages had one thing in common—opium farms. Opium was the only cash crop, and opium trade was the only major connection with the outside world since the beginning of colonial times.

At the bottom of the village, the other path led straight down like a worn-out ladder toward the well-known colonial Route 7, which was at the bottom of the mountain slope. On a clear day, we could look below and see a small portion of the gravel road with our naked eyes. The road, constructed with largely free labor during the French colonial era, provided a linkage between the provincial town of Xieng Khouang on the west and the small town of Nong Het on the east, near the Vietnam-Laos border.

At the bottom of the slope, the path to our rice fields

merged with Route 7 and went together for about two hundred feet before it exited on the other side into the woods. Hence, we had to walk barefoot on the unpleasant gravel road for a short distance.

Every time we approached the road, even though there were no cars passing by, my mother would be sick from the emission smell and she would vomit. She would run by everyone and quickly leave the road. The smell was foreign to our natural world.

I, on the other hand, would wish a car would pass by. If I were lucky enough and one would pass by, I would freeze like a deer to watch it until it went out of sight. Sometimes, I would continue watching it even a few minutes after it was gone and still find myself walking backwards. My mind had drifted away with the strange mechanical creatures of different sizes and colors.

"Go! Hurry!" my dad would yell.

We would leave the road and follow the dirt path into the jungle toward our rice field miles away and stay there for a week or two before returning to cross the road again. My grandparents and my parents had repeated this pattern of trips along that path for years before I was born and even before the gravel road was built. The road was wide, flat, and clean compared to the muddy and steep path we traveled every day.

Some of the villagers would stay in the fields for three or four days or sometimes up to ten days to finish the daunting farm work. Some would return home daily to feed their animals. They would go back the next day to resume their work and repeat the same pattern throughout the rice planting and harvesting seasons.

I sometimes would stay with my blind great-grandmother. Although she was old and blind, she was not exempt from the laborious daily work. She had to prepare food for the pigs, including shelling corn and rubbing dirt off yams.

Both paths were steep and narrow. They were also muddy and slippery in the rainy season. Traveling was not easy for the villagers as well as for visitors coming to the village. Horses were the only viable source of transportation in the area's rough terrains.

My great-grandfather, Song Leng, and his uncle, Pa Ger, of the Xiong clan settled in Namnya in the early 1900s, more than a century after their grandparents left China as immigrants, fleeing atrocities. The settlement in Nanya was a hope that they had ended a brutal immigration trail their parents and grandparents had endured, not across visible boundaries and checkpoints, but rough jungles, mountains, valleys, and dangerous rivers.

Despite the atrocities their grandparents faced in China and the unfriendly treatment toward them by the ethnic lowland Lao, the people in Namnya still believed in a world created for peace—a natural world without boundaries of races. Past experiences were rarely communicated and were almost completely forgotten. Instead, productivity and self-reliance were frequently discussed, ensuring every generation followed the same principles.

Although Namnya was only a small village, with only a half dozen houses and far remote from civilization, its residents—like the Hmong elsewhere in Laos—believed in self-sufficiency in that they produced their own food for their families. The vast surrounding lands and resources belonged to no one and were ready for anyone to claim ownership until they were temporarily exhausted of fruitfulness.

A new piece of land would be available for a new rice field or cornfield. The old one would be left to be replenished by nature and made ready for a new owner. Like all members of the Hmong society, my parents believed that everything—lands, creeks, rivers, rain, clouds, air, and jungles—belonged to no one, and no one had permanent ownership of everything in our natural world.

A barter tradition of free exchange of goods and labor which had been practiced for hundreds or even thousands of years was only recently replaced by cash purchases and trades. Opium demands, coming from thousands of miles away, provided the Hmong with cash for trade and purchase of goods made outside of their world. This had given them an understanding of how the world is interconnected.

Phou Duu, a well-known village in French colonial times during which the Hmong played an important role hiding the French from the Japanese, and the provincial town of Xieng Khouang were within a day's walking distance away. Route 7 was only half of an hour walking distance down the mountain slope, giving easy access to the many local and provincial administrative towns along the colonial road.

My great-grandmother, my grandmother, and most of my uncles' wives were from the Moua clan of Phou Duu. Many of the prominent Hmong leaders of the Moua clan were no strangers to my grandparents and parents. The people in Namnya were familiar with the French, whom they called *Fakee*, and had eaten their bread, which they called *mov mog*, or soft rice.

They had taken part in building Route 7, a requirement they could not refuse. Every family had to contribute at least fifteen days of free labor annually toward the construction and maintenance of the road or face a heavy penalty. They had known and met Haje, a Frenchman whose real name they did not know, and to whom they had sold cabbages and potatoes.

The French, the Japanese, Route 7, the mechanical creatures whose exhaust fumes had sickened my mother, and the growing towns along Route 7 gave the people in Namnya a vague understanding of the world of men in which the heat of men's competition for power had been gradually felt in their natural world. Far more complicated and dangerous aspects of human factors which the next generations of the people in Namnya would face had begun to emerge and make them realize how vulnerable they were on the face of the earth on which they walked every day. Their perception of the natural world without boundaries was about to be challenged.

My grandfather, Yia, was the eldest son of Song Leng. He married my great-grandmother's distant nephew's daughter. A year later they had their first child—a boy. They proudly named him Ber, meaning "round faced." My grandfather died when my father was only seven months old. My grandmother was forced, by Hmong tradition, to marry her husband's younger brother, Thong, who was still single. He later was given an adult name, Chia Thong. My grandmother's life was short. She died after giving birth to my father's half-brother, Heu—the only child she had with Chia Thong. My father was only three when she died. My great-grandmother had to shoulder the upbringing of my father and Heu.

Chia Thong remarried five years later to a woman of

the Vang clan from the neighboring village of Hamkheu. She had married twice before. Her first husband was from the Xiong clan and died shortly after they had their second child. Her second husband was from the Lee clan and she divorced him shortly after their marriage.

Shortly after Chia Thong remarried, tragedies struck again. His youngest brother, Tong Ger, died from eating poisonous mushrooms, and his pregnant wife died shortly thereafter, after giving birth to a girl who only lived for a few days.

Childbirth-related death was the leading killer of women in that part of the world. They left three children—two boys, Kai and Xa, and one girl, Mai. Xa was the youngest and only about two years old. He was mute. Chia Thong's new wife brought her two-year-old daughter, Bee, with her. Her eldest son, Ying Pao, was left with his father's family—a tradition in which women did not have a choice.

Chia Thong and his new wife never had any children together. All six children—Ber, Kai, Heu, Xa, Mai, and Bee—lived under one roof. Ber, Kai, Mai, and Xa had no parents. They only received care and love from their grandmother, who was a strong, determined, and decisive woman. Ber and Heu Never called their new mother "mom." They only called her "Bee's mom."

Because of the many losses in her family within a short time period and the heavy burden of caring for her grandchildren, my great-grandmother lost sight in both of her eyes. Although completely blind, she continued to give unwavering love and care to her grandchildren, and her indisputable voice of wisdom continued to guide the union of our family for many years—even after I was born. Within her hearing distance, she used her ears and instincts to assure justice and fairness in the family.

Chia Thong's new wife was a shaman. She was unusually intelligent and manipulative for a Hmong woman. She only respected one person—my great-grandmother—in part because she was from the prominent Moua clan of Phou Duu. In front of my great-grandmother, her words and voice were sweet and sounded as if she was the most caring and honest mother. However, the reality beyond my great-grandmother's keen sense of hearing was far different. The children knew it well, and everyone in the village frowned at her action, but dared not to confront her.

Unfortunately, being visually impaired, my great-grandmother's ability to assure justice for her parentless grandchildren only extended to the limits of her hearing power. She was especially concerned about Ber—the oldest who carried the brutal burdens of caring for his younger siblings and of doing everything else.

Chia Thong, on the other hand, was quiet and never disputed his new wife on anything. Being one of the men who built one of the two largest wood-shingle roofed and wooden-plank walled houses, he never sat idly for one moment, except when he drank his bowl of hot, fresh green tea and when he was asleep. He never wasted his time; even when he went to the bathroom in the woods, he would come back with a fire log on his shoulders.

A heavy-built man, round faced, bald on the forehead, and slightly taller than most Hmong men, he would walk, with both hands on his back, around the fences of his orange grove garden every morning, inspecting any damages or suspicious break-ins. He was most concerned with his second-eldest brother, Nao Cha, who was an opium addict and who sometimes snuck in during the darkness of the night to fill up a large bamboo-woven back basket with fresh, ripe oranges to trade for opium at the Laotian villages along Route 7.

My father, Ber, had never seen his real father, nor did he know that his father was a different man than the person he always called father. He had no knowledge that the father he knew was only his stepfather—his father's younger brother. He also had no memory of his mother. Only years later did Uncle and Aunt Nao Cha tell him about his real parents and what had previously transpired in the family. This was not what his stepfather and even his grandmother wanted him to know. It was later confirmed to him by his mother's younger brother, Choua Dang Moua.

His rough hands and feet, and his complexion that was darker than the rest, were clear indicators of the rough and brutal life he had endured under the brazing sun since childhood. He did not have the nurturing care and support that a child needed for positive social and emotional development. He was quiet and always ridiculed by unthoughtful kids, including some of his siblings, for his lack of opinion on anything. He smiled slightly sometimes when people laughed loudly.

His only companion was a crossbow made by Uncle Choua Dang, an expert in crossbow making, who visited him only occasionally. Uncle Choua Dang lived in Ban Xouan, a neighboring village about eight miles to the northwest. Although many years had gone by since his sister had passed away, he tried not to let the relationship become completely broken and forgotten. He always had wanted to know how his sister's son, the child who had lost both of his parents, was doing. He had always been concerned about the boy whom his sister had brought to see him frequently when she was still living. His sister was now gone like a broken bridge that had tumbled down into the water, and the boy who had turned twelve had no way of coming to visit him, unless he went to see the boy.

Uncle Choua Dang had made a crossbow and carefully crafted it with the best hardwood and the oldest piece of bamboo split and some arrows. He had tested it for accuracy and perfection. He had sent a message with some relatives in Namnya who had gone to Ban Xouan a few days earlier that he would visit his nephew in a few days.

Everyone stayed home expecting a visitor as the days passed. Appearing at the door was a curved-faced man in dark Hmong dress.

"*Tuaj los, dablaug!*" Ber's stepmother greeted, meaning, "You come to visit, brother!"

"Yes, good day," Uncle Choua Dang replied.

"Hello brother," Ber's stepfather greeted from behind his wife.

"Good day, brother," Uncle Choua Dang replied.

Ber's stepmother dominated the conversation as usual. She invited Uncle Choua Dang inside. He had a brownish crossbow, darkened by fire smoke, tucked in his right armpit and a bunch of arrows in his left hand.

Before he sat down, he looked around and asked, "Where is my son, Ber?"

"He is here behind me," his stepmother said loudly.

"My son, you have grown so much since I last saw you with your mother. Do you remember me, your uncle?"

"Yes, Uncle," Ber replied hesitantly.

He presented a beautiful crossbow to Ber and gently rubbed the top of his head—a touch of genuine love.

"Do you want to try it?" Uncle Choua Dang asked.

They both went outside and other boys followed. Ber put a piece of tree leaf, larger than a thumb, on the drop-edge where the dirt house platform was dug. They stepped away about twenty yards. Ber handed the crossbow to Uncle Choua Dang and stood back. Uncle Choua Dang put his knees against the bamboo strip and pulled the string, pressed it onto the cross groove, and put an arrow on the top along a groove, secured by soft honey wax. He aimed it at the target and pressed the trigger. The arrow flew at bullet speed and hit the target right in the middle. Everyone shouted.

"This could hit a dove on the top of a tree!" Ber said loudly.

"Now you try it."

Ber put his knees against the strip and pulled the string just like his uncle did. He pulled it with all his power. He could not pull it. The strip was elastically too tough for him.

"Sit down and put your feet against both sides of the strip, my boy."

Following his uncle's advice, he made it this time. He put an arrow on it, aimed at the target, and pressed the trigger. The arrow hit the target almost as good as the shot taken by his uncle.

"Good shot, son. I hope you like it."

After several more good shots, Uncle Choua Dang went to the orange grove garden with Ber's stepfather. After several hours of visit, a good welcome meal, and good talk, he returned home.

By 1949, all the children in Chia Thong's family became young adults. The Japanese had been gone for a few years and the French had returned to Xieng Khouang. The Hmong traveled to Xieng Khouang and other towns along Route 7 without fear of the Japanese.

There was news brought from Phou Duu that, with the support of the French, Hmong leaders had gained ranks in the Lao government in Xieng Khouang. The Hmong in Namnya, as well as the Hmong elsewhere, wished only two things: peace and freedom.

Life in the Chia Thong family had changed dramatically. All six children, whose ages were only a few years or even months different, had become adults. My great-grandmother noticed through their voices that the little children she had seen before she was blind were now grown up and would soon have their own families.

Ying Pao, who was slightly younger than Ber, was brought in to join Chia Thong's family by his mother. His mother devoted all her attention to her son and gave him everything. This had greatly concerned my great-grandmother. She maintained and asserted her principles of fairness by declaring to everyone that Ber must be married before everyone, for he was the oldest.

Following her order, Ber was pressured to find a girl he would marry as soon as possible. Ber was shy and had difficulty engaging in conversations with girls. His younger siblings, who had more outgoing personalities, became impatient. They offered him help. They just had to look for a girl that he liked. In a society where forced marriages were acceptable and commonly practiced, it did not matter whether she liked him or not.

Ber shyly hinted he was interested in the youngest daughter of Dang Vue of the Ly clan in the nearby village of Hamkheu. Her name was Xee, and she was only about sixteen. Her mother was a widow whose husband (the younger brother of her first husband, Chia Chue) died when Xee was only five.

Although without a father at a young age, her situation was completely contrary to that of Ber. She was the youngest and received all the love, care, and support from her older half-brothers and sisters. She did not even have to cut meat or clean a chicken—a duty traditionally expected of a girl or woman. Her mother still saved her the best pieces of meat and the chicken drumstick, mostly reserved only for young children. She had everything her mother could afford. She enjoyed the special treatment and did not worry about not getting what she needed.

However, as a woman in a society where men dominated every decision-making process, she was just as vulnerable as any other girl when it came to selecting a life partner. If she had the freedom of choice, she would not have married Ber. She had seen him visiting Hamkheu many times and had known him well from her mother. Her parents had known the people in Namnya all their lives.

Ber, on the other hand, was the oldest, without both of his parents, and had to bear the responsibility for everything, including cooking and cleaning. Other than the caring love from his blind grandmother, he was deprived of love and nurturing support. His sense of pride, confidence, self-esteem, and assertiveness had been hurt and damaged by verbal abuse from an early age.

The only things he believed he owned were the faded and worn-out traditional clothes presented to him by his stepmother for his hard work and the shiny crossbow given to him by Uncle Choua Dang. He did not dare to ask for time to engage in courtship with girls in neighboring villages. He spent his spare time going dove and squirrel hunting with his crossbow in his arms. He would be praised if he came home with birds or squirrels or otherwise yelled at for wasting time.

Ber knew Xee would not marry him, and there was only one way—forced marriage. Hence, one night, when Xee's mother was away from home, Ber brought his two cousins and his half-brother, Heu, with him to Hamkheu. They waited outside in the dark. When she went outside to fetch firewood, they grabbed her and carried her to Namnya. When they had gone far enough where they were sure her mother would not pursue her to bring her back, they sent the two cousins back to her house to inform her family—according to Hmong tradition—that Ber of Chia Thong in Namnya had taken her to marry.

Her mother was furious and wanted to go to Namnya and take her back, but her eldest half-brother, Ka Thai (Ga Thai), calmed his mother down.

"A girl has to start her life somehow, somewhere outside her family, and there is no guarantee that the man she chooses would always turn out good," he said.

In fact, two of her three older half-sisters were also married to members of the Xiong clan—one of whom had lived next door to her family for many years. The wedding ceremony took place within three days, according to Hmong tradition.

Unlike Western Christian culture in which a wedding ceremony is a pleasant presentation of a formally recognized union through ring exchange, bride-groom pledge, cake cutting, and joint picture taking, a Hmong wedding is a serious negotiation, investigation, and membership-transfer ceremony. The groom and his family must pledge they take the bride with earnest love and care, and that she will henceforward endlessly be a member of their family. The most respected uncle and brother of the bride would give her their best counseling and advice. The most common counseling words are as follows:

> From this day forward you are a member of your husband's family. His parents will be your parents; his ancestors will be your ancestors; and his house spirits will be your house spirits. You will pray to them and worship them to the day you die and you will become a member of the ancestors of your children and grandchildren. As you walk out of this house which used to be your home, you don't look back. The house of your husband will be your home from now on and forever. As a member of your husband's family, you will live in their way of life, support them, respect them, and nurture them. You will not gossip to us or anyone about what they do. You will defend them even if you don't agree with them. You will cook even if you are not hungry and invite them smilingly, even if you are not happy. In the event that your husband lacks responsibility, engages in unproductive routines, or abuses you, you talk to his parents, not us. If they fail to neutrally resolve the matter, you go to their most respected elder. If all efforts fail to result in a productive solution, you come to us. You are like a rope which we give one end to them, but still hold the other end. We will inquire about the truth of the matter.

For my mother, a woman who was forced to marry a man whom she did not love and choose, such a moment was not a happy one. But she took her eldest brother's advice, "The man who loves you more might be better than the man whom you love more," and accepted my dad to be her husband.

The way of life in Namnya was not different from that of Hamkheu. There was nothing completely alienating to my mother. The only difference was that there were so many siblings of nearly the same ages living under one roof. Her sense of maturity was greatly challenged. The man whom she relied upon to make her feel at home and protected had lost his sense of ownership of everything, including the place in which he was living. He did not seem to be aware of how much his young and shy wife needed from him to feel comfortable in her home. He was shy and he rarely talked to her. It looked as if she were to be the one who would protect him and bring back his sense of confidence and self-worth. But she was too young and immature. She was shy, lonely, and hungry. Everything happened so quickly and so suddenly.

She had gone back to her mother three times, protesting she could not spend her life with the man who not only lacked the ability to provide her with a sense of feeling at home, but also lacked the understanding of what they had become—husband and wife. Each time she went back she was told the same words.

"You only marry once. You don't want to come back and live as a divorced woman and hope that a good young man of your choice would want to marry you. Your second marriage will most likely be that you would be a second or third wife of someone."

She had attempted to commit suicide once by taking a dose of raw opium, but was discovered before it had taken effect. Her last return to petition to divorce my father was after I was born. Having a child in this state of relationship was not really a proud moment for her. This time, however, she was told, "You would not want to leave your lovely son to the man who you have just described as lacking a sense of awareness of someone's need for love, defense, and care."

Hearing this, my mother said no more. She wiped away her tears and decided to return.

A year after I was born, my dad was given an adult name, moving him up to an adult status. The honor of adult name selection is, by Hmong tradition, given to the parents-in-law (the wife's parents). My father was given a new name, Cher Pao. Some would call him Cher, for short.

The ceremony is almost similar to a wedding and is even called a second wedding, except this time it's done in the son-in-law's house. In a situation where an illness is the cause for a name change, a shaman would perform a ritual and determine a new name. In this case, a similar ceremony would be held to give the wife's parents the honor to affirm the selected name.

Kai, Heu, and Ying Pao were all renamed later, and had earned their adult statuses, except Xa, who never married. Kai became Wa Kai; Heu became Youa Pao; and Ying Pao became Nyia Vaj. My grandfather, Yia, died before he was given an adult name. In some cases, shamanic healing rituals determine the need for new names for boys or girls. Some men who already have adult names, even those who don't have any children, may be renamed by a shaman.

Adult names are aimed at giving young married men the status of honor, respect, and wisdom. The Hmong call this process "broadening the names and widening the roads of men from boyhood to manhood." Their wives are largely responsible for making sure the new names are widely known and used.

Ironically, some Hmong men who had attained their prominent status before they received their adult names were never given adult names. Vang Pao, Lee Tou Bee, Yang Dao, Lee Teng, and Moua Tou Lue had only been called by their young names. They had never been given or called by adult names, even if they had them. Perhaps, their statuses did not require adult names to broaden their wisdom and respect.

Like the Chinese, the Hmong call each other by last names first, like Vang Pao. This has only changed recently. Most Hmong only tell their first names when asked. If you need to know their last names or clan names, you have to ask. The Hmong from Laos have eighteen common clan names. They are: Cha or Chang; Cheng; Chue; Fang; Hang; Heu, Her, or Herr; Khang; Kong or Song; Kue; Lee or Ly; Lao, Lo, or Lor; Moua; Pha or Phang; Thao or Thor; Vang; Vue; Xiong; and Yang. As listed, some people in the same clan call or spell their last names differently.

Many boy or man names are preceded by Tou, as in Tou Pao or Tou Lue; Tou stands for proud son. Likewise, many Hmong parents love to call their daughters Mai before their names, such as Mai Yia or Mai Lee; Mai stands for lovely daughter.

Traditionally young Hmong names are monosyllabic, with a few exceptions, such as Ying Pao, Vapao,

Chueneng, or Vaneng. Recently, many Hmong have given their children long and creative names.

Hmong women are never given adult names. When they marry, their names are never used again, to the point they become forgotten. They become known by their husbands' names. My mother, Xee, has been called Mrs. Cher Pao, to this day. She would feel embarrassed if she was called by her young name.

Two years later my parents had their second child, another boy. They proudly named him Teng—meaning "lamp." My mother looked at the two boys whose lives would be hinged upon her protection and care and never returned to petition for a divorce again.

Having two children in a lifestyle where everything had to be carried on their backs, mostly up hills, my parents had an increased burden. My father would carry a load on his back and put me on top of it with my legs hanging on his shoulders. My mother would strap Teng on her chest with a baby carrier and carry a load on her back. They had a young male horse, named Boj Liab, meaning "red," that helped them carry rice, corn, and other livestock feed, including grass for itself.

The lives of the Hmong in Namnya and in neighboring villages were heavily hinged upon two things—rice and opium—neither of which they could decide not to have. Thus, the people in Namnya split their time between their rice fields down the valley across Route 7 and opium fields upon the hills of Phou San—a fog-covered mountain range about six miles northwest of the village. Phou San was covered by clouds nearly year round and was the region that had one of the largest opium productions in Laos during the French colonial era. The ground was wet year round under majestic trees. The only winding trail under big and furry trees was joined by paths from all nearby villages.

Using horses as primary vehicles to transport needed supplies and harvested crops had caused step holes on the trail, which made it resemble a ladder laid flat on the ground. The holes were filled with muddy water; some were nearly a foot deep. The adults would walk with big steps to avoid stepping in the holes. Four- and five-year-old children would take a big step and still have one foot land in the hole and mud up to their knees.

Carrying my brother and me to Phou San was difficult for my parents. Hence, I was often left with my great-grandmother in Namnya. My parents would be gone for two weeks or more before returning to get more rice and check things at home.

"Leaving you alone with your great-grandmother," Grandma had told me years later, "your parents would put up a big wooden board about your chest height to block the door and prevent you from going out without her notice. She would let you open the door to look outside, but you couldn't go out."

According to Grandma, there was a giant cauldron full of pig feed on the fireplace about my chest height. The feed was cooked early in the morning and was still warm. I reached in with both hands to scoop the warm pig feed, threw it out to the pigs, and watched them fight.

All of a sudden, Grandma showed up and she screamed.

"Ge! What are you doing?"

Hearing Grandma scream, my great-grandmother also screamed.

"Ge! Where are you? What happened?"

Grandma told me she realized that if she told my great-grandmother about what had happened, she would be mad.

"Oh, nothing happened," Grandma said as she calmed down and softened her voice. "I saw the door open and didn't know you were at home."

My great-grandmother greeted her. She went inside and the two old women talked.

"His parents have been gone for ten days now and have not come back," my great-grandmother said. "The boy has been good, but he surely misses his parents."

"I've just returned from there last night," Grandma said. "The poppies are at their peak. They won't come back for ten more days. I was afraid Ge would miss them, so I am coming to take him to be with them."

At three and a half, I could not walk on the narrow, steep trail that followed the top of the narrow mountain ridge to Phou San. My grandmother had to carry me on her back with a baby carrier. We were alone, on a narrow trail surrounded by grassy hills and narrow valleys of arching bamboo clumps, so she was glad that I was a little talkative for my age. She said I asked her to give me a gun. She grabbed a dry wooden stick about the length of an arm and gave it to me.

She said I told her, "Grandma, you should not be afraid of tigers because I have a gun and I will shoot them. Bang! Bang! Bang! I shot a tiger."

I had seen Hmong flintlock guns and heard stories about tigers attacking horses and even humans.

My grandmother was tired. She let me down, and we rested for awhile before we continued. When she was too tired, she would let me walk for a short distance, but that slowed us down. Fearing we would not get to our opium fields before dark, she put me back on her back.

We walked for two hours before entering into the Phou San's thick forest where the trail began to become wet and muddy, even in the dry season in December. We had to walk for another two hours to get to our small thatch hut. There were two other huts—one belonged to my mom's eldest half-brother and the other belonged to her other older half-brother.

In Phou San, the air was cool and humid. The vegetation looked completely different from that of Namnya. Around the rim of the old opium fields, there were majestic trees with green and gray furs hanging down like giant mustaches and beards. Giant red wild banana trees with hanging red blossoms loomed in the distance. Nearby was a small creek from which we brought our water supply. On tree branches overhead, above a bamboo water line where clear water ran down like a running faucet, there were wild grape vines decorated with green and purple grapes hanging here and there.

About two miles away, ethnic lowland Lao and Chinese merchants set up a market camp on the same spot where they had been doing business for many years. They had tents full of merchandise and food service to collect the freshly harvested opium. A combination of smells of chopped onion, cilantro, and ground black pepper could be sensed from one hundred yards away. The farmers worked hard harvesting opium sap from thousands of poppies that they had scratched the day before and that had to be collected before noon, or the hot sun in the afternoon would dry it up and harden it. They did not have time to cook.

Going to the market camp to purchase bowls of

freshly cooked rice noodle soup for their families was rewarding and convenient. After eating, they would tour the marketplace for a few minutes, buy a few candies, and then hurry back to scratch more poppies to harvest the next day. The market camp continued every year, like a festival, until the peaceful farming life was shaken by the intensifying Communists' takeover in the 1960s. Later, opium trade became outlawed.

In March 1958, at four and a half, I became too big to be carried on my parents' back, but I still could not walk on the rough, muddy, and slippery trails. I stayed home with my great-grandmother for up to two weeks in a row or longer.

One sunny afternoon, the village was quiet; there were sporadic cocks' crows here and there; the pigs rested as if they were in hibernation in the shade under a rice storehouse; the cows chewed their cuds vigorously under a large tree nearby; the wind blew dust into a swirling spiral and disappeared over the bushes; and over the treetops, mommy bugs sang endless songs, "Mommy, mommy, mommy . . ."

"Mommy bugs are calling their mommies. Where is my mommy?" I lamented.

My great-grandmother heard me. She came to hug me, assuring that my mommy would be back soon. She shared my laments with a relative who came back for supplies. Tears rolled down from her eyes as she talked.

The relative went to my parents in Phou San and told them. Two days later my grandmother came down from Hamkheu to bring me to my parents. She was really concerned about the growing number of children in my parents' family. She was especially concerned about my great-grandmother caring for my younger brother and me. My parents decided to move to Hamkheu in early February 1958 to live with my mother's folks: her mother, her three half-brothers, and her two older half-sisters—one in the Thao clan and the other in the Xiong clan. There were other families, all of whom were interrelated in some way. Their traditional way of life had begun to be interrupted by the long and bloody war.

CHAPTER 2

A NATURAL WAY OF LIFE ENGULFED BY FIRE

A seemingly peaceful life during the period between the end of World War II and the end of the French colonial era was about to change as Laos began to plummet into another internal conflict intensified by the raging fire of the Communists' expansion.

There were twenty-six houses, most of which had thatched-grass roofs. Hamkheu, a dirt-barren village, was four times larger than Namnya. Phou San, one of Laos's highest mountain peaks which stood at 2,218 meters, was less than four hours walking distance to the north. Hamkheu's location was less difficult to understand than that of Namnya. It was situated in a flat valley and at the foothill of two grassy mountains—Phou Kheou (a two-thousand–meter beautiful mountain peak soaring from a low plateau south of Phou San) on the northwest and Phou Kong on the northeast.

The Namfun Creek—a crystal-clear creek coming out of Phou San—passed through Namfun Village, hitting and splashing over giant boulders, before it ran through the middle of Hamkheu. A small creek flowed from the east, joined the larger creek at the bottom of the village, and flowed toward Ban Xouan—about two miles to the south. Across the Namfun Creek to the west and at the foothill of Phou Kheou, giant pine trees whistled in the wind and sounded as if they were whispering all the time.

At a glance, a visitor would notice that Hamkheu's first settlers had unmistakably selected its location for its natural beauty. However, its location and natural beauty had a less important purpose. There was a hidden and complicated purpose that could not be described in one sentence.

The way of life of the Hmong in Hamkheu was not different from that of those in Namnya or elsewhere. The climate in Hamkheu was too cool for rice, but the soil was too dry and not rich enough for opium. Rice was the main food dish; corn was for livestock; and opium was for cash. Corn could be planted around Hamkheu and Phou San. Rice could only be planted in the Ban Hang area which was located about six miles to the south. Opium, on the other hand, could only be planted around the slopes or near the summit of Phou San. Hamkheu was the middle ground for all three—none of which could be selected out.

My parents arrived in Hamkheu in early February—just in time for the slash-and-burn season—the time during which lowland ethnic Laotians rested from the rice planting and harvesting season. The Hmong, on the other hand, finished one season to immediately start another.

The slash-and-burn process required slashing bushes and cutting down trees to make new fields. For those who reused existing fields, the process of slashing old rice stalks and weeds needed to start in early March. My mother's eldest half-brother had two used rice fields which they had opened the year before and were still good and fertile for another year or two, at best. He gave her one, which saved my parents from having to open a new field and permitted them time to build a thatch-roofed house before the busy season started.

With the help of my mother's folks, the house was built quickly. A small horse stall was built next to the house for Red. A chicken coop was also built about twenty feet away for five hens, some little chicks, and a red rooster, brought from Namnya. A long trough was made of a tree trunk for three pigs—two mothers and a small male. These were all that my parents had—the least for a Hmong family—but they hoped life would improve in the new village.

"By the middle of March, all fields must be burned," my father had said, "or they will be hit by the first monsoon storm and will become difficult to burn."

Corn planting started when the fields were freshly burned. For those whose fields didn't burn well, branches needed to be cut and brushes needed to be cleared, piled, and burned. Rice planting season started in late April. The nonwritten seasonal calendar was on everyone's mind as villagers watched every move of nature.

The first monsoon rain was coming on the horizon as dark clouds rolled closer like giant piles of dirty cotton. Wind gusts blew from the southwest; big drops of rain splashed on dusty ground; thunders roared across the sky, commanding nature's unforgotten duty; lightning affirmed nature's might; water rushed down mountain slopes and dirt paths toward rivers and streams; the rain stopped; the sun returned and shone brightly in satisfaction; and the murky air polluted by smoke from the fires of slash-and-burn season became clear, providing a relief.

Hmong farmers rushed to their corn and rice fields, with the best seeds they could get, and frantically worked throughout the months of the monsoon rains, weeding their rice and corn fields. They had virtually no time to rest between the end of opium harvest season and the beginning of a new slash-and-burn cycle.

By early November, Hmong farmers started harvesting rice. They would cut the stalks about two feet from the ground and would lay each hand-full bunch on the stalks from which they were cut. They would be left to dry for a week before being collected to make a cone-shape pile with the heads in and the stems out. They would carefully stack each arm-full bunch, making a circle shape about ten feet in diameter (more or less depending on the size of the field and the quality of the crop). After each ring, they would fill the inner hole to make a strong and solid pile. The pile was smaller at the bottom with a gradual increase in size toward the middle, then a gradual decrease toward the pointy summit. Some of the piles would be as tall as twelve feet. They would use a wooden paddle to pat around the pile until it was nice and smooth. Some people would decorate their piles with a pointy stick or a straw wreath at the top. When done, the family would stand back and proudly admire the beautiful pile of crop—feeling ensured the family would not be hungry for the year.

Traditionally, the Hmong New Year celebration is held on the first lunar day of the first lunar month of the year, which usually falls in the middle of December. By the end of November, rice harvesting must be done to just barely allow enough time to prepare for the weeklong New Year celebration. To this day, New Year celebration is the only event which the Hmong celebrate together communitywide. The quiet and empty Hamkheu would become lively with human voices and animal sounds for a short period—maybe up to two weeks.

Most often, the people in Hamkheu stopped their New Year celebration early—even though young people would wish to continue their ball-tossing courtship for a few days longer—to start harvesting opium in Phou San. They had been checking their opium fields periodically and had projected the timing closely.

After the New Year celebration and the harvest of opium, the Hamkheu farmers would return to open the rice piles to thresh the rice off the stems. This process was called the rice beating or *ntaus nplej*. When finished, they would start the laborious winnowing process. They would carry a basket full of newly threshed rice up to the top of a ten-foot ladder and slowly pour it down so the wind would blow away the unwanted chaff. The last and even more laborious process was hauling the rice home to put in storage. Horses were critically important for the uphill rice-hauling process.

The villagers had the annual farming timelines all planned out in their heads. In the ensuing busy seasons they would watch the lunar cycles closely to make sure everything started and finished at the exact time or they would fall behind the process sequence. They knew they would have no time to maintain their main home in Hamkheu as they split their time between Ban Hang and Phou San.

Some families would move everything, including pigs and chickens, from Ban Hang to Hamkheu and from Hamkheu to Phou San, then move everything back in a reversed sequence. Hamkheu would be left nearly empty. Only those who had large numbers of family members could have one or two persons stay in Hamkheu, and the assigned individuals would then travel back and forth to bring food and supplies.

Upon arrival in Hamkheu, I was paired with my cousin, Noo, whose real name, Vapao, was not heard until I discovered it from his school friends in 1967. He was three years older than I.

There were great differences between us as he was the youngest son of my mother's eldest half-brother, and I was the oldest child of his father's youngest and only half-sister. Our childhood experience was completely opposite. He had everyone in the family taking care of him. I, on the other hand, helped my parents take care of all my younger siblings.

At eight, he did not go to school, because Hamkheu and other Hmong villages, except Phou Duu, did not have schools. None of the children in Hamkheu, whose parents were poor rural farmers, went to school, even though the French had issued a school attendance mandate aimed at promoting education in Laos. No one had given any thought about school.

Our parents would have something planned every day—eating a big breakfast and going to the rice or corn fields before sunrise. Every day, they would repeat the same routine.

There were no names for the days. Every day was the same and counted by the shapes of the moon. Thirty days would make a month or a "moon," by the Hmong way, and twelve "moons" would make a year, divided by different seasons of the slash-and-burn cycle. The New Year celebration would mark the end of an annual cycle and the beginning of a new one.

We lived in the way of life guided by the tradition of

our ancestors. I was dressed in my Hmong clothes that looked the same every day—loosely fitted black pants and black shirts with blue cuffs made by my mother. And, I wore a small silver necklace with snake heads on both ends for protection from bad spirits. It was brightly exposed on my neck—a good match with my collarless shirt and the fashion of our era.

My parents were very proud to have a son, for I would be the family's security in the future, carrying on my dad's spiritual practices. My mother, only for the short-term help, would have preferred a girl. However, for the long-term security, she preferred a boy—a notion I did not agree with. I believed then and still do now that there should be no preference of one gender over another.

There were many boys in the village, but we chose not to have any connection with them. Since Vapao was older, they tended to be friendlier toward him than me. Perhaps that was the reason he chose not to associate with them, I thought.

The other boys had fighting roosters and they carried them around the village to have them fight with other people's roosters. Neither one of us liked cockfights.

The French had been gone since early 1955 and had not been present in Hmong villages, including Phou Duu. There had been gossip about the Americans replacing the French, but they had not been seen in Hmong villages.

"The only American some Hmong had met was one who was wounded and was saved by Chong Toua Moua and the Hmong Maquis in Phou Duu many long years ago, and who smiled with thumbs up despite his severe wound," my father had said.

Since there had not been any confrontation between Major Vang Pao's forces and the North Vietnamese (whom the Hmong called *Nyab Laj*) in the area, except for reconnaissance news about occasional sighting of Pathet Lao soldiers in the region, whom the Hmong called *Nplog Liab,* meaning "Red Lao," everything seemed peaceful. High ranking Laotian government officials stayed only in the big towns, having no plan for the country, but enjoying their princely status and not getting along with each other. People who visited them had to kneel down at the door and walk on their knees toward them, according to stories we had frequently heard from the elders.

There were lowland Lao villages about ten miles to the south, on low plateaus and flat valleys along rivers. The Hmong visited them frequently. The lowlanders, too, visited Hmong villages often. The Hmong would trade opium or silver coins for salt. They would buy one or two basket containers—each weighing twenty kilograms—at a time. The lowlanders would bring steamed spicy fish and cane-sugar tablets to trade for opium or silver coins. The lowland residents in Xieng Khouang called themselves Thai Xieng Khouang, meaning Xieng Khouang people were more familiar with the Hmong, thereby sharing better relationship compared with the residents elsewhere in the country.

The lowlanders and the Hmong addressed each other as *Sahi*, meaning friend. *Pho Sahi* meant "Mr. Friend" and *May Sahi*, meant "Mrs. Friend." These terms were, perhaps, the best they could use to address their distant friendship. But, at least, they treated each other with respect. Most Hmong spoke Lao, but none of the lowland Lao spoke Hmong. The Hmong called the lowlanders

A NATURAL WAY OF LIFE ENGULFED BY FIRE

Nplog (*Blaw*)—a term to which they never paid attention or were aware of. And, the lowlanders called the Hmong *Meo*. The term was later rejected by the Hmong, who said it was derogatory. In a politically correct term, the Hmong were also called "the highland Lao" or "highlanders." The two ethnicities had always been foreign to each other, even though infrequent intermarriages had drawn closer relations in the 1970s.

There were distinctive lifestyle differences between the Hmong and their lowlander counterparts. While the Hmong had to look for new fields to clear and burn, and had no time to rest, the lowlanders concluded their rice harvesting in January and rested until May, when they started their rice paddy fields again.

Life in a lowland Lao village not far away seemed quiet and peaceful in this relaxing season. Water buffaloes grazed busily on empty rice paddy fields, occasionally whipping flies away with their tails. Men relaxingly weaved bamboo baskets under the cool and well-shaded house platforms.

Having rice paddy fields, they did not have to look for new fields every year. They could plant rice on the same field for generations.

Vapao's parents had two rice paddy fields in Nam Kout (Nam Koot), about five miles south of Hamkheu and four miles west of Ban Hang, where they also had non-paddy rice fields. The two fields were about a quarter mile apart from each other, separated by the joining of two creeks. The smaller field, which was given to my parents, had been left unplanted for a couple of years. Some of the dirt ridges had been damaged by water buffaloes.

A paddy field may consist of as many as fifty mini

fields or subfields ranging in sizes from 10 by 30 to 40 by 60 meters, depending on the terrains. Each small field was surrounded by a foot-high dirt ridge to hold water in. With one or two overflow openings, each field would let water flow to the field below, and the last ones would let water flow out back to the same creek from which it was diverted. Fish would travel from the canal into the fields and back and forth through these channels. A lot of fish would stay in the fields until we drained the water and caught them. Catching fish when we drained the fields was the part I liked the most.

Time had gone by quickly. In April, my father and I went to Nam Kout to begin working on repairing the paddy rice field.

Making and repairing a paddy rice field was very labor intensive. My father spent more than a month repairing the irrigation canal to irrigate the field and building dirt ridges around each small field. There were thirteen small fields filled with water, and the field looked like a fish farm with multiple ponds.

My father worked until dark in the evenings. I stood close by him and watched him scoop hundreds of shovels of mucky and heavy dirt to repair a ridge. Mosquitoes and bugs were bad during the evenings, but he refused to stop. He worked until we could not see his shovel. We stayed with my uncle and my cousin in their small farm cabin for over two months while my mother stayed in Hamkheu taking care of my younger brother who was three and my newly born sister. There were also pigs and chickens for her to feed.

After one and a half months of hard labor, we finished the paddy field, just in time for the planting season. With the ridges finished, the water level in each pond rose high above our ankles, and the ground was soft, ready to be plowed. The next thing we needed was a water buffalo and plowing tools. My father had to borrow everything from my uncle, including a buffalo. He gave my father the needed help and training, and the seedlings to plant.

The estimated three-acre field, which only provided sticky rice, did not yield very much in the first year and did not provide enough rice for our family. We traveled frequently between Nam Kout and Ban Hang to work on the dry rice field that produced regular rice.

With my father spending more time in Nam Kout, I traveled daily to Ban Hang with my mother. My job was to take care of my three-month-old sister. My mother would put her on my back and wrap her on me with a baby carrier. Fearing I would fall, I held on tightly to a stump, making me look invisible from a distance. She only wore a thin baby blanket and no diaper. When she urinated, it would run down from the lower part of my back and down on my legs. First, I would feel warm, then cold. My shirt and pants were soaked and wet all day until we went home at the end of the day and changed them.

Children as young as six had their roles in the family farming, no exception. There were no labor laws, only a hard-working principle for self-dependence and survival. We did enjoy our way of life and have fun in our natural way, not knowing if life was better or worse elsewhere in the world.

My mother's other half-brothers also had rice fields in Ban Hang, next to ours. Vapao was either with his mother in a different field, a mile away, or stayed in Nam Kout with his father. I was alone with my other cousins—Chong, ten, and Bee, six.

While the adults were frantically collecting bundles of rice to make piles, the girls were playing flutes made of hollow rice stalks. They seemed more talented than us—boys who were frequently yelled at for playing rough and throwing rocks.

The Viet Minh had intensified their attacks on the northern provinces. In 1959, two of Laos's northern provinces, Phong Saly and Saneua, had been under Communist Pathet Lao and Vietnamese control. Far from the political turmoil in Vientiane, the people across our region appeared to have a peaceful life. Not far away, however, people in villages and towns in Xieng Khouang province were under fear of being attacked by the approaching Pathet Lao and Vietnamese forces. Through word of mouth, we had noticed something going on somewhere in the world.

While working in the rice field in Ban Hang, on cloudy days, we would hear thunder-like sounds from above the clouds. The adults would tell us, "Those are the sounds of thunder-sound airplanes."

On sunny days, we would see tens of shiny airplanes flying high up in the blue sky over our rice fields like flocks of geese. In each flock, there were four or five big ones, each of which was followed by four or five little ones. They resembled mother geese and their babies swimming in the blue water. We had no idea where they were coming from or going to, and we never talked or questioned about why they flew in such a formation.

Hours later, we would see them return, flying across the sky to the other side of the horizon. We did not know how many of them did not come back, and who had lost a father, son, or brother in a war somewhere in the world. Such a phenomenon never occurred to our minds that something was about to drastically change our way of life.

In 1960, during rice harvesting season, we enjoyed watching black airplanes flying in flocks of four or five over our heads. They flew low, compared to the shiny thundering little ones. They flew from the southwest to the northeast or sometimes in the opposite direction. This time, these big, dark airplanes flying every day sent chilling messages to my parents and other adults who stood motionless as they watched the giant dark birds until they disappeared into the horizon. The adults called them Soviet airplanes and discussed that a major war was imminent—although they were not fully informed of the details of what had been transpiring.

Cherpao Moua, who lived in a lonely and large corrugated tin-roofed house in Ban Hang, two miles northeast of Ban Khai—an ethnic lowland village—and who was chief district *Tasseng* of Phou Duu, knew about every detail of the situation. He had been working with Lt. Col. Vang Pao on establishing Bouam Loung—a military camp about twenty miles northwest of Hamkheu.

One day in July 1960, Cherpao Moua traveled past our remote farm house in Nam Kout—soaked and wet up to his waist. He traveled on a muddy path in the rainy season toward a Hmong village, located two miles south of us—the last Hmong village before the ethnic Lao villages along Route 7. The lone traveler stopped by to change his wet Hmong clothes and let them dry in our house. All the adults were not home; they were busily working on the paddy fields.

"When your parents come back, tell them that a Hmong man had stopped by and left his clothes here," the man said. "And tell them he will come by to pick them up tomorrow." Actually, he had walked past our paddy field and talked to my parents.

The next day, he returned.

"Did you tell your parents that the Hmong man would return to pick up his clothes?" he asked with a forced smile.

Shyly, we simply said, "Yes."

He thanked us and left toward the direction he had come the previous day. He became the commander of Bouam Loung two years later.

In January 1961, right before the start of a new slash-and-burn cycle, news came from newly promoted Col. Vang Pao, alerting that North Vietnamese forces had taken Xieng Khouang town and all towns and villages along Route 7, and they were on their way to villages south of Phou San. Hamkheu villagers panicked and took hiding in Nam Tong, the thick jungles behind Mount Phou Kheou.

The hiding had no meaningful purpose and provided no guarantee for safety because the villagers (still naive at the beginning of the war) traveled every day between the villages and their hideout camps to check and feed their animals anyway. After a month of hiding, there was no sighting of Communist forces near or around their villages and the villagers decided to open corn fields around the hideouts.

The connections with neighboring ethnic Lao villages had been completely cut off. There were no Chinese merchants coming around to trade opium. The opium farming in Phou San suddenly stopped. Cherpao Moua had left his house in Ban Hang and moved to Bouam Loung. My parents had planned to discontinue the rice field in Ban Hang and stay only in Nam Kout.

Cherpao Moua set up military outposts on the summits of Mts. Phou Kheou and Phou Kong. The jungles around our corn fields in Nam Tong became ammunition hiding places for Cherpao Moua's forces. Empty cartridge clips, brass bullet cases, and unused green cartridge clip sashes became children's war toys in their imitation of soldiers. Green camouflage parachutes were conveniently used in whole for temporary shelters and in parts for rice sacks, mosquito-net canopies, bedroom door drapes, and many more household necessities. Parachute ropes became useful for animal leashes, tent ropes, and sewing threads. And artillery shell carton tubes became convenient salt storage containers.

Local villagers became caught in the middle as intelligence informants for Col. Vang Pao, as well as the Red Lao forces, expected to report activities of their adversaries—an expectation that put them in a difficult position. In fact, the villagers had been in constant contact with Col. Vang Pao's intelligence units that roamed the jungles of Phou San. By 1961, many of the men from local villages had already served in guerrilla forces commanded by Col. Vang Pao.

One afternoon in March 1961, Vapao, my two other cousins, and I were playing next to a giant boulder by the Namfun Creek. While playing a war game with empty cartridge clips, brass machine gun cartridges, carton grenade cases, and soft woodblocks used as pretend soldiers, we looked up toward the dusty path across the creek toward the giant pine trees on the west, and there were twelve Red Lao soldiers wearing green uniforms and fluffy caps, walking in a column toward us. They walked with varied steps according to spaces of rocks laid on the shallow water, for there was no bridge; their eyes were alert and their guns pointed down with straps hung on their shoulders, ready to be raised and fired at any time.

Fearing they would come toward us and see our toys, we shoveled them into the waist-high bushes—still leaving plenty exposed—and stood motionless as we watched them approach. As they neared, they stopped and looked straight toward the houses to check if any houses had their doors open. My grandmother's house had its front door wide open. They walked straight toward her house, with only a brief glance at us. We breathed deeply with relief, grabbed all the military items, and buried them in the soft and dusty dirt under the giant boulder. We never dug them up again.

"That was close," Vapao said, wiping his forehead. "They almost saw our toys."

The soldiers, three Hmong and the rest Red Lao, crowded in Grandma's house, sitting everywhere—on short stools lined up on the dirt floor, on the open guest bed, and on the wooden-treadmill beam. The leader, whose name was Pa Ma Thao, whom Grandma called son, was the cousin of the son-in-law of my grandfather's second wife. He spoke vigorously, calling Vang Pao's forces "the enemies" and themselves the *Nao Lao Haksat* or "the Lao Patriots."

"You should not fear and should work hard on your corn and rice farming," he assured and encouraged. "The Nao Lao Haksat are coming to liberate you from the imperialist Americans and their ally, the American hunting dogs. If you see them, you should report to us at once."

My grandmother was blunt in her question.

"Son, we had been told that the Nao Lao Haksat would create a common property system and that everyone would co-own everything together, including the women," she said in a stern tone. "Is that true?"

He denied and protested bitterly.

"Those accusations are not true. You should not believe the imperialist Americans."

My grandmother invited them to stay for a meal.

"No, no, no, thank you. The Nao Lao Haksat never put burdens on people."

They left in the same formation toward the direction they came from. The war escalated in every corner of Laos, more heavily in the northern part of the country, drawing its citizens to fight each other with deadly weapons. The new weapons were brought in and paid for by people from thousands of miles away as the Hmong and Lao paid for the fight with their legs, limbs, and lives.

CHAPTER 3

THE AIRPLANE RICE AND THE SINGING BOX

As they became refugees, uprooted from their farming tradition, their lives became dependent upon airplane rice, whose smell they rejected months earlier. Hmong children became exposed to war materials and the killing talents required in the wars.

Leaving behind a more than three-decade–old ally with the French, in which the Hmong played an important role in helping the French against the Japanese and the Viet Minh, the Hmong became involved in a different era of war with the Americans. Although a long war loomed ahead, they naïvely remained hopeful for peace.

Neatly grazed pastures, wild pink and purple turmeric flowers blooming under giant oaks, and crystal clear streams and creeks gave Nam Kout an unmatchable natural beauty. It was a place where we believed we had everything for our simple way of life. Every day, we spoke our natural language that sufficiently described everything in our world.

In 1961, our paddy rice field was in full operation, and my dad bought a male water buffalo and plowing equipment. The buffalo worked well in the early morning up until around 10 a.m. After that it needed time to rest, eat, and bathe in a nearby mud pond, called a buffalo pond or *hawv twm*, in Hmong language.

"When the sun is about an arm span over the tree tops, the buffalo must be released or it will be very angry at you, and will not follow your orders," my father had said.

"Buffaloes are smart animals," Uncle Ka Thai had said to my father. "They can recognize and follow commands, such as Go, Stop, Slow Down, Turn Right, Turn Left, or Back Up. A good female is better than a male."

My father made a mistake by buying a well-trained male. When it was tired, its eyes would turn red and it would start blowing its nose and shaking its head. My father sold it and replaced it with a trained female. A trained buffalo was much more expensive than a regular one. Buffaloes loved mud baths, for they helped cool their bodies and protect against flies. They would lazily soak themselves in muddy ponds for hours each day, especially during the middle part of the day, leaving only their eyes uncovered with mud.

With the help of a buffalo, my father was able to handle the work on the paddy rice field by himself, except for the planting and harvesting seasons. My mother and I continued commuting back and forth between Ban Hang and Nam Kout until 1962. Each day, from dawn to dust, we were in the rice field, working.

With two more children—both girls—Mee, a little over two, and Kia, two months old, our burden had increased. Sometimes, just my mother, Kia, and I were in the rice field. It was quiet, except for the occasional sounds of baby cries. When I was bored, I would talk to myself. But the sounds of bugs and birds from a distance were louder than mine. My mother occasionally coughed from a distance, telling me that she was still there, not far away.

My parents had opened a non-paddy rice field in Nam Kout and we no longer traveled to Ban Hang. I thought that was a smart move. Our life in Nam Kout was more relaxing and enjoyable since the opium farming in Phou San had stopped. Vapao and I had more time together, playing, fishing, and enjoying whatever nature provided.

Hmong children under ten had already learned so much about wars. During our free time we liked playing war games. We loved making two- to three-inch block cuts of *kav qos nphoo*, a soft and spongy tropical plant that had a cylindrical shaft which could grow up to six feet in height. We called the blocks soldiers. We would line them up in groups of ten or fifteen. Each group would be led by a bigger and taller block called the leader. We would use bamboo tubes as guns and soybeans or acorns as bullets. One would blow a bean at the other person's block lines. When a block was knocked down, a soldier was hurt or killed. The person who knocked down more of the other person's blocks would win the battle. Sometimes we would leave the ground littered with game blocks, but we were not in trouble for the mess because there were limitless outdoor spaces to play. The blocks would rot away in a few days.

Corn planting still could not be abandoned, for it provided feed for the animals and sweet corn for the family when it was young and freshly harvested. Ancestors were always called to join the new-crop meals, a tradition practiced for centuries which could not be neglected.

My parents boiled a large pot of sweet corn that

sent a fresh smell throughout the house. I was sick and was only allowed to eat rice gruel or rice drenched with water, nothing else for fear that eating something else would make me sicker and could cause death. The Hmong still believe in this notion to this day.

The steam of freshly boiled corn smelled too good for a sick child—who could not eat anything, but plain rice—to resist.

"Mom, can I eat a corn?"

"Ask your dad!" my mother said in a despising tone. "Ask if he would let you eat it. Your dad and his folks are very strict on what you can eat when you are sick. Sometimes, he almost won't let me eat rice when I am sick."

"No, you can't eat it," my dad said, confirming my mom's scorn. "Wait until you feel better. Okay?"

"Dad, what if we only have corn and no rice?" I asked and started crying.

My father raised his head abruptly, a bit surprised.

"All right, go ahead and eat it. Eat just a little."

The tradition that was not taken lightly has begun to face challenges as we began to intermingle with different people in a world that was larger than we thought. The wisdom which was once indisputable in the tradition of our small world had begun to face questions that we never thought existed.

In 1962, Vapao and his parents visited Bouam Loung during a New Year celebration. Bouam Loung was a village newly established by Cherpao Moua since he left Ban Hang. It was a military base with an airstrip, located about twenty miles northwest of Hamkheu. When they returned to Nam Kout, they brought back some items: ten kilograms of sticky rice, which they called airplane rice, three empty giant rice sacks, and three green gun cartridge sashes. They had foreign odors. When my mother smelled the airplane rice, she quickly turned her nose away from it.

"It smells awful!"

Vapao's parents gave about three kilograms of the airplane rice for us to try. We could not eat it, even after rinsing it several times before cooking it. The hemp sacks also had a sickening smell.

Vapao talked excitedly about what he had seen in Bouam Loung. He spoke of how big Bouam Loung was—about three times the size of Hamkheu. It made me wonder if Hmong villages were growing bigger every day.

Bouam Long had an airplane landing field, a marketplace, and lots of airplane rice. He had listened to a singing box which we later discovered to be a radio.

"A lady was singing in the box," he said. "She was breathing heavily and laughing sometimes."

"How big was the box?" I asked.

"Not very big," he tried to explain. "Only this big," he said, providing hand gestures of its shape and size—about a foot long and four inches thick.

I was completely puzzled.

"Was she really in the box?" I asked. "Did you see her?"

"No, no, I did not see her. She was just talking inside the box."

For days, I tried to understand what he was talking about. Two years later, I found out about the "singing box" when my mom's brother in-law, Uncle Song Chai, brought out a radio to listen to news and entertainment broadcast on the newly installed radio station in

Long Cheng. Radios and radio news and entertainment broadcasting became the newest technological features reaching the remote Hmong villages as the war escalated and had broadened our view of the world.

As Communist forces increased in numbers, the latest outpost was established north of Namfun Village, about four miles north of Hamkheu. It had a small airstrip and three artilleries: a 106mm, an 81mm, and a 60mm. Empty carton-tube shell containers were thrown and littered the ground around the big guns. On our way to Phou San, Cousin Chong Moua, Vapao's eldest brother, Uncle Ka Thai, and my father decided to stop by the outpost for a visit. Vapao and I were fortunate to accompany the three adults on that day to have a firsthand experience of the modern military ammunition.

The soldiers in green uniforms at the outpost, some of whom were from Hamkheu, welcomed us warmly. They showed us around and demonstrated how the big guns worked. They shot each gun three times. The two smaller guns were stationed firmly on the ground at a forty-five–degree angle. As they fired the 60mm, a not very impressive sound sent out the mortar which exploded a distance away in fewer than ten seconds. The 81mm was much larger and more powerful. Its loud sound and noticeable kick on the ground produced dust at its base as it was fired.

The 106mm sat on a large, round base with legs spreading out, making it look impressive. Its power was visible as its legs pushed the ground each time it was fired, deepening its footprints on the ground. A soldier dropped a large shell into the hardened steel barrel; he stepped away about ten feet from the gun with two fingers plugging his ears as the gun ejected its bullet-shape mortar. It sounded as if lightning had struck something nearby. About a few minutes later an explosion was faintly heard from a distance. There was no declared military restriction zone for the exercise. However, because of the area's thin population density, there was no concern that someone might be in the target area.

The guns were new to the recently recruited Hmong soldiers. The daily shelling exercise, evidenced by the piles of carton-tube containers, was not a wasteful use of ammunition, but rather a training effort for the intensifying war—a required killing skill that Hmong soldiers had to learn.

In Bouam Loung, for the years that followed, airplane rice sacks became household rice storage as carton-shell tube containers became household salt containers. Unable to read warning signs of hazardous materials, health hazards were completely ignored. Airplane rice sacks and airplane fuel barrels became so abundant that every household could have one or more and there were still a lot more, enough for some people to cut open and use for house-wall panels. The strange smell became familiar, and it was no longer noticeable.

In 1963, many more people in Hamkheu and surrounding villages had been recruited to serve in the CIA-funded Special Guerrilla Units (SGUs) and had moved to Bouam Loung. Empty houses and spaces in various parts of the villages sent chilling effects throughout the region. Close-up views of silvery Helio planes and green helicopters flying low over the treetops became new experiences. The Vietnamese and Pathet Lao soldiers who once marched on villages in the Hamkheu region had been pushed back to the Xieng Khouang area. They would, however, prepare for another attack soon.

In June of that year, the Vietnamese and Pathet Lao launched another attack on Mount Phou Kheou, killing Za Teng Moua, nephew of the well-known Hmong leader Chue Ker Moua, and six other soldiers. The post was seized and we were the last people to leave Hamkheu. The other two posts were also lost to the Pathet Lao. The people of Hamkheu and surrounding villages moved to Phou San and eventually moved to the small village of Houayhom about ten miles east of Bouam Loung, where they became refugees for the first time.

My father and everyone hid away their personal hunting guns—old French semiautomatic rifles—in caves, fearing they might be caught by the Red Lao and Vietnamese while fleeing.

Cherpao Moua, now in the rank of lieutenant commander of Bouam Loung (Lima Site 32), had ordered an attack to retake Mount Phou Kheou and to regain control of the Phou San region. But the inhabitants of the region who had lived there for decades never returned. The once noisy Hmong villages became flea- and rodent-infested ruins and were slowly reclaimed by nature, leaving only remnants of human tools and utensils beneath thick underbrush.

Houayhom, a small, remote village surrounded by limestone karsts, suddenly became a noisy place. The newcomers arrived in an unprecedented number and settled in temporary shelters across the creek from the village. An old grassy rice field, in which remnants of banana trees and sugarcane remained in abundance, was filled with new human voices. Another old rice field about a half mile away became the rice-airdrop field.

While Hmong from other areas of Xieng Khouang

province had moved from their homes and become refugees a few years earlier, it was the first time that the Hmong from Hamkheu and surrounding villages became dependent on airplane rice to survive. The foreign smell they rejected a year earlier became what they depended on every day and changed their way of life forever.

In Houayhom, my family lived in a 20-foot by 12-foot thatched-grass–roof and chopped-bamboo–wall hut for three months. Lt. Moua vigorously recruited boys as young as thirteen and men under sixty to retake the Phou San region. But the Hmong were outgunned and outnumbered. Phou San was within range of the North Vietnamese forces' long-range artillery from Ban Ban and Ban Khai.

Lt. Moua required that all males in the specified age range must register or face arrest. My father wanted to move to Phou Vieng, a village about twenty miles west of Bouam Loung. My mother wanted to join her older half-sister whose husband—whom I called Uncle Song Chai—was the Phou Vieng district chief. My parents' hope was to move far away from the raging fire.

My father and Chong Moua left in the middle of the night, leaving behind my mother and five children; Vapao's family, including his parents, Vapao, and two sisters; and Chong Moua's wife and two children. Uncle Pa Xiong, my mom's youngest half-brother who was disabled, his wife and four children, and my grandmother were also left behind. My mother went to Pa Xiong Vang, the chief recruiting officer, and reported that my father had gone to Phou Vieng and that we would move to live with her sister's family.

My mother, my grandmother, and her half-brothers' families spent an entire day killing and preparing the last little pig and chickens that we had brought from Hamkheu. The meat was deep fried and put into bamboo tubes for the three-day journey. We started at 3 a.m. on the first day. Dried bamboo torches were prepared the night before and used for light.

Like a herd of migrating African antelopes, we walked across mountains, steep hills, and valleys, and sometimes along creeks and rivers. My father came back to meet with us after we had walked for a day. The journey of our migration had begun as the war intensified throughout the remaining decade and into the next.

On the first day, we rested on a sandy bank of a clear creek before sundown and were already exhausted. The atmosphere was calm and peaceful, and the environment was filled with unmatchable beauty. The gentle currents sent soft sounds as they hit against smooth rocks standing in their way. Melodious singing of tens of species of birds was a resonance of the natural beauty of a wild kingdom in which its members called each other to rest for the night.

We quickly gathered firewood before sundown and were barely able to make a fire before dark. My mother and my aunts took out a large rice-cooking pot, some bowls, and spoons. They went to clean the dishes and get a half-pot full of water to cook rice for supper.

My father and Uncle KaThai cut wild banana leaves, which were abundant, near the sandy-river bank to make bed for the nine adults and eleven children. Since November was the beginning of the dry season, there was no need to build a shelter for a one-night stay.

Before eating, my father scooped a half spoon of rice and filled it up with the deep-fried meat. He stood up facing the upstream of the small river and called upon the spirits dwelling in the surrounding mountains, rivers, and trees to join us for supper and to protect us.

We slept on banana leaves, using our clothes for pillows. Our eyes gazed at the stars in the clear sky before falling asleep. The night was quiet, for there was no village nearby, with the exception of millions of cricket sounds, occasional frog jumps in the water, sporadic owl hoots, and gargling sounds of the creek.

When we woke up in the morning, before our eyes was the beauty of scenery that looked as if we were in paradise. The unparalleled beauty of steaming water associated with the morning fresh air, hundreds of colorful birds, and the streaks of morning mist was a complete irony to the approaching storm of human destruction from which we were running.

We quickly prepared breakfast and enough rice for lunch for the tiring journey. Before eating, my father would not forget to perform the same ritual as he did the night before, inviting the spirits who dwelled in the local natural structures to join a meal with us and to protect us. He would do the same before every meal until we arrived at our final destination. This is a Hmong tradition passed on from generation to generation. When the Hmong are on a journey or a mission outside their homes, this ritual must not be neglected before eating a meal.

"We need to start moving quickly," my father said as we started getting ourselves ready to move. "We have to get to Nam Sai before nightfall. The slopes before Nam Sai are too steep to sleep."

Nam Sai Valley was about six miles north of Bouam Loung. We had to walk across the slope of Mount Phou

Kang, a high and rugged mountain range across a deep valley from the Mountain of Bouam Loung, overlooking golden rice fields on the mountain slopes and pleated narrow valleys and hill ridges.

The small and winding trail ran through thick jungles, along creeks, and across countless small valleys and hills. My grandmother, at seventy plus, was still able to walk without assistance. She carried nothing but a five-foot bamboo stick to assist herself. At ten, I was only able to carry her three-foot–long bamboo smoking pipe, weighing about four pounds, and a hen with seven chicks.

Grandma was one of a few Hmong women who smoked tobacco. The majority of older men and women smoked pipes instead of cigarettes. However, during the Vietnam War, cigarettes were distributed to Hmong men who served in the CIA-funded guerrilla forces. The number of cigarette smokers had significantly increased, including some boys as young as thirteen. Smoking at a young age, which was previously criticized, became increasingly acceptable or at least ignored.

I walked closely with Grandma, although I was not able to be of much assistance to her. The trip was rough and difficult for her, especially walking up and down across the rough terrains of valleys and hills. We had to move quickly to pass the mountain's steep and rough slopes before nightfall. We started walking at sunrise, and I started feeling hungry. None of us had a watch. Feeling hungry was the only sign that it was about noon or lunchtime. We came upon a rocky valley where clear water dropped from a stair-like cliff and flowed under giant and furry boulders.

"Let's rest for a while and eat lunch before we go,"

my father said.

He knew it would be a long distance ahead before the next place where we could eat lunch, because he had previously traveled on that trail. There were yellow and brown banana leaves lying under nearby bushes, which indicated previous travelers had eaten lunches there before continuing their journey in either direction.

"Put some water in the pipe for Grandma!" my mother said loudly.

I took the pipe to the waterfall and filled it with water about four inches from the bottom. I handed it to Grandma. She took out a pack of tobacco wrapped in a dry banana leaf that she had tucked in the sash around her waist. She opened it and took out a small amount, the size of a fingertip. She put it on the tip of the small bamboo spout, the size of a finger, jutted down at forty degrees into the side near the bottom of the pipe. She put her mouth against the hole of the pipe and inhaled while she lit the tobacco with a match. I could hear the water bubble inside the pipe. Then she exhaled the smoke. She repeated this twice and put another amount in and did the same one more time. She stopped just as the food was ready. My father never neglected his ritual before everyone could eat.

The rice had been prepared early in the morning and the deep-fried meat did not need to be heated. So the meal was quick, and we continued our journey. The trail started descending toward the Nam Sai Valley. As we approached the low elevation, the change in vegetation was noticeable. Trees were not as thick and bamboos became more dominant, particularly *xyoob mov raj* or rice cooking bamboos. This type of bamboos was popular because it had long sections between joints and a thin paper coat inside, and it was good for cooking sticky rice. When peeling off the bamboo pipe, it would leave a good sausage of cooked rice.

The trail was not frequently traveled. We had walked for almost two days and never met any travelers from the opposite direction. The trail became smoother and soon we heard sporadic cocks' crows in a distance. The trail passed directly through the middle of a lowland Lao village. There were more than twenty houses, all of which were built on wooden-plank or flattened-out bamboo platforms. Underneath the platforms were good and dry spaces for animals and storage. The houses were better built than those in most Hmong villages, although the village was far remote from civilization. It was an indication the lowland dwellers had a more stable life than their mountain dweller counterparts.

The remote inhabitants might have been living in the village for generations. Interestingly, the thick jungles on the surrounding mountain slopes remained intact. Near the village, there were paddy rice fields on the strips of flat land along both sides of the Nam Sai River. This had prevented the Nam Sai villagers from the slash-and-burn cultivation which the Hmong practiced on the mountains that would have depleted the surrounding jungles.

The Nam Sai villagers used push carts and horse wagons to transport their crops, thereby significantly reducing the labor of carrying everything on their backs. To this day, many of the Hmong living on rough mountainous terrains in Laos still continue carrying everything on their backs.

One interesting aspect of this remote community was its members seemed unaware of what happened around them, particularly the fall of Xieng Khouang, the provincial capital town, and the approaching Communist forces in Phou San. It was later discovered, while Cher Pao Moua mandated every man under sixty and boys as young as thirteen must serve in the military, the Nam Sai villagers were never contacted.

Even though Gen. Vang Pao knew he was short of Hmong men and boys, he left it up to the lowland Lao leaders to decide who they would recruit to serve in the military. Local administration boundaries were drawn along ethnic lines, not geographical boundaries. One ethnic administration district had no jurisdiction over another.

We traveled past a rice paddy field where a herd of water buffaloes stood near a muddy pond, staring at us.

"Don't make noise," my father said. "Some water buffalo bulls are vicious."

Having lived in Nam Kout for years, we were familiar with water buffaloes and their behavior. We walked past them cautiously without incident.

We came upon a nice spot where the Nam Sai River turned into an elbow shape, making a sandy beach inside the elbow water bank. This place was similar to the one we slept the night before as it had an abundance of firewood and banana trees.

Like the night before, we had just enough time to gather firewood and banana leaves before dark. Schools of fish swam up and down and were clearly visible in the crystal clear water. The clean sandy beach, smooth pebbles, and shallow clear water could have made the place perfect for enjoyment if it were three years earlier. The situation had changed the life we once had enjoyed. My parents were only concerned about what they would do next to keep our family alive. And that was clearly visible on their sad faces.

The fire burned warmly and it looked as if we were having a campfire. None of the adults, including Grandma, was in the mood to tell stories like they used to when we spent nights in our farm huts as recent as eight months ago.

On the way, we had cut some rice-cooking bamboos and brought them along. We filled each tube with water about half full; then we slowly stuffed it with uncooked airplane rice, leaving room about six inches to the top, enough for it to expand almost to the top after letting it soak overnight.

Tired from the long day's walk, everyone slept on the prepared bed with just banana leaves underneath us, right after supper. Our eyes stared at the bright stars in the clear sky.

"Do you see that bright star up there?" Cousin Chong asked.

"Where? Which one?" I asked. "There are so many."

"Up there!" she answered, pointing her finger.

"Be quiet and go to sleep," my dad said. "We will get up early tomorrow."

Everyone was quiet. I turned to my left side and pulled the thin blanket over me, up to my right shoulder, and was soon falling asleep. Everyone slept quietly, not far from the fire which still burned warmly with yellow flames and occasional cracks of sparks.

The fire burned in huge yellow and orange flames. My father had put more wood into the fire. It was still dark. All the adults were up, and Grandma sat by the fire smoking her pipe. The bamboo pipes, which we had stuffed with rice, were in the middle of the fire, propped up on a large fire log at a forty-five degree angle. There were eight of them. It was the first time that we cooked rice in bamboo pipes because these bamboos did not exist in the Hamkheu area.

Each of the children got up and went right to the burning fire to curiously look at the steaming bamboo pipes. Soon everyone was up. Each would walk drowsily towards the shallow water, which barely flooded the smooth rocks and pretty pebbles, to wash his or her face.

"We have to start early." We had heard this phrase every day, for three days, without a clue of how far ahead we had to go. My father wanted us to arrive in Phou Dou Noy, a village about three miles west of Phou Vieng, before sundown. It seemed as if the journey had been divided into equal segments, each with well-calculated timing.

Our food supplies were running out as felt by the weight of some of our loads. That was the concern over anything else. We had to get to our destination or we would be without food. So we started even earlier than the previous day. Everything was ready at dawn. My mother and my aunt cooked some rice for lunch. My father and Uncle KaThai peeled the bamboo tubes of rice. We ate the sausages of rice and the deep-fried chicken, which was nearly empty.

"Hurry! Get everything ready and let's start moving," my father said, rushing everyone again.

Starting on the trail again before sunrise, the journey seemed to continue forever. The trail followed along the Nam Sai River which flowed toward the Nam Khang River, one of the major rivers in Laos and a tributary of the Mekong River. The trail split into two: one followed the Nam Sai River and the other turned up to the Bouam Mou slope, a low mountain range that lay between Bouam Loung and Phou Vieng. By late morning, we arrived at the Bouam Mou village where Uncle Ka Thai's kin folks lived and where Chong Moua had traveled with my father days before and had stayed there waiting for his family. Uncle Ka Thai had planned to settle there.

The rest of us, including Uncle Pa Xiong's family, would go to Phou Vieng after stopping there briefly. We would become separated after years of living close by each other. How far we would be separated from each other would depend on how far our journey would continue from there. We would visit each other only if necessary.

Bouam Mou was a freshly established village with fewer than a dozen houses. Aunt Ka Thai's older sister, Mrs. Zong Koua Lor, her eldest son, Vang Neng, and other children—who were natives of Hamkheu—had moved there a year earlier. There were also families of Uncle Ka Thai's folks and other families of the Xiong and Thao clans who had moved there a year earlier because of the escalation of the war and the threat of the Communists' takeover of their homeland in the Phou San area.

We continued our journey, following a winding trail down toward the Hoy Hom Creek. Grandma also continued the journey with us. By lunch time, we were at the bottom of the long slope where the trail followed the zigzagging creek and crossed it several times before turning uphill. It looked as if Phou Vieng was not too far ahead because there were rice and corn fields alongside the trail, which were believed to belong to the people of Phou Vieng. We stopped for lunch before leaving the creek and continuing our exhaustive journey.

The trail left the creek and led up toward the Phou Vieng Mountain. Where the trail split into a Y, we took the left fork. We did not go to Phou Vieng. We went to Phou Dou Noy instead.

As planned to arrive on time, we arrived at Phou Dou Noy before sundown. The red giant fireball still hung like a glowing charcoal over the horizon as we arrived at the edge of the village. People were returning from their fields after a long day of farmwork. Some people held ropes in their hands, guiding their horses behind them with heavy loads on their backs. The scene reminded me of our old way of life back in Hamkheu.

"*Nej tuaj los?*" a woman asked, meaning, "Hello, did you come to visit?"

The Hmong always greet visitors with a question.

"*Peb los hos,*" my mother answered, meaning, "No, we've come to stay."

In Hmong language, *tuaj* means "come to visit" and *los* means "come to stay" or "come home." The unique subtleties of Hmong language frequently confuse Hmong children. A boy had once mistakenly told his father that his mother had come to visit, whereas he'd meant to say his mother had come home.

"*Kuv niam tuaj lawm,*" the boy said, meaning, "My mom has come to visit."

"*Hais tias kuv niam los lawm no mas, ruam,*" the father corrected and laughed, meaning, "Say 'My mom has come home,' dummy."

I had wondered whether if I were to learn Hmong language as an adult I would have an enormous difficulty understanding its nuances. Fortunately, we had no communication barriers with our new friends and extended relatives with whom we shared the same language.

Phou Dou Noy was a midsize village of about two dozen houses. There were only four or five big wood-shingle–roofed houses. The village was on a curved bowl-shaped hilltop between two mountain hills. There were houses on both sides of the slopes, but none at the bottom of the curve. Perhaps there was a good reason: good drainage in the rainy season.

There were no standing trees in the village, providing a good view of sunrise and sunset, but no shade under the blazing sun at noon. Cow, horse, and pig manures littered the barren ground. The wind stirred dusts of animal waste into the air creating spiral clouds in the dry season. The rain pushed dirt and animal waste into a layer of dark green manure in the bottom of the curve. It had been five months since we had left Hamkheu and lived in temporary camps and shelters. The smells of soot and animal manures had become unfamiliar and quite unbearable.

My father led us past all the houses on the northeast side of the curve and toward a big, perhaps the biggest, house on the middle elevation of the southwest side of the curve. It belonged to Boua See Xiong, the eldest brother of Song Chai Xiong, my mother's brother in-law.

"*Nej twb los txog lawm lod*," an old woman said (she was later known as Mrs. Boua See Xiong), meaning, "You have arrived."

I wondered if she knew we were coming. Then I remembered, my father had been here just days ago.

"Yes, we are coming," my mother said with a slight smile. "I am afraid we will put a burden on you tonight."

We had lost everything. We only had what we carried on our backs.

"Come on in and feel at home," Aunt Boua See said, affirming they were not strangers. "Don't say that. You never put a burden on us. Your sister's family is our family."

The windowless house had a few logs burned faintly in the open fireplace in the middle of the smooth-dirt floor. There were no chairs, but plenty of little round and rectangular wooden stools, enough for us, and many more for everyone, to sit on. We put our loads down and were greeted by everyone in the house.

Like a good Hmong family, a lot of people were in the house, including two newly wed sons, Tong Pao and Cha, and their wives; one unmarried son, Ker; two young daughters, Der and Bao; and Uncle and Aunt Boua See.

In Hmong culture, grown-up and married children continue to live with their parents under the same roof. Families that are able to maintain harmony and live under the same roof for generations are widely praised by community members.

At nightfall, the only things that illuminated the house were pine sticks, split from blocks of fat pine wood. They were lit and placed on a metal rack hung on a wooden beam in the middle of the house. Although without windows, the loosely fit wooden-plank walls let plenty of air through to ventilate the smothering black smoke.

Since his grandpa, Song Leng, had settled in Namnya, this was my father's first long migration, repeating what his ancestors had done a century ago. The brief stay with Uncle Bouasy, although burdensome and chaotic, was filled with a warm spirit of reception of the long-separated distant cousin. We were warmly welcome. Perhaps no one had thought much about what would happen next as the war began to intensify and spread like a wildfire. Most would feel assured that they had the upper hand, for they had the Americans on their side.

My mother and the women talked and laughed loudly about their women issues as they cooked supper, although they did not prepare anything special. They only cooked plenty of sweet leaf soup and plain pumpkin soup. Sweet leaves were picked from trees in the woods, which grew soft stems and shiny leaves in the early dry season.

Sweet leaf soup had a sweetish and delicious taste, even without meat. This was our first time eating sweet leaf soup. Sweet-leaf trees were not found in the Hamkheu and Phou San regions.

Plain soup, especially pumpkin soup, has been, even to this day, the most respected dish in a Hmong family. The Hmong frequently say *pluas mov zaub tsuag,* meaning a meal of rice and plain soup. When there is nothing else to eat, a humbly served bowl of rice with a bowl of plain soup would make an appreciated meal.

The food was served on a small table, a bit bigger than a coffee table. The men ate first. Then the women ate. Each of the children was given a bowl of rice mixed in soup. They did not join the adults at the table.

It was around 9 p.m. by the time we finished supper. Most people in Hmong villages went to bed around this time, for they had to get up at the first cock crow in the morning. Everyone in Uncle Boua See's family was tired from the long-day work and we were exhausted from the long-day walk.

There was a bedroom for each of the married couples, including Uncle and Aunt Boua See. There was also a bedroom for Ker. Der and Bao slept with their parents. There was an open guest bed called *txaj qhuas*, large enough for four people, but there were too many of us.

My father and the other men talked loudly about what had happened in Hamkheu and Phou San and seemed unaware that it was bedtime. The women, including my mother, made beds with plaited mats on the floor along the back wall—an area where Hmong usually stock pig vegetation. Aunt Boua See took out brand-new green military blankets for us. They still contained the foreign smell that made us sick two years earlier. Tong Pao and Cha were soldiers at the outpost in Phou Vieng. They received blankets and other allowances in addition to their salaries of fifteen thousand kip or about two dollars a month.

"Grandma and four children can sleep on the guest bed," Aunt Boua See said.

"I want to sleep with Grandma," I said.

"Me too; I want to sleep with Grandma," Bee said.

Chao also wanted to sleep with Grandma. The rest slept on the floor.

The women were up early to prepare breakfast. We were awakened in the morning by the clanking noises of pots and pans. It was still dark outside, but the women had already made the fire and had started cooking for the big family and, especially, for us.

"You are up already," Aunt Boua See said in a soft voice. "It's still too early. Go back to sleep."

I could not go back to sleep. I got up and grabbed a round stool to sit near the fireplace. There was a kettle full of boiling water on a three-leg iron stand on the fireplace with steam and hot bubbles coming out of the spout. My mother put some boiling water in a big bowl and added some cold water.

"If you don't want to go back to sleep, then wash your face," she said.

I washed my hands and my face and returned to my stool. There was nothing to enjoy except for listening to the competing cocks' crows outside.

Everyone woke up and got up one by one. Everyone was up before daylight and soon the plaited mats and blankets on the floor were rolled up and put away. It was a very busy morning, especially for the women. Besides cooking for the people, they also prepared food for the pigs and brought water from a quarter mile away.

The men got up later. Instead of going out to bring in two or three loads of firewood or fire logs before breakfast as they usually had done, they stayed home and talked. It looked as if they never talked enough or maybe they just wanted to make us feel welcomed. It was the way Hmong treated their guests. Ker grabbed four or five big bundles of horse grass and chopped them for the horses.

Daylight soon came to reveal a clear day in early November. Streaks of smoke from the morning cooking fires lingered over the village.

"Kooroo kooroo kooroo kooroo—" They were the sounds of a woman calling her chickens at a nearby house.

It was the chicken and pig feeding time.

An old man, named Tong Ger, came to the door.

"*Los txog lawm los, Txawj!*" the man said loudly, meaning, "You have arrived, Cher!"

"*Aws, los txog lawm os,*" my father answered,

meaning, "Yes, we have arrived."

Another man arrived and joined the men who were already positioned in a circle. They argued if Tong Pao or my father was older. In a society where actual birth dates were not recorded, who was younger or older was only guessed based on physical looks.

"I am sure Cher is older," Uncle Tong Ger proclaimed.

The discussion then focused on our destination.

"It will take you almost a day to get to Keouvanh," Uncle Tong Ger said. "You will have to start early."

Keaouvanh was the village where Uncle Song Chai lived. I thought my father had told us that Uncle Song Chai lived in Phou Vieng and thought we had arrived. I was tired and didn't want to walk anymore, especially up and down on rough foot trails. It was even harder for Grandma and Uncle Pa Xiong, although walking was our expertise.

Breakfast was served. In Hmong culture, breakfast is a big meal for the hard work ahead. The men, again, ate first, especially when there were guests.

By the time breakfast was over, it was already late. Sunlight had already flooded most parts of the village. Most people had already left for their rice fields.

We gathered ourselves for the seemingly endless journey as we had done for the last three days. We had completely run out of food supplies. Aunt Boua See wrapped two big packs of rice in banana leaves. She also packed some pickled mustard greens sprinkled with ground chili pepper. It was the best they could provide for us. We had to arrive in Keouvanh before nightfall or we would have no food for supper.

We headed up toward the top of the village following a small trail badly eroded by rainwater. My father had already traveled on the trail days earlier, and he knew the way.

"*Mus nej ho tuaj xyuas peb nawb,*" meaning, "Come back to see us," Aunt Boua See called loudly behind us.

CHAPTER 4

A MOVE THAT CHANGED MY VIEW OF THE WORLD

I ran away to attend school and had to confront the cultural values to which education presented multiple fear factors.

Keouvanh was on a narrow plateau of a mountain ridge. The top of the ridge was about five hundred feet wide—just wide enough to build houses on both sides of the edges, leaving enough space for the path in between. The village was quite clean because the white sandy soil absorbed rainwater quickly, preventing the ground from being muddy and slippery, and the slopes on both sides provided good drainage.

Arriving at the northeast edge of the village, we walked past several houses on both sides of the path. We came upon a wood-shingle–roofed house whose barren surroundings were cleaner than those of others. A flat grassless ground was in front of the house, where it looked as if people had had frequent meetings.

"Is this the house?" my mother asked.

"This is his house," my father told everyone, pointing his finger. "This one right here, on our left, belongs to his eldest daughter, these, on our right, belong to his son-in-law's folks, and the rest over there belong to his cousins."

A MOVE THAT CHANGED MY VIEW OF THE WORLD

We had, finally, arrived at the village of Song Chai Xiong, the Phouvieng district chief who was my mother's brother in-law and whom my father had frequently spoken of. Uncle and Aunt Song Chai came out to greet us as if they had been expecting us.

We all crowded in the windowless, smooth, and well-packed dirt-floor house. It was late in the afternoon on a sunny day in November 1963. The war was intensifying in South Vietnam; President John Kennedy was assassinated in the United States; and Xieng Khouang province was engulfed by the fire of the Communists' invasion. The situation was as if the world was on fire.

The rice harvesting season had started in earnest. The village was quiet and empty because everyone was working harvesting rice in the fields a few miles away from home, mostly down the slopes of the ridge. Uncle and Aunt Song Chai had stayed home, expecting our arrival.

Cocks crowed sporadically everywhere in a seemingly peaceful Hmong village. After having walked for nearly four days, Keouvanh seemed far away from Hamkheu and Phou San—our homeland—which had become a human killing field. We felt a great relief and hoped we had moved away from the violent human killing storm and we would be there for a long-lasting settlement. In reality, Bouam Loung was not far away. We had simply walked along deep valleys and around high mountains of thick jungles.

Lt. Cherpao Moua had been informed of every moment of the Communists' movements. Our understanding of having moved far from danger to a peaceful land was only a false assumption. Our trail of fleeing the fire had simply moved to the north, slightly turned to the east, then to the west, and then back to the south. The trail had made almost a half circle loop—not far from where we started. Actually, Keouvanh was only hours walking distance from Ban Yai—a lowland Lao village not far from Song Hak Muong Kheung—where Capt. Kong Le, the head of the army of the Lao Neutralist, stationed his Soviet-supplied 130mm long-range artillery.

The Pathet Lao and North Vietnamese forces had begun to intensify their attacks on the Hmong forces like a raging fire and could soon reach Phou Vieng in a matter of days. Not realizing that Keouvanh was within a few days' walking distance from enemy territory and could soon be abandoned and become a flea-infested ghost village, we were in an upbeat spirit about life in the new village where we would no longer depend on airplane rice.

"Gong, gong, gong!" sounds of a shaman gong came from a distance.

"A shaman is performing ritual today?" my father asked.

"No, Brother Seng Ber Lee is making shaman gongs," Uncle Song Chai explained. "He is cognitively disabled, but very talented. He cuts out fuel barrel lids and makes gongs out of them. The Americans parachuted barrels of fuel in Phou Vieng for their helicopters. The empty barrels become very useful. We use them for water containers or cut them open for house wall panels."

These were new to us. In fact, Phou Vieng was not different from Bouam Loung in that its residents had been dependents of airplane rice a few years before we had.

Lunch was ready—nothing special—a bowl of rice, a dish of tree fungus and squash-vine–tip soup, and a

A MOVE THAT CHANGED MY VIEW OF THE WORLD

dish of plain pumpkin soup. There was plenty for everyone. Again, the men ate first, then the women.

While the women were eating, the men went outside. A dog came sniffing my father and Uncle Pa Xiong on the legs, his tail waving.

"Hma, go away!" Uncle Song Chai shouted.

Hma was his name, meaning "wolf."

"He and those two down there are good hunting dogs," Uncle Song Chai said, pointing to the other two dogs lying in the shade under the rice storehouse about thirty feet away.

Dog-deer hunting and guns had become the talking topics. There were a lot of deer down the mountain slopes and the men in Keouvanh had frequently conducted dog-deer hunting.

"Using dogs to chase deer," Uncle Song Chai said, "the men station at different points in the woods, waiting for the deer scared by dog chase to run toward them."

My father was very excited because this type of hunting was rarely practiced in Hamkheu. But he had no gun since he had hidden away his old French rifle in Hamkheu. Uncle Song Chai went back inside the house and quickly came back out with an automatic carbine rifle—a shorter gun, not as powerful as my father's old one. They had recently been distributed to the Hmong in Bouam Long and Phou Vieng by the Americans for them to use in the intensifying war.

Their service as soldiers in the US-funded Special Guerrilla Units (SGUs) was to prevent the North Vietnamese from taking over Laos and using its caves and jungles as ammunition depots for their takeover of South Vietnam. The Hmong in Phou Vieng and Keouvanh were not exempted.

These automatic rifles replaced the old French five-shot semiautomatic rifles. The Hmong had seen different types of guns in the different wars in Indochina. They had known the power of different gun models since the French's arrival in Laos. They frequently talked about the long three-shot rifles which were the most powerful guns received during the time of the French Maquis. My father had used the eight-shot semiautomatic rifles, called the M1—a different model provided by the United States. But he had never used a carbine automatic rifle. These powerful weapons had replaced the Hmong's old flintlock hunting guns and had changed their world.

"Cher, I am giving you this gun," Uncle Song Chai said. "It's automatic. The barrel holds fifteen shells and you can empty the whole barrel without manually retrieving the empty shells and reloading. It's very accurate. You can hit doves and squirrels on the top of a tree every shot." "You give it to me," my father said in disbelief, "you won't have a gun!"

"Oh, I have another one. We all have to have guns, even civilians."

My father held it in his hand and rubbed it gently. He held it up and aimed it a couple of times, pretending he was shooting, and wholeheartedly thanked Uncle Song Chai as he held it against his chest.

"It's beautiful! I can't wait to go hunting!"

"Yes, we can go tomorrow if you want."

At sunset, the villagers returned from work, each with a load of horse or pig feed on his or her back. Some walked with their horses behind them, carrying two baskets full of yams and golden pumpkins. As soon as they let down their loads, some women hurried down the slope following a trail toward a shallow well (the only well shared by the village residents) to get some water before dark. Others scooped buckets full of prepared food to feed their pigs. The horses had been grazing all day. They were given only a few pounds of corn or finely chopped pumpkin were left to rest in their stalls for the night.

Some women came to greet us and talk briefly. After supper, five men came over to talk. Everyone seemed to be aware of our arrival.

"Would anyone like to go deer hunting tomorrow?" Uncle Song Chai asked.

They all said they would be willing to suspend their rice harvesting for a day and go hunting. They had not done any hunting since the dry season started in the beginning of October.

The women would be glad to stay home for one day, for they had plenty of things to do. Having a day off from the dawn-to-dusk fieldwork would permit them to do laundry, mill rice and corn, sew clothes, and much more.

Having a brief opportunity before breakfast, Uncle Song Chai brought out a box that fit the description of the "singing box." He turned it on.

"This is Long Cheng Radio," a man spoke in Hmong in the box.

He continued giving news about government affairs in Vientiane and the Communists' movements and activities in the front lines in Xieng Khouang. After the news came the entertainment part in which men and women alternately sang Hmong folk songs. It reminded me of the woman who sang in the "singing box" which Vapao was talking about when he visited Bouam Loung a year earlier.

Listening to the news every morning, Uncle Song Chai might have been informed of what went on around the country, I thought. The Hmong part ended and the Thai Dam followed with their ethnic programming. Then other ethnic programming sessions followed in succession in the same order every day. There were Lao, Hmong, Thai Dam, Khmou, and Yao or Mien.

Not included in the Long Cheng ethnic radio programming schedule were the Chinese and Vietnamese, who were mostly merchants. Although counted as part of Laos's ethnically diverse population, they did not take part in fighting against the Communists' invasion. They lived largely in Vientiane and major towns far from the front lines, earning money through trades, despite a desperate need for men to defend the country.

The box was put away after the Hmong session ended. Everyone ate breakfast early as usual. The men met on the dirt-barren ground in front of the house. Two more men came to join. There were seven men and six dogs in all—plenty of dogs, although some men didn't have dogs. Uncle Song Chai laid out the logistics. Two men were assigned to hold the dogs once they were down the mountain slope until the five men were situated in their stations. My father was known to be a good shooter, so he was among the five and was given a good spot.

They started walking down the slope. Soon, five men were given orders to spread out and walk directly to their positions. Two men led the dogs down the slope—holding tight on their ropes until they estimated the five men had stationed in their positions. They let the dogs go and commanded them the way they had been trained. The dogs scattered, sniffed, and barked—

using their finest sense.

Ten minutes later, they spotted fresh deer tracks and started going after them. A young female ran toward my father. He shot it and broke one of its front legs. Before he knew, he had emptied the barrel—all fifteen shots. The dogs chased and killed the little deer. When the men arrived, the dogs had eaten half of one of the hind legs. The other man killed a buck. It was a success. When they came home, they talked and laughed about my father. It was the first time he had shot an automatic rifle.

"It just kept on going!" he said. "I couldn't stop it."

The men laughed again. They skinned the deer and divided the meat. In a war-ridden society, there were no wildlife conservation and protection laws. Therefore, hunting was limitless. The entire country was without laws and regulations of any kind.

December was approaching. Rice harvesting needed to be finished soon to have just enough time to prepare for the New Year celebration. Uncle Song Chai's house was unbelievably crowded with all of us living with him. More urgently, my mother was expecting a baby soon.

In Hmong cultural belief, Uncle Song Chai's unforgiving house spirits would not like a woman other than his wife and his sons' wives to have a childbirth in his house. Even his married daughters would be considered outsiders. And when they gave birth to children, they would not enter his house for at least thirty days.

While my mother was helping Uncle Song Chai on the rice harvesting, my father was preparing wood for building our house. The men in Keovanh also took time out of their busy work to help build a small school in Phou Houa Xang village—two miles to the southwest.

My father was not excluded. Uncle Pa Xiong was exempted, for he was disabled and could not do much, even to help himself. My parents had to help build a house for his family.

With the help from Uncle Song Chai and people in the village, a thatch-roofed house was built for Uncle Pa Xiong's family, and Grandma lived with them. In Hmong culture, parents never live with married daughters, unless they don't have sons. This, to this day, makes girls feel as if they were outsiders from birth.

Shortly thereafter, and with the help of everyone in the village, a small wood-shingle–roofed house was erected just in time for the New Year celebration. A few relatives of Uncle Song Chai had kindly contributed three chickens and some rice to my parents for the New Year celebration. It was the second year in which the New Year celebration was simply a spiritual tradition and not an event of happiness and enjoyment for our family as well as Uncle Pa Xiong's. In any case, we were grateful for the help and support from our new friends and relatives.

In the time that our family had virtually nothing, having three chickens for the New Year was a soul healing for everyone in the family. Two of the chickens were used for the soul-calling ritual. My grandmother would call the soul of everyone in the family that might have been lost, frightened, or saddened by the constant moves from one place to another to come home and enjoy the New Year celebration and the abundance of food. It was the time of happiness and love.

The third one was sacrificed to the spirit of the house altar for the blessing of fortune and prosperity. The meat of the other two chickens would be served as a feast for the New Year that everyone could enjoy. But the latter must be cooked and left by the altar for three days to be fully blessed. In a time when most children were deprived of meat and nutrition, they looked forward to this special occasion for good food.

On the third day, when there was nothing left, the blessed chicken was served. My two young sisters, Mee and Kia, were hoping to have a piece of the last chicken. My mother told them they couldn't eat it.

"Girls and outsiders cannot eat this chicken. It's for men, married women, and boys in the family only."

"Why, Mom?" I asked.

"Because girls will marry men outside the family. If they eat it, they will bring the fortune to outsiders."

"That's not fair!" I protested and started raising my voice. "Mom, they are your children, too! Why do you want your sons to be rich and your girls to be poor?"

"Son, it's not that we want the girls to be poor," Mom tried to explain. "Girls will have their fortune from their husbands' families. That's the culture and the tradition."

"Mom, they are your children! I don't think this is fair! This chicken is not going to make anybody rich without working hard to earn! Are the dogs that eat the bones . . . ? Are they going to be rich, too? I am not going to eat this chicken if the girls cannot eat it."

I started getting angry.

"Everybody can eat it," my father said.

Our family had broken the tradition. The curse was broken, thanks to my father.

My mother, who was a vulnerable woman, had taken the tradition without question as it had been practiced and passed on for generations.

"This is the way we have always done." I had heard my mother say these words all the time. "This is the Hmong way," my mom had said, even though some traditional practices had deprived her of choices and equality.

We have accepted tradition without questions and without exploring better ways. Sometimes it made me wonder. We had eaten so many blessed chickens, but continued to endure hardship.

After the New Year celebration, my mother gave birth to a boy. He was proudly named Chue. He became sick after ten days and died two days later. Without medical examinations, the illness was unknown. It could be caused by the stress my mother endured—moving constantly from place to place without adequate nutrition. Or he could have suffered from a common early-childhood disease which had affected and killed countless young children in Laos. But, leaders of the country paid no attention to this issue. The war was the only thing on everyone's mind.

The loss of the baby had caused tremendous emotional distress for all of us, especially for my mother. When I went with her to Uncle Song Chai's rice field to pick sweet potato leaves for our only pig nearly a month later, she mourned the baby and started wailing loudly. Not knowing what to say to comfort her, I sadly watched her cry. My parents' mourns of the tragic loss of Chue in conjunction with the loss of everything had a profound effect on us. It was a dark and depressing moment for my family.

The unforgiving clock had ticked at every breath toward a new slash-and-burn season. Although my father had not shown a smile since the loss of my brother, he had gone to look for a good piece of woodland not far from home which was good for both rice and corn fields. The clearing process was begun without delay.

We finished the clearing process. The next process was cutting down big trees. Sometimes, just my father and I went to the newly cleared field to cut down big trees. Only men could do this part. Using a heavy Hmong ax, he cut down a big tree as I stood nearby, watching.

He paused occasionally and sighed heavily to recoup his breath. He was tired. He did not feel well or still had not recovered from grief, I could tell. I wished I could help him, but I couldn't. Some men had big sons, and they helped each other.

In April, just as the villagers completed burning all the newly opened fields, the brand new wood-shingle–roofed school was complete—a joint effort and partnership of the people in Phou Houa Xang and Keouvanh. Benches made of long, hewed wooden planks were planted in rows on the dirt floor. Each seat was long enough to seat four students.

All school-age children were enrolled in the school, except for girls and eldest boys like me. I was kept at home because I was the eldest child in my family and was needed to stay home to help my parents. Girls were kept from attending school for the same reason, eldest or youngest. In a culture where luck and fortune were largely measured by a house full of children, eldest boys and all girls bore the sacrifice of keeping the families from being hungry.

Every morning, just as the other children left for school, I went to the freshly burned rice field with my parents. I glanced at them several times until they disappeared around the corner. They talked and laughed and seemed to have a lot of fun.

We came back from the field in the evening at the same time the children returned from school, talking, laughing, and teasing each other, the way kids always do. Three of those kids were Uncle Song Chai's nephews who lived just next door. I visited them after supper. Three boys, ages from six to nine, were sitting around the fireplace whose flame burned faintly—providing the only light that dimly illuminated the house. They all were on the very beginning page and none could read. The boys' father, Uncle Xia Foung, Uncle Song Chai's cousin, watched them proudly. I stood behind one of the boys, curious to see what they held in their hands.

"Why didn't you go to school?" he asked loudly. "Look at them, they are reading."

I stood and watched them quietly for about fifteen minutes as they flipped the pages without reading. I went back home and went to bed with a lot of questions. What is school? What was in the books that the three boys were reading? Why can't I go to school? I went back to the rice field with my parents and watched the other kids go to school as usual. I wanted to see what a school looked like.

A few days later I planned to go with the kids to see the school. I knew if I asked my parents for permission, I would, for sure, be disappointed. That morning the children left for school before my parents left for the rice field, providing me with a good opportunity to sneak out. I just joined them and lied to them that my parents had let me go to school.

"My parents let me go to school now," I said.

The children were happy. We danced and we ran. I

A MOVE THAT CHANGED MY VIEW OF THE WORLD

knew I had lied, feeling a bit guilty.

Soon we were more than a half mile away from home. My parents found out I was missing just minutes after the children left for school. They knew I had gone to school with them, but did not try to come after me and bring me back. In the evening when my parents came back from the rice field, I came home with the children. I told my mother I had enrolled myself for school.

My mother was not happy as she paused and gave me a long look.

"Son, if you go to school, who will help me and your dad on the rice field?" she asked with a stressed voice. "The other children have their older brothers and sisters helping their parents. You are our eldest son, we really need your help or we will not have rice to eat."

I was disappointed, but could not argue. I stood quietly for five minutes. My heart sank heavily, not knowing what to say. There were more than a thousand things going through my mind. Questions were popping up in my head for a few hours before I finally fell asleep. Why do the eldest boys have to do everything for the younger ones? Why can't girls go to school? Is it because girls have to stay home to do everything, too? Is going to school a bad thing? Is school only for the younger boys in the families?

The next day my father went with me to school to talk to the teacher and to withdraw me. We left home long after the other children were gone. We arrived at the school while the teacher was teaching reading. He wrote a page in the book on the blackboard. He read the consonants and vowels separately, then the combinations that made the sounds of words. The children repeated after him. Some of the children looked sad as if they had just stopped crying.

The teacher stopped abruptly to greet my father as we stopped at the door, then turned briefly to the students sitting in the front row and asked them to go, following in order one by one, to the blackboard to read.

Sitting behind his bench and not mentioning why I was late, he said to my father, "Brother, you are one of the few lucky parents."

He pointed at me while I attentively watched the children read.

"Look at his big eyes staring at the blackboard."

After listening calmly, my father said, "I am coming today to let you know that we want our boy to stay home to help us watch our younger children. We would like him to come to school, but since he is the oldest, we need him very badly."

The teacher looked a little unhappy and said:

"Brother, I understand your situation, but let me explain to you. There are a lot of good men like you and my father who work hard on rice fields to feed their families. There are men like me who are lucky to have some education who also work hard to feed their families using knowledge. And there are some men who are luckier than I am and have more knowledge than I do who are able to raise better families than I. Your son is making the choice of which of the type of men he wants to be. Every kid in this room is making his choice of what he wants to do in his future. Some of those kids have just stopped crying because they don't like school. Parents are important in helping their children make the right choice—especially at this young age. I strongly recommend that you not pull him out."

My father stammered, trying to explain his reason

further, but did not finish his sentence. He hesitantly agreed to let me stay.

"But we did not prepare lunch for him today," he said.

"Yesterday the kids happily shared their lunch with him," the teacher assured. "You don't need to worry about that."

He called a student sitting in the third row.

"Lee, do you have enough lunch to share with Ge?"

"Yes," the boy said.

The teacher turned to my father and assured him.

"See. No problem!"

My father reluctantly extended his hand and shook hands with the teacher. He walked out the door and down the straight path under tall pine trees toward the path that linked Phou Houa Xang and Keouvanh. He looked back and seemed sad. I felt both happy and sad, thinking I would no longer be able to help him on the rice field, except for weekends.

I came home in the evening. My grandmother, who loved me so dearly, carried me on her back from Namnya to Phou San, and visited me every two weeks in Namnya, was in the house. She hugged me and gave me a long talk.

"My son is going to school to be a town boy, sitting in the town far away and leaving Grandma behind, huh? No . . . My son, I want you to be like my son, Yapao."

She referred to the eldest son of my mother's second-eldest half-sister, who was about eighteen and had already been married.

"Yapao is a good boy. Every morning he brought home a load of horse grass before breakfast," Grandma added. "I am so proud of him. I want you to be like him.

He fixes the roof, cuts fire logs, and arrives at the rice field before his parents."

Grandma tried to explain the characters of many good men she knew in her world. In her perception, a man with an education would keep his hands off dirty work; would not help his parents fix the roof; would not believe in his parents' spiritual practices; would not raise hardworking children; and would be forever separated from his parents. Education has presented many fear factors to Hmong parents, even to these days of modern times.

Grandma had acknowledged that education would bring people to live in town. But, it was for rich people; it was for people in the upper class who were leaders, and it was not for us.

Listening quietly to Grandma's counseling, I sternly adhered to my decision. The next day, I got up and prepared my lunch for another day of school. Grandma finally stopped counseling me, but called me "my town boy" and continued calling me that ever since.

I was glad about the move that I had made which changed my view of the world. I believed then and still do, to this day, that good education provides the skills for successful pursuits of careers that match individuals' strengths and interests.

My reading had progressed extraordinarily well. Within a month I had turned and read a lot of pages. I had nearly finished the book while the other kids struggled with the first few pages.

Everyone talked about how well I did in school. My mother became proud of me. In a society where people believed in spirits and reincarnations, my mother believed, perhaps, I still remembered almost everything I had learned in my past life.

My mother thought my rapid progress in school was attributed to something good that I had done in my past life—a notion widely believed in Animism, Buddhism, and a lot of other religions. She blamed her hardship as a Hmong woman on something bad she might have done in her past life. She blamed the injustices in her society on her own sins. She believed she had sinned in her past life, and that's why she was born to be a Hmong woman. Girls are not as lucky as boys because of their sins from their past lives.

When she talked about her life, her explanation and solution were simple.

"God gave me a bad map of life—a cursed paper for this life. When I die, I will remember to appeal to God for a better paper for my next life."

I did not accept the belief of luck as an inescapable path of life. I had taken the choice that had changed my view of the world and taught me to believe that human potential cannot be predetermined by sex or race or being rich or poor, but it can be explored through equal opportunities. And that success, to a large degree, is attributed to efforts, not luck or anything done in anyone's past life. Therefore, the world of learning has no boundaries, if everyone were given the same opportunities.

I thank my parents for giving me the opportunity, but still feel sad for my sisters who have been confined in the traditional boundaries. I thank the teacher who saw my potential and convinced my father to let me stay in school. I had been given the opportunity to see the world from outside the boundaries. Otherwise, I would have grown to become a man blinded by traditional boundaries.

The school was small and only taught beginning-level first grade, which I nearly finished within two months. The teacher said if I continued learning at that rate, I would be sent to Phou Vieng in the next school year. This news had affirmed my grandmother's fear that I would be going away. My progress became a concern to my parents. Phou Vieng was only ten miles from Keouvanh. However, in my parents' view, it was a long distance which extended past the visible horizon. At eleven, my parents believed I was too young to be away from home.

Besides, I had never been away from my parents for any period longer than ten days. Well, I had stayed with my great-grandmother in Namnya for two weeks in a row or longer when my parents went to the opium farm in Phou San. But, that was with my great-grandmother. Staying with someone in Phou Vieng whom I had never known was something completely different, my parents would say. Thus, the good news became bad news for my parents.

Many days had quickly passed by and the school year would end within two weeks. The monsoon season had begun and, as nature had programmed, the monsoon rains had increasingly intensified. The teacher had been thinking about whether we needed to have an out-of-school potluck lunch or some sort on the last day of school.

During Tuesday morning recess in early June, three T-28 bombers flew low across the sky and disappeared over the treetops. As we gazed at the horizon, hoping the planes would reappear, the empty brass-cannon mortar-shell bell rang. Everyone went back to class as usual.

A MOVE THAT CHANGED MY VIEW OF THE WORLD

A parent wearing black Hmong clothes—the village chief—came to the school and talked to the teacher. The loud conversation was in Hmong and heard across the classroom. Everyone understood it clearly, for the student population was entirely Hmong, although the instructions and curriculum were strictly in Laotian language. It was a mandate from the Ministry of Education, requiring no other ethnic language be spoken while in school.

The man spoke, gasping for his breath.

"Teacher, the situation in our country is hot now," he said. "Laotian villages around Muong Seng and Ban Yai areas are now flooded with Pathet Lao and North Vietnamese forces. Our village will be overrun in a few days. We received orders from Phou Vieng to evacuate to Phoukoum, across the Nam Khanh River. People in our village are in the process of packing and we plan to evacuate tomorrow; some are leaving today."

The teacher looked obviously dismayed as he listened.

"You have just built this school and we have just been in school for over a month," he said. "I have so much hope for your children. I have a feeling that we may not come back to this school again."

He thanked the man for their support of him since the beginning of the school. The man looked obviously sad as he left the school in a hurry.

The teacher turned to the class and spoke, surprisingly, in Hmong:

"Today is our last day of school. Do not come to school tomorrow. Your parents may have already known this situation. I will see you in Phoukoum. You will go to school there."

The class was immediately dismissed. We all left the tiny and newly built school. The playground, under tall and whistling pine trees, was still fresh and covered with thick and brown needle leaves—the place that had changed my life forever, which I vividly remember until this day.

Map of Laos 1975

A MOVE THAT CHANGED MY VIEW OF THE WORLD

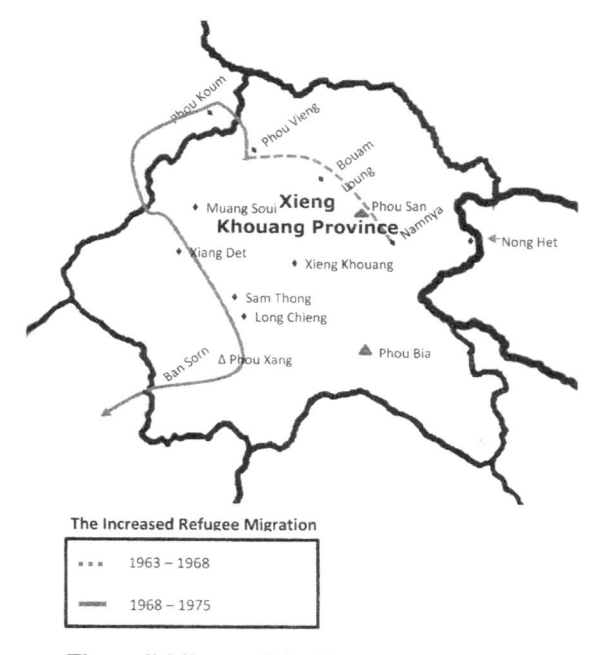

The Increased Refugee Migration

- ▪▪▪ 1963 – 1968
- ▬▬ 1968 – 1975

The solid line trail indicates a massive increase in refugee movement.

CHAPTER 5

FLEEING THE HUMAN KILLING STORM

The war not only escalated like a raging fire and outpaced our run, but also tripled the number of refugees running for their lives and enduring unimaginable suffering.

It was an afternoon in early June 1964. None of the people in Keouvanh went to work in their rice fields. There was a big crowd standing in front of Uncle Song Chai's house, talking about the unexpected development of the situation.

The Red Lao and North Vietnamese forces had occupied Ban Yai—stunning news. Some men from Phou Vieng had just gone to Ban Yai fewer than two months ago. Everything was normal then.

"I hope this is a temporary evacuation," a man, who was a relative of Brother Seng Ber, said. "The good thing is we have the help from the sky," he added, referring to the T-28s seen briefly flying over the horizon and the Americans who had wings.

"How long are we going to be gone?" my father asked. "If we are to be gone for three months, when we return, our fields will be covered with weeds and brushes. This is the third loss for me."

"We may not return to this village again," Uncle

Song Chai said in a commanding voice, because he knew the situation from listening to the radio newscast. "We have to evacuate by noon tomorrow. Kill all the chickens and small pigs and deep fry them for extended preservation. Let's do what we need to do now to prepare for evacuation."

The men returned to their homes to pack what they could bring with them. In a chaotic scene, they called their pigs and chickens and caught as many as they could. There was no time to catch and kill big animals.

My parents and Uncle Pa Xiong, the two new families, had been refugees for almost two years and had lost everything. As newly settled residents, we had one small pig and half a dozen small chickens, and ourselves, still alive.

After having lost everything, there was nothing more to lose, except for the rice and corn fields on which they had worked so hard in the spirit of hope that everything was going to be okay. It was unthinkable that the destructive human killing storm from which we had run away would catch up with us so soon.

The village was noisy and lively as if everyone was preparing for the long-awaited New Year celebration, but there was no invitation for a thankful meal. Bamboo-woven back baskets were filled up and strapped as securely as they could be. Fresh giant bamboo tubes were cut and stuffed with deep fried meat for the unknown and goalless journey. It was the first time for most of the people in Phou Vieng region to become refugees, although they had tasted airplane rice—since the airstrip was built—two years before we had.

Horse baskets were also filled to the maximum, even though the load bearers did not have a clue about what the human situation was. Red was waiting to accept his load without question and take the journey as he was guided. By noon the next day, the village would be empty and quiet.

Every day, as was their way of life since they settled in Keouvanh more than a decade ago, the residents returned home before nightfall to illuminate their houses. This time, when darkness took over, the village would be dark, quiet, and cold. The remaining animals would wonder what had happened to their not so friendly companions who fed them every day. Some said good-bye to their left-behind pigs, dogs, and chickens with teary eyes. We had done the same when we left Hamkheu more than a year earlier.

Uncle Pa Xiong, who had endured a physical disability since childhood and had nothing much to pack, started the journey before everyone—following the same trail toward the same direction we came from almost exactly six months earlier. This time we would go past Phou Vieng toward a destination we had never been.

Down the slope, at the bottom of the Keouvanh Mountain, the residents of a peaceful lowland Lao village—where we had come to join their Buddhist holiday celebration a month earlier—did not panic and lived peacefully, as if the world was perfectly fine. The storm only affected the Hmong, because we had made our choice of which side of the war we would be on, while they took no position. They might have been forced later to serve in the Pathet Lao forces, more likely fighting against the Hmong.

The trail followed the crystal clear Nam Hang River—crossing several curves and loops. Walking in the water on slippery rocks, we had been soaked and wet up to our thighs or higher for children before the trail started climbing up the slope of Phou Dou Noy Mountain. We were back into Uncle Boua See's house again before dark. This time they were not welcoming us; they were preparing to leave as well.

This time we did not eat sweet-leaf soup, we ate feet, heads, and toes of chickens and ducks—not as a welcoming feast, but as part of finishing up what they had before leaving their home. They, too, would lose everything just like we did. This time we all would go to no one's house, but temporary grass lean-tos or parachute tents, at best.

By dawn, we were up and ready to set out on the trail. We were not their guests. We would all become refugees going together toward an unknown destination where no one would welcome us and where we might be competing for food if there was not enough for everyone.

Nothing was unpacked the night before. Everything was ready. Red was given the grass that he had carried on top of his load. The good horse quietly accepted his load and followed us for as long as we kept on walking.

We arrived at the top of Phou Vieng village, a red-dirt, barren ridge where houses were built on both sides, leaving the middle clear straight down toward the dirt airstrip. The house of Uncle Song Chai's eldest son, Neng, a third-grade teacher, was on the left. Uncle Song Chai's thatch house in which he had frequently stayed when he came to visit or on his job mission was down below next to Neng's. His family would stay there for another night. People greeted him warmly, calling him *Tasseng* or "district chief."

He invited us to stay, but we needed to move on, for there was a lot of commotion and everyone needed to go sooner or later anyway. We traveled past all the houses and toward the airstrip. The smell of airplanes and airplane fuel was fresh, and the power of Americans was obvious. The world's most powerful superpower from the sky was on our side. Why do we need to flee? Can the Americans do anything? These questions went through my mind as I walked through the long, flat, and straight unpaved airfield.

As we walked past the airstrip, the trail was narrow and human walking traffic was heavy. Some people carried heavy loads on their backs; some were piled up higher than their heads. The grass-overgrown trail, which ran past the dirt-mound cemetery on the left, became slippery due to the monsoon rains and unusually heavy traffic. A weary old man, carrying only a tightly rolled striped blanket hung from his shoulders with a dark pink waist sash, sat by the trail to replenish his breath. A partially naked two-year-old boy sat on his dad's neck with both feet dangling without shoes.

After about five miles of up-and-down and slow-pace walk, we reached the Nam Khanh River, which flowed west toward the Royal city of Luang Phrabang where it joined the Mekong River.

There was a peaceful lowland Lao village with houses on both sides of the riverbank. The river had already swelled up due to monsoon rains and could only be crossed by rowboats, ferrying only four or five at a time. There were three boats going back and forth and the line was long—a once-in-a-lifetime and unprecedented opportunity for the boat owners. For the passengers, it was a life and death situation. They were all Hmong, not only from the six villages in the Phou Vieng region, but also from other villages in Bouam Loung, Keou Leuk, and Phou Vei regions, who came to meet unexpectedly at the river.

"Hold on tight, boy!" a mother yelled at her five-year-old boy as half of her family climbed on the wobbling canoe-shaped boat.

Again, the residents of this lowland village obviously had nothing to panic about. It was all a Hmong problem—not theirs. They had lived peacefully in their natural way of life with rice paddy cultivation and fishing along the abundant river for generations. Their houses were built on bamboo woven platforms supported by large hardwood posts and with thick layers of thatched-grass or chopped-bamboo–shingle roofs. These were structures built to last, which indicated a stable and permanent settlement. Their paths were large for cattle wagons.

At the edge of the village where the trail led to Phoukoum, there was a clean and well maintained Buddhist temple from which monks in their yellow garments stared at us, wondering what was happening to the "Meo." Not very far beyond, a clear and slow-moving creek flowed toward the large river. In the knee-deep water, Hmong men and women, partially naked, bathed vigorously, for they had been walking on rough trails, not having time to bathe for days. Human voices and sounds of babies' cries echoed through the valley. Yet, what loomed ahead was not known.

It was only late in the afternoon, but we realized we would not reach Phoukoum village, near the summit of the four-thousand-foot-high mountain, by nightfall. We decided to rest for the night. The children innocently had fun splashing and bathing in the shallow water. Fire smoke blurred the views of arching bamboo tops in the flat-valley bottom—a flawless beauty of nature.

Everyone was up early and ate breakfast quickly. We had been informed that the trail up to Phoukoum village was steep and without water until near the summit. We had to set out early and bring plenty of water. Some people had already started moving.

"Hurry, we need to get moving," my father said softly in a near-whispering voice—it was a phrase heard too many times since we left Hamkheu. "When the sun is up, it's going to be hot to climb up the hills."

There were many unfamiliar faces in the crowded camp. But the adults talked as if they had known each other well.

"Hello, you are coming, too," an old man said to another middle-aged man.

"Yes, don't know when the life of being displaced by war is going to end," the man replied.

"Where are you from?" the old man asked.

"Oh, we are from Phou Vei," the man said.

"Nice meeting you," the old man said as he hurried to catch up with his family.

In Hmong culture, we usually don't introduce ourselves by name, unless asked for it. The situation was hectic and there was no time to ask for names. The people were moving in commotion. Some looked around and called to make sure no child was left behind. Others looked around to make sure nothing was lost or forgotten.

The trail led up the hill in gradual steepness through thick, brushy, and chalky bamboo groves. The soil was dry, even in the monsoon season. Grass on the rocky hill struggled to grow, distinguishable by their brown leaves and the spotty, barren ground.

Up to the higher elevation—halfway to the summit—the vegetation started to become greener with taller trees. The soil became richer as evidenced by patchy rice fields along the sides of the trail. It was a sign indicating a Hmong village was near—maybe up on the top of the hill.

Is this the natural place the Hmong choose to live? Or is there another reason for the choice of this place? Was it true the Hmong chose to dwell on the mountains because they love cooler climate? Many questions had run through my mind, searching for answers, as I traveled on these hills.

There was a two-level plateau near the summit of Phoukoum. The steep trail led us toward the lower plateau on the east where there were about ten houses. A steep and rocky trail slightly turned to the left, past a thatch house on the right, and linked between the lower and the upper plateaus.

The upper plateau's features consisted of about twenty houses, a church, a school, an airstrip, a medical house, and an air guide system with a generator. Areas around the airstrip, the medical house, and the generator house, including the rice airdrop area, were well maintained—bushes were neatly cut by the residents as part of their undeniable responsibilities.

The new refugees settled on the outskirts of the existing village and around the airstrip. We walked past the village, the airstrip, the rice airdrop area, and the medical house toward a newly opened area where giant trees were freshly cut down on top of thick underbrush.

It was 3 p.m. Using knives, slashing sickles, and

axes, we cut branches, vines, and briar bushes, and cleared the floors with garden hoes to make lean-tos and parachute tents. Human talks, shouts, babies' cries, and kids' laughter echoed through the jungle.

"I've told you not to climb too high!" a mother said loudly following loud cries of a boy. Then laughter and soothing phrases of comforts followed.

"Stop crying. You'll be okay."

We ate rice and deep fried meat brought from Keauvanh for supper, and we ate it conservatively for the next few days, not knowing what we would eat for the days and weeks after that.

The refugee population not only outnumbered the existing residents but also swelled in an unprecedented magnitude. People lined up to get drinking and bathing water from shallow wells dug by the village residents.

The first airdrop of rice had been delivered on the second day of our arrival, meaning Mr. Edgar "Pop" Buell—known as Mr. Pop, a highly respected and fatherly figure American who oversaw the refugee relief program—had been aware of the situation.

Life had already become unimaginably bad within the first few days. Overcrowding, sickness, human waste without proper sanitation, and lack of food and water were only the least of our problems. There were too many people to be sustained by the local natural resources. The wild bamboo and edible plants on surrounding hills could not produce enough shoots and roots for the sudden influx of the refugee population. Young children and pregnant women suffered from malnutrition, resulting in an unprecedented rate of death. Each day one or two dirt-piled graves were added to the growing dirt-grave cemetery. Funeral drums sounded angrily in all directions in combination with sounds of men and women wailing.

The tragic events were beyond what the isolated medic could do. His job was simply to distribute basic medication such as aspirin, quinine, and cough medicine to the refugees. The only option to escape death was to spread out, allowing space and good air to help heal some of the illnesses.

Uncle Pa Xiong's only son, Chao, was critically sick. His mouth was open; his eyes were closed; his breath was heavy; and his chest was up and down. Uncle and Aunt Pa Xiong wailed loudly—a sad and terrifying moment for us. As children, we helplessly clung to each other and watched with teary eyes. He died the next day. At eight, he was a smart and good-looking boy. It was a tremendous loss for all of us. I was also sick and coughing heavily. I feared that I, too, was going to die. At night I had a fever and huddled tightly next to my grandmother, listening to voices of men and women wailing, funeral drum beats, and sad ceremonial melodies played in Hmong *qeej* (Hmong bamboo-pipe instrument) throughout the night.

We moved to the grassy gentle slope on the northeast side of the village, a mile from the airstrip and near the summit where we shared the same well with the lower village residents. Nearly half of the people from Phou Vieng built temporary thatch huts along a trail, not knowing how long we would be living there.

The summit, which exposed its hanging orange round-rock cliff toward us, was clearly visible like a face, about a half mile up. It was during the months in which schools were closed. All school-age children took their family horses to the coarse-grass field near the summit. The sudden increased number of horses had grazed the tough grass neatly down to its roots, exposing the mountain slope up to the hanging cliff.

"When you boys take your horses out every day, you should not go up to the summit," Uncle Boua See warned.

"Why, Uncle?" one of the boys asked.

"No one dares going up there because there was a legend saying that it was the dwelling of a powerful spirit."

I had been curious about what was it like on the top of the summit, but did not dare going up there, for it looked scary. The Hmong, who believed in spirits, took Uncle Boua See's warning seriously. No more questions were asked, and there was no encouragement for exploration. It was a place one should not go near because legend said so.

Rice airdrops came on a weekly schedule. When a silvery C-47 Dakota cargo plane arrived, hovering in the sky above the hills, the refugees hurried toward the airstrip with their bamboo-back baskets bouncing on their backs. Airplane rice, brought from Thailand and paid for by people halfway around the globe, was the only thing that kept them alive. Without it, they would all starve and die.

Local leaders would make sure they were the first to arrive at the site to make sure no rice was taken prior to distribution. Airdropped rice was counted by pallets as they were dropped and inventory was taken immediately to ensure every sack was accounted for before distribution was calculated.

The distribution was calculated by the number of sacks per village based upon the per-person-ration formula. Chiefs or representatives of villages had a handwritten list of every family in their respective jurisdiction, including numbers of family members of each family, and were responsible for distributing rice to members of their respective groups.

Sometimes one or two sacks of salt were airdropped, which would be measured and distributed by cups per family. The refugees were responsible for finding everything else to eat with their rice. There had been a few deliveries of canned meat and noodles by small porter planes.

Because younger men and teenage boys served as soldiers, stationing in outposts along the front lines or staying behind to guard outposts in their home villages, the refugees were largely women, old men, and children, with more than 98 percent illiterate. Teachers were instrumental in helping calculate rice and salt distribution.

The three-classroom school was increased to seven classrooms, ranging from first to fourth grades. Because educated men consisted of a small fraction of the population, young men with only third to fifth-grade education were recruited to become volunteer teachers, paid by USAID.

In late August, orders came from Bouam Loung announcing that all refugees may return to their villages. By early September, nearly all refugees returned home, crossing the Nam Khanh River once again, but leaving some of their older children in Phoukoum to attend school, which began September 1.

Uncle Pa Xiong, still grieving the loss of his only son, moved back to join his eldest brother, Uncle KaThai, in Bouam Mou village, where the residents did not follow the evacuation orders. Grandma returned with him. We moved to a different settlement on a plateau in the lower elevation—a mile east of the airstrip—to live in a larger thatch house left by some refugees who returned to Phou Vei. Five other families moved with us, including four of Uncle Song Chai's brothers and cousins from Keouvanh and Phou Dou Noy who decided not to return. Uncle Song Chai returned to Phou Vieng, leaving behind in Phoukoum his eldest son, Neng—the third-grade teacher—his twelve-year-old second son, Xao, and his second son-in-law, Houa Lee—also a teacher.

The new location seemed quieter and more peaceful. There was a clear spring creek coming out of the foothill, just three hundred feet away. Suddenly, a family of the Xiong clan—a father, a boy, and three girls, one of whom was critically sick—moved in and settled in a small lean-to erected between our house and the spring creek. The man, known as Uncle Cha Thao, had lost his wife and one child within a week.

Uncle Cha Thao, a shaman, performed his rituals using all his spiritual power and banging his shaman gong almost constantly for three days. Shamanism is a widely practiced and highly respected spiritual tradition in Hmong society. Uncle Cha Thao had done all he could, but he could not save his daughter. She died. He had lost three people within a short time.

Suffering unbearable grief, he threw away his shaman tools in anguish, abandoned his dead daughter's body for my parents and other families to bury, and moved to join the Christian church near the airstrip.

Most people had returned home, leaving behind only their older children to attend school. The health crisis had subsided. September had nearly passed and the school had already started, later than usual. Lee, who shared lunch with me at school in Phou Houa Xang, and his older brother, Lo—a third grader—had been going to school for three days. My parents had not said anything to me about school.

Neng, the school teacher who was also my cousin, came down looking for me on Tuesday evening.

"Aunt Xee, I have not seen Ge in school!" he said loudly. "What happened to him? Why has he not been in school?"

"Oh, we didn't know anything about school," my mother said.

"He should start tomorrow. Don't worry, just send him to school and I will take care of everything."

I was so happy. I washed my hands and cut and cleaned my nails, because teachers routinely checked students' hands and nails. I ate a ball of warm sticky rice for breakfast; I had been ready since dawn that morning, waiting for my father. We walked up the hill toward the school, which was only a quarter of a mile before the airstrip. Neng was waiting for us at the front of the school.

"Do you have a notebook and pencil?" he asked.

"No, not yet," my father said.

We went to the house of Dang Moua, the head teacher, where his wife had a small shop of candies and school supplies. Neng picked up a notebook and two pencils.

"How much?"

"One hundred fifty kip," Mrs. Moua said.

Neng handed her 150 kip. My father gave him 150 kip in return. He didn't take it.

"Don't worry. It's taken care of," he said.

My father thanked him for the book and pencils. He returned home and let Neng take care of me.

"Let's go," Neng said.

I followed him to the school. He led me to the first classroom at the end of the long thatch-roofed school building. The name of the beginning-level first-grade teacher was Vang of the Lee clan—a slim-built twenty-three-year-old man. He endured a slight limp as he walked.

"Lee Vang, here is a new student," Neng introduced in Laotian language. "His name is Ge Xiong. He is my aunt's son."

The teacher, Mr. Lee, took me in and seated me with three other students in the second-last row near the back wall. He wrote down my name. There was no registration form to fill out and no question asked about birth date or age. Those were not important. In a society of oral tradition, parents wouldn't be expected to know their children's birth dates. But some smaller students would be asked to use their right hand to reach over the top of their head and touch their left ear. This was a way largely used to measure if a child was at least six years old.

Searching and reconstructing my birth date was one of the most laborious inquiries in my life. It was a society where everything was simple without complicated reasons and purposes. Everyone was born, grew up, grew old, and died. That's the way of nature.

The classroom was packed with students, ages ranging from as young as six to as old as sixteen. At eleven, I was small for my age. There were four big boys, whose ages were between fourteen and sixteen, sitting in the last row, behind me. They were bullies and mean. They talked and laughed all the time. They hit me and those who sat in the same row with me on the head with their knuckles three or four times a day. When we turned around to see who did it, they laughed and acted as if they had done nothing. They hit us again for violating the classroom rule. Our days of school were filled with miseries.

At reading time, the four bully boys silently stood at the blackboard, unable to read. The teacher, who only completed third grade and had no teaching training, used harsh punishment by having the students who could read hit on the heads of those who could not. He had me hit nearly half of the class every time, including the big boys. They threatened to beat me up when I was alone somewhere.

Fearing for my safety, I told my mother about the boys. She told Neng. He was concerned, and he talked to the head teacher about my progress, and I was immediately promoted to the advanced level class, only after being in school for a month.

I was promoted to second grade at the beginning of the 1964–65 school year and promoted again to third grade after only three months into the school year because the teacher who only completed fifth grade could not keep up with me on mathematics. I was able to solve multiple-digit long division problems. I caught up with some students who were in third grade when I started first grade. I passed the transitional exam to enter fourth grade at the end of the school year, ranking number four. While some of my third-grade classmates were retained for failing the exam, I went on to fourth grade, leaving them behind.

In early 1966, right after the New Year celebration,

daily morning news from the Long Chieng Radio announced critical situations in the front lines. Nakhang, which was Gen. Vang Pao's most forward post, in Sam Neua province, was under heavy Vietnamese and Pathet Lao attacks. News came from Phou Vieng saying that Gen. Vang Pao was wounded and Nakhang had fallen to the hands of the Communists. Hmong residents throughout the region were alarmed by the Communists' advances.

A soldier who had returned from Nakhang shared frightening stories about the North Vietnamese's new deadly weapon, B40 cannons. He also talked about the Hmong's new battle tactic to minimize casualties.

"We could not use our guns in the fight," the soldier said. "Whoever used a gun that showed sparks on the gun tip would be dead instantly by the enemies' B40. All soldiers were ordered to only throw hand grenades. Guns were used in a close encounter situation only."

From then on, all outposts throughout Vang Pao's Military Region II were supplied with plenty of hand grenades. Trench complexes, zigzagging throughout every post, were filled with cases of the metal balls of explosives. The North Vietnamese, who suffered heavy casualties from the new war tactic, protested that there were American military personnel in Laos. They claimed that the primitive (Meo) Hmong soldiers would not have known how to use such a tactical counterattack and that they must have received training from their foreign boss—the imperialist Americans.

My parents and two of Uncle Song Chai's cousins were the last families to return to Phou Vieng. They moved in early February to start the slash-and-burn farming cycle, leaving behind Lao and me to stay with

Neng and his wife. There were five of us—all teenage boys—living with Neng. We all depended on airplane rice.

In the beginning of the monsoon season, Gen. Vang Pao—with his arm still supported by a sling hung from his shoulder—walked past the school ground several times a day with his accompanying radioman and officers, commanding the operation from Phoukoum to retake Nakhang. Lacking local facilities to accommodate his team, the Christian church was offered for his stay. They slept on green stretchers lined up in rows across the packed dirt floor.

At the airstrip, green American helicopters and big Chinooks were on standby to rescue American pilots shot down on the Lao-Vietnam border. Barrels of aircraft fuel were parachuted, providing more water containers to the locals. Aircraft fuel barrels left in abundance by the airstrip were extremely dangerous.

A Hmong man, who lived between the school and the airstrip, rolled a barrel full of fuel into his house. While he poured the gaseous fuel from a small container to fill up his lamp one afternoon, it caught fire at twenty feet from his fireplace and burned his thatch house in flame. While the teachers and students rushed to help put out the fire, a big explosion sent the barrel up about four hundred feet into the air. Luckily, the man escaped unharmed.

In September 1966, the school was expanded from grades 1–4 to 1–6 and became a full group school (*Groupe Scolaire Premiere de Phoukoum*). Mr. Dang Moua was replaced by Mr. Ying Yang as the school principal. All students who finished third grade in surrounding villages, as far as Phou Vei, had to travel over twenty miles and lived away from home to continue fourth grade or higher in Phoukoum.

An unprecedented series of violent thunderstorms had hit Phoukoum in 1967. In early April, a seventy-mile-per-hour thunderstorm hit Phoukoum, lifting rooftops and knocking down houses. The entire three-hundred-foot thatch-roof school building collapsed during lunchtime, except the new sixth-grade building.

Fortunately, all students had gone home for lunch. Three of the fourth graders who returned to school early after lunch hid under the teacher's desk and were unharmed. All the first, second, and third graders were dismissed for the year—nearly two months before the school year ended.

The fourth and fifth graders were sent to the two-room corrugated-tin-roof school in the new Phoukoum village—a mile down below, southwest of the airstrip where a new airstrip was constructed. The sixth graders stayed in their one-room building which was still standing next to the collapsed building for the remaining school year.

Meanwhile, Lt. Cher Pao Moua ordered the construction of a brand new twelve-room school in Bouam Loung and proposed to Moua Lia, the provincial school superintendent, that the Phoukoum Group School be moved to Bouam Loung starting September 1, 1967. The request was approved and local carpenters used their best skills to finish the two-building—one-hundred- and three-hundred-foot—corrugated-tin-roof and wooden-plank-wall school just before the school year started. It was bad for the people in Phoukoum, but since the refugees had returned home, the once crowded village was left with a small population that could not support a large school. In addition, Gen. Vang Pao gave Lt. Moua, the "Northern Warrior," any support he needed.

PART TWO
THE RAGING FIRE

CHAPTER 6

FACING THE WORST FEARS

Among those who had come face to face with their worst fears were my 60-year old uncle and aunt, and my 80-year old grandmother. The gruesomeness of the war was evidenced in the Sam Thong Hospital where I accompanied my grandmother for a grenade-wound surgery.

The school year in Phoukoum Group School had concluded in early June and all the fourth through sixth graders would not return to Phoukoum in the coming school year. They would go to Bouam Loung to attend the grades to which they had been promoted—good news for those who lived in Bouam Loung.

Hmong children who had been away from homes for months would, no doubt, be happy to be home. Their parents, too, would be happy to see them home, especially because they were needed to help in the rice and corn fields during the wet monsoon season. I looked forward to giving my parents the badly needed help. Teng and I would go fishing along the Hoy Hom River below the village, where there was an abundance of snake-head fish.

Phoukoum had become quiet, as it once was. Most of the people living north of the airstrip on the plateau near the summit had moved to the new village in the lower elevation after the violent storm—leaving the whole upper area a ghost village. House posts left standing in areas where the mass refugees had settled two years earlier served as a vivid memory of the human storm far more destructive than the violent natural one that collapsed the school. All the refugees who once flooded the airstrip and built temporary shelters in Phoukoum had returned home to resume their slash-and-burn cultivation. Nearly all men who returned to their home villages had the duty of maintaining their home-defense posts or being assigned to the front lines to defend their homeland and fight against the Communists' expansion—the United States' main concern during the Cold War era.

When refugees returned home, although the situation was presumably safe, they continued to be haunted by the ugliness of the war as tall weeds and grass grew around their houses during the months they were gone. American green and gray choppers, delivering military supplies, constantly reminded them that the Communists could come back to launch another attack anytime.

The goal of the war was to win by any means, including causing as much destruction as possible to the opposing side, and torturing and killing human beings—often the innocents. Many had met face-to-face with their worst fears.

A few weeks after we returned home from school, Uncle Ka Thai got up before dawn as he always did and traveled on the grass-overgrown and wet trail in the monsoon season to get horse grass. As usual, everyone in the family expected him to be home before sunrise to eat breakfast.

Sunlight had flooded the village and he had not returned. Aunt Ka Thai, Chong Moua, and Vapao started worrying and wondering if something might have happened to him. They talked loudly and became restless. Grandma, who lived just next door, heard them talk.

"What have you just talked about?" Grandma came out and asked.

They told her what happened.

Grandma went inside the house, grabbed her shiny bamboo stick, and walked as fast as she could toward the trail on which she watched her eldest son walk home with a load of horse grass every morning. Chong Moua ran to get help from all the men in the village, preparing for the worst. Before Aunt Ka Thai noticed, Grandma had already disappeared over the edge of the village. She ran after to catch up with her on the grass-overgrown trail—the only trail that linked Bouam Mou and Bouam Loung.

They walked for about a mile into the woods with their eyes scanning everywhere, over thick grass and under giant trees, to see if he would be somewhere doing something. There, they saw a load of horse grass laid on the side of the trail. But he was nowhere making noise or to be seen. They started calling.

"Ka Thai!" Grandma called.

No sound or response.

"Ka Thai!" she called again.

No sound again, except for her echo.

"Ka Thai!" Aunt Ka Thai called.

She repeated twice. It was quiet.

Grandma became more concerned and agitated. She strode forward as a thousand things went through her head. He might have been lying in the tall brush somewhere waiting for help. He might have been bitten by a snake, or attacked by a bear or other vicious animals. He might have fallen into a hole or fallen off a slippery log and broken his leg or fallen unconscious. The unthinkable was none of the above.

Aunt Ka Thai had sensed the smell of cigarette smoke in the fresh air. She suspected something unusual might have happened and stopped for a moment while Grandma moved forward about thirty feet from her. A large line of hand-grenade trap was stretched across the trail, hidden in tall grass. Grandma was walking fast and she tripped on the line. She fell forward with her face down.

"Boooom!" The explosion blew grass and dirt in all directions. The black smoke darkened a radius of vegetation. Metal fragments cut tall grasses as if they were slashed by a sickle. Small grenade fragments cut Aunt Ka Thai on the face, neck, and shoulder, but none penetrated deep inside her flesh.

A large fragment hit Grandma behind her foreleg, barely missing her bone and causing a bulging bump on the front of her foreleg. She lay on her face, moaning as blood spewed out. Aunt Ka Thai also had blood running down her body, soaking her clothes.

The explosion was heard in the village, a mile away. The men, who were not far behind, ran toward them. Aunt Ka Thai sat in bewilderment in the middle of the trail, soaked with blood, and Grandma was still lying on her face, blood running down and soaking the ground. Uncle Ka Thai was nowhere to be found. His fate was unknown.

The remote village had no medical personnel or medic. The outpost—about three miles away—had limited supplies of bandages and pain medicine. The men did their best to help. Some ran to the outpost. Others ran to the village to bring two blankets to make stretchers with which they brought the wounded old women to the village.

Soldiers at the outpost radioed Phou Vieng where there was a medic and limited medical supplies. My grandmother was brought to Phou Vieng with a handmade stretcher. Aunt Ka Thai stayed in Bouam Mou and was treated with medication available from the outpost. We were informed of the horrific news. Uncle Song Chai and my father gathered some men to head toward Bouam Mou to meet halfway the men who carried Grandma.

Her wound needed to be treated by a surgeon to remove the metal fragment from her leg. The medic in Phou Vieng not only did not have the equipment but also was not trained to perform surgeries. She had to be transported by airplane to Sam Thong. But she arrived late in the evening—too late for the airplanes that landed there daily. She stayed in the medic house for the night and was given painkiller by the medic.

People in the village crowded in the small medic house, but none could do anything to help. With Aunt Ka Thai's wounds and Uncle Ka Thai's unknown fate, their families were in a state of shock. As for Grandma, they were sure that she would be taken care of in the hands of my parents and Uncle and Aunt Song Chai. They discussed who would be going to Sam Thong with Grandma. No one wanted to go. The smell of car emission and, worst of all, the smell of the hospital was what they wanted to avoid.

"I only want my town boy to take care of me," Grandma said.

Everyone laughed and the decision was easily made—a relief for everyone. Barely fourteen, but small for my age, I agreed to go with Grandma—the person who loved me more than anyone on earth.

By sunrise the next morning, we were waiting by the dirt airfield. At 9 a.m., a silvery single-engine Helio was approaching like a hungry mosquito. It landed and pulled to the side where we were waiting. Noticing that there was an old woman on a stretcher with a wound on the leg, after dropping off some boxes of unknown supplies, the American pilot gestured to bring Grandma on board and I followed. Grandma and I were the only passengers. I sat by her side on the floor. The pilot turned around to look at us with his thumb up. Within minutes, we were over the treetops and above the jungles and deep valleys below.

Not having flown on an airplane before, the forty-five-minute trip was long. The rises and falls of the vulnerable plane upset my stomach. It was a strange feeling.

The pilot radioed Sam Thong and talked in a language that seemed rolling without words. Perhaps he informed headquarters about a wounded old woman on board. Looking down before landing, it looked as if Sam Thong was big—about twenty times the size of Phou Vieng. Is this why no one wanted to come to Sam Thong? Were they afraid of big towns and their smells? I asked myself as I busily looked down through the plane's glass windows. It was the war that brought me to Sam Thong.

We landed and the plane moved slowly toward the USAID building—a large, round, metal-roofed structure on the side of the airfield. As soon as the airplane came to a stop, a green jeep was backing up toward the small plane. Two people came out with a green stretcher. They carefully took Grandma down and put her on the stretcher and placed her on the open back of the jeep. I climbed on and sat by her, and they drove slowly toward the large open foyer of the hospital.

The men brought Grandma into a small room on the left of the front foyer. The surgeon, known as Dr. Khammeung—a young doctor who was ethnic Lao—was waiting as if he had expected the arrival of a patient. Grandma was moved from the stretcher onto an adjustable bed. He looked at the wound and the bulging spot.

The doctor asked, in Laotian language, if Grandma knew how old she was. The young nurse translated in Hmong. Grandma looked perplexed, since she did not know her age nor had she ever thought numerically about it.

"This grandma is very old," she said in half Hmong and half Laotian languages. "During the Meo War, I already had three children."

The doctor understood. Grandma was referring to the Hmong's uprising against the French in 1921. He calculated and said to the nurse:

"Put eighty years old."

A nurse took an X-ray and it showed no broken bone and the metal fragment just below her skin.

The doctor began the surgical procedure immediately. I was in the room, watching. He gave her a shot of painkiller near the bulging bump. Then he took a cotton ball soaked with orange disinfectant liquid and cleaned the area. He checked to see if Grandma felt any pain. She said she did not. He began cutting on the bulging bump, and I watched the knife cutting through her swollen skin into her flesh. Dark brown blood was oozing out; the young Hmong nurse wiped it away with clean cotton balls; the doctor grabbed a pair of clean curved needlehead stainless steel pliers, inserted them into the two-inch cut, and pulled out a black bullet-size fragment. He rinsed it in a bowl of clean water and showed it to Grandma. She looked at it.

"Damn," she said.

Everyone laughed.

"Grandma, you are okay now," the young nurse said to Grandma in Hmong. "We will take good care of you and soon you will go home. Okay?"

Grandma smiled and simply said, "Yes."

The cut was sewn, a clean pad was put on, and the wound was cleaned, disinfected, and securely bandaged.

She was rolled out to the hallway and down on a long open corridor past three or four doors, then turned left on a platform walkway connecting to a parallel building, and turned right on a corridor past some doors toward the last one on the left. The nurses put her in a prepared bed, and I was given a stretcher next to her.

Beds were lined up in perpendicular to the wall—from end to end—on both sides in the open-truss building with ceiling fans spinning tirelessly, leaving a walking aisle in the middle and spaces between beds. There were critically sick patients who moaned loudly throughout the night—every night. Next to me, a critically sick man moaned loudly and rolled his head side to side. He was accompanied by his younger brother, who was about my age.

"Brother, what am I going to do? Our parents are not here. Fight hard to get better. Okay? We will go home soon, brother."

His brother gave no response.

The only hospital for the war-ridden region was so overcrowded. Hence, there was no room for privacy. The overwhelmed doctor came to check the man. A young nurse accompanied him. They opened up the patient's gown in plain view of other patients (young and old) and inserted a urinal tube into his genitals to prevent him from wetting the bed. His condition worsened, and he died the next morning.

Along the corridor of the next building, recovering wounded soldiers—some of whom had amputated legs—sat motionlessly. Young nurses, mostly Hmong, walked hurriedly from building to building—connected by wooden-platform walkways—looking pretty in their white uniforms.

There were very few Hmong girls who could read and write to become nurses and teachers. They could not escape the expectations that girls should stay home helping their parents just like eldest boys who had to do the same—a tremendous and, to a large extent, unfair sacrifice they had to bear.

Grandma's condition improved every day. Despite her wound, she never forgot her bamboo smoking pipe. With my help, she got up and smoked. It was a good sign.

The hospital provided food for all the patients. Every day they served steamed sticky-airplane rice and fish and pickled bamboo-shoot soup or beef and pickled bamboo-shoot soup—neither of which Grandma could eat, especially when she was sick.

Up to this day, the Hmong have a belief that when you are sick you should avoid pickled bamboo shoot and other spicy food, for it could make you sicker and could result in death. She would only eat softly boiled plain rice. It had to be naturally harvested regular rice only, and not airplane rice. We had prepared naturally harvested rice from home, knowing that Grandma would not eat anything in the hospital. But what could a young boy my age do to find a place where I could cook rice in Sam Thong? I needed a place, boiling pot, and fire.

We were lucky. Neng's wife's grandmother, Chue Ker Moua's sister-in-law (whom I called Grandma Moua), worked as a cook in the hospital. She and Grandma had known each other in Hamkheu, long before her son, Za Teng, was killed on Mount Phoukeou. In 1964, her granddaughter married Grandma's grandson, Neng. Their relationship became even closer. She came to see Grandma when she learned we had come to Sam Thong Hospital.

She offered to cook the rice for Grandma. She also cooked chicken soup without pickled bamboo shoot for her. I had to go to the kitchen—a brown building about three hundred feet to the southwest of the hospital—to pick it up.

There were ten women—mostly Hmong—working in the kitchen. When I went there, she introduced me to all the women.

"This boy is the son of Neng's aunt, his mother's youngest sister," she said as if everyone knew Neng. "He is here because his grandmother was wounded by a hand grenade."

"Oh, no, is she okay?" a woman asked.

"Dr. Khammeung did a surgery and removed the grenade fragment," Grandma Moua replied. "She is okay now."

"Good. Dr. Khammeung is a good doctor," the woman said.

"Are you hungry?" another woman asked.

"No, I already ate the food they brought for Grandma, but she didn't eat," I said.

"From now on, you can come and eat here every day," Grandma Moua said.

She gave me the rice and a small bowl of chicken soup to take to Grandma. I ran between the hospital and the kitchen three times a day. Within a few days I had become very comfortable with the whole complex. I walked up and down the parallel buildings and the walkways that connected them.

When I had a little time between meals, I would walk up to the front foyer and stay there for about twenty minutes, watching airplanes landing and taking off. The round-roofed USAID building where Chue Ker Moua worked with Mr. Pop was just about 1,500 feet away from the foyer. There were corrugated-tin–roofed buildings and houses everywhere. From the hump, where the hospital was located, there was a pretty view toward the provincial administrative building about a mile away. The school buildings were closer on the left, partially obscured by large trees.

There were no paved roads, and the dirt roads were muddy except for the gravel airfield and the short road that linked to the hospital. From the foyer, I had a good view of Sam Thong. It looked as if it was a big town in a flat valley, with a four-hundred or five-hundred–foot-tall limestone karst, standing in the middle and towering over the airfield like a giant skyscraper.

Grandma was able to get up by herself and talk to other patients and their accompanying relatives next to her and across the aisle. She would ask their names and where they came from, the way people always do. Neither Grandma nor I had any news about Uncle Ka Thai. Chue Ker Moua had not come to give us any news either. The remote villages had no telephones except for the military communication devices, but they were for military use only. Everyone across the region was obsessed with concerns about the movements of Communist forces and their attacks on positions around Bouam Loung, Bouam Mou, and Phou Vieng.

After five days in the hospital, good news came. Dr. Khammeung told Grandma that we could go home within a day or two, depending on when a plane would be landing in either Phou Vieng or Bouam Loung. The arrangement was made with Mr. Pop. For Grandma's sake, Bouam Loung would be a better choice, for there would be more military helicopters delivering supplies from Bouam Loung to Bouam Mou than from Phou Vieng.

Two days later, Grandma was prepared to leave the hospital. Two nurses came in the morning gathering her belongings and medical supplies, including a bedpan. They put her in a wheelchair and rolled her out to the corridors toward the front foyer. Fifteen minutes later, a Porter—a more powerful single-engine transport plane—was approaching from the USAID building and stopping in front of the foyer. A male assistant gestured that I go first. I climbed on. An older Hmong woman was already on board. Two men lifted Grandma and sat her on a pillow next to me with her back against the wall. It was tight for the three of us, sitting in a row.

The plane started rolling past the USAID building and up the runway. It turned around, took off, and flew toward Bouam Loung. After a forty-minute flight high above the low clouds, resembling thick layers of cotton below, we arrived in Bouam Loung. The plane descended, making an attempt to land, but there was cloud cover at the low end of the rough and short airfield. The plane hovered above the village for about thirty minutes, making several attempts to land. The pilot could have decided to return if Grandma was not on board. This might not be unusual for a pilot who might have had far worse situations in his career of flying airplanes in northern Laos, but for the residents of Bouam Loung, this was really unusual.

Grandma and the other woman started vomiting after so many droppings and risings. The hospital had prepared some plastic bags for her. That was a good thing. I started feeling sick in my stomach when the plane landed. I was praised for being brave and not throwing up.

The soldiers at the outpost by the airstrip helped bring Grandma to the medic house, which was about two hundred feet from the airstrip. Grandma was recommended to stay in Bouam Loung for extended care because her full recovery was slow due to her age. She had relatives in Bouam Loung who came to see her as soon as we arrived. The medic, La Xiong, also had families in Bouam Mou where Grandma lived and where his older brother was killed in a Communist attack on the village two years earlier. He told Grandma that Uncle Ka Thai had returned three days after he was captured by the Communist Red Lao. It was good news and a big relief for Grandma.

Five days later, Chong Moua, Vapao, Aunt Pa Xiong, and Chong came to visit. Chong came to replace me and stay with Grandma. I went to Bouam Mou and stayed there for ten days before going to Phou Vieng.

Uncle Ka Thai gave a detailed account of what had happened. Using a sickle, he slashed the tender and green grass in the wet morning in June. He tied each of the hand-full bundles securely with a small portion of the bundle and laid them down, scattered behind him. Then he collected them and assessed if he had cut enough. He put them on a firewood carrier and started walking home. There were noises as if someone was walking behind him.

He turned around and found ten Red Lao soldiers in green uniforms and fluffy caps, approaching from the slope. The first soldier in the front yelled in Laotian language with his gun pointing at him.

"Stop!"

Uncle Ka Thai jerkily stopped. He was so scared that he felt as if he had lost both of his legs.

"Lay down your load, old man!" the soldier yelled again.

Uncle Ka Thai complied slowly.

"How many enemy soldiers are there in the outpost near your village?"

"I don't know," Uncle Ka Thai replied in broken Laotian language. "I am just an old farmer."

"You're lying, old man!" the soldier yelled. "We know you are lying!"

Uncle Ka Thai begged them and said he was really just a farmer all his life, and he was not involved in the war. So he really didn't know anything.

The soldiers were angry, saying he was not telling the truth. They tied his hands behind his back and took him up the hill and down the slope toward the lowland Lao village of Moung Seng, ten miles to the southwest.

They kept him in a house and used different tactics to interrogate him, including threats and coercion.

The sixty-year-old man, who had very little interaction with ethnic lowland Lao, was not fluent in Laotian language. He could not provide much information. The Red Lao and Vietnamese soldiers saw no gainful benefit in keeping him or killing him, but maybe more political gain in letting him go. They pretentiously apologized, sent him home up the hill, and gave him a farewell after two nights and three days of captivity.

He walked alone up the hill on a trail only traveled occasionally by North Vietnamese and Pathet Lao soldiers, scared and without any time to sleep and not knowing what had happened back home during those days and nights that he had been captured and taken away without a trace.

Grandma was sent by helicopter to the outpost and went home after I had gone to Phou Vieng. After Grandma came home in the middle of July, a thanksgiving ceremony was held for the safe return of Uncle Ka Thai and for Grandma's recovery, and to thank all the people for their support.

The two-and-a-half-month school break had gone by quickly. In late August, it was time for me to prepare to head for Bouam Loung to continue fifth grade in the newly built school. The war continued in greater intensity and the Vietnam War was reported daily in the news as the world's dominant event in the Cold War era.

CHAPTER 7

A SOCIAL/POLITICAL CULTURE OF DESPAIR

Leaders of Laos divided the country, coercing citizens to fight on their sides and promising local and low-ranking leaders positions that would elevate them to ruling status. The ruling class would secure permanent places for their descendants—the seeds of rulers—to enjoy privileges, leaving the working class no opportunities to elevate themselves. The fire of war raged on.

The situation in northern Laos, particularly in Phou Phathi and Na Khang, became increasingly critical. Many men in the Phou Vieng region, including Uncle Song Chai's younger brother and four nephews, were sent to support the defense of Phou Phathi and Na Khang, deep in enemy territory.

Nearly every able Hmong man was required to serve in the US-funded irregulars to defend the front lines against the advances of Communist forces. The Hmong in small remote villages just didn't have enough men. Somehow, the Hmong's freedom-loving nature got them trapped in a mutual agreement with the United States that cost them more lives than they had realized.

Neng had left his teaching job to continue a two-year teacher training program. Uncle Song Chai's second son-in-law, Lee Houa, who was my second-grade teacher in Phoukoum, was assigned to continue teaching in Bouam Loung.

The situation in Bouam Loung and Phou Vieng was temporarily calm despite the Communist soldiers stationed in lowland Lao villages—fewer than fifteen miles away—only separated by brushes, mountains, and valleys. Bouam Loung, deep in enemy territory, had been isolated from Long Chieng and could only be reached by planes. The expansion of the school was a strategy, in part, to provide the isolated residents a sense of morale.

Days and nights in August had gone by quickly and the school year was approaching. To leave home and go farther away to attend school in Bouam Long was a mixture of excitement and worry. The most fearful challenge was to find a place to live, particularly in a village far away from home. A twenty-mile distance didn't seem really far in today's world. But a day-long walk on a grass-overgrown trail, following and crossing turns and curves of creeks and rivers, and climbing up steep hills, was like traveling to a different world.

Most of us would not return home until the end of the school year. There would be no communication between our families and us. Even a letter could be delivered only by a walking human. In a society where 99 percent of adults were illiterate, finding a person who could read was hard when all the fourth- and fifth-grade students were away from home. In extreme situations such as death in the family or enemy attacks, contacts could be made through military radios.

A thatch-roofed house would be built for Lee Houa and his wife by the community, and it would be the place where we planned to live. There were eight of us, including Lee Houa, his wife, his daughter, two brothers, his cousin, his brother-in-law, and me.

There were more than twenty students, from Phou Vieng and nearby villages, going to Bouam Loung to attend fourth grade or higher. Some had to stay with friends or relatives, and most of the arrangements were not even made by parents. In a best case scenario, parents simply wrote a letter for the child to take to inform the relatives with whom their child would stay. In some cases, the children looked for the relatives themselves. In other cases, older teenagers would build small thatch houses and younger siblings would stay with them.

Life was hard for children living away from home, attending school, and lacking parental support for finding food, although airplane rice was provided. Located on a plateau at nearly five thousand feet above sea level, Bouam Loung was surrounded by coarse grass-covered hills and was not different from Phoukoum. There was nothing in the wild that could be used for food.

Nearly 100 percent of families had at least one person stationed at one of the outposts surrounding the village and airfield as a soldier, and the families depended upon airplane rice. Few families had rice and corn fields miles down the mountain slopes. Bouam Loung was far from large creeks and rivers, providing no access for fishing. There were a few small creeks running down the steep and rough slopes, dropping thirty feet or more at some points. It was impossible for fish to come up.

Bouam Loung was cold. Temperatures could drop below freezing in December and January, killing fish in the ponds. It was extremely hard for children, especially for poor children, going to school without shoes.

Bouam Loung's location was selected for its natural

fortress for fighting against the Communist Pathet Lao and Vietnamese expansion and not because it had plenty of natural resources that made it an ideal place for a long-lasting village.

Most of the outposts surrounding the airfield and the village were within the range of machine guns, a perfect natural setup for them to support each other in an attack—day or night. Any enemy attempt to attack the village and the airfield in the bowl-shaped plateau at the bottom of the hills would mistakenly enter into a deadly trap.

The brand-new school was about five hundred meters from the end of the airfield, providing a good view for us as we watched airplanes landing and taking off every day. We feared that an airplane failing to take off would slam into the school.

Mr. Ying Yang, the school principal in Phoukoum, became my teacher in addition to his stressful job. A heavy-built man and taller than most Hmong men, he was a good teacher. Despite his overwhelming responsibilities, he maintained a good sense of humor. His student-interest–centered teaching approach worked well for me. I ranked number one in his all-male class every month. Female students in fifth- and sixth-grade classes were rare in remote Hmong communities.

When he asked a question, I was almost always the last one he called, because he wanted other students to think hard instead of listening to answers. He liked to call me Mr. Ge. Other students believed I knew as much as he did.

French, math, and science were my favorite subjects. I hated penmanship class. It just wasn't my talent, and it was where I found my weakness. But, I enjoyed writing stories and drawing.

Despite some hardships, the school year had gone well. I was promoted to sixth grade. Some of the students, including Neng's younger brother, Xao, who was in second grade when I started first grade, were retained. They had to repeat fifth grade in the coming school year or for as long as they kept on failing.

In September 1968, Lee Houa left his teaching job to attend a two-year teacher training program in Sam Thong. We had to find our own place to live. Xao, his cousin, Yaj, five other new students, and I crowded in the home of a relative whose name was Cherpao, the same as my father's, also of the Xiong clan.

Mr. Ying Yang was my teacher again in sixth grade for three months until a newly graduated teacher came to relieve him after the New Year celebration. He became a full-time principal and provided full support for the teachers.

After a bloody battle, killing some Americans and a large number of Hmong soldiers, Phou Phathi fell under the Communists' control. Among the soldiers who survived the battle and returned home to tell their horrific stories was Lee Houa's uncle, Lt. Lee Ge. Other Hmong soldiers who were killed defending the site and the Americans were never recorded. Their names were never mentioned in history as if they never existed. Their heroic actions never earned them recognition as heroes. They were simply cheap mercenaries who died without burials and graves.

Although perceived as the homeland-defense fortress, Bouam Loung only had a small and weary force consisting of fathers, sons, uncles, and nephews of families who had drunk the water of binding agreement.

A SOCIAL/POLITICAL CULTURE OF DESPAIR

Each had sworn his life for the defense of Bouam Loung, not realizing their ammunition and forces alone could not win the fight against the Communist forces of over 15,000—more than three times their entire village population.

Bouam Loung had been prepared in anticipation that enemy attacks would come anytime. The preparation was evidenced by frequent airdrops of ammunition and routine deliveries of supplies to surrounding posts by Air America choppers. Heavily surrounded by razor-sharp barbed wires, each post must be defended until the death of the last man.

Cherpao Moua, who had recently gained rank of major, had ordered every family to dig holes and create bunkers near their homes to protect them from enemy shelling mortars or in case their soldiers had to help them from their surrounding posts.

Most students from Phou Vieng had gone back to participate in the New Year celebration. The rough trail between Bouam Loung and Phou Vieng was still open, although the risk of being captured by Communist soldiers was not only a fear, but could have been a reality. With Phou Phathi already under Communist control, Na Khang felt the heat of the approaching enemy forces and the imminence of their attack that would happen anytime.

In January 1969, an increased number of Air America choppers landed in Bouam Loung. The days preceding the slash-and-burn season were hazy and would only get worse until the arrival of the monsoon storms.

In February, families of Hmong farmers started working in earnest, opening new rice and corn fields, although the war had intensified and the situation in Na

Khang had been broadcast daily like an approaching storm. It had become increasingly critical as days went by. If Na Khang fell, would Bouam Loung be next? Concerns and questions were expressed among teachers in school, folks in rice fields, and vendors in the village's marketplace.

In March, Air America choppers landed in Bouam Loung and stayed for hours, doing nothing. American pilots were standing and talking, perhaps on standby to be called to rescue downed fighter pilots in northern Laos, along the Lao-Vietnam border.

News spread confirming Na Khang had fallen, and all the men from Phou Vieng, including Uncle Song Chai's brother, Chong Leng, and nephews Ka Cheng, Tong Pao, Lia, and Tou, were reported missing.

Fearing Bouam Loung, Phou Vieng, Bouam Mou, Keou Leuk, and Phou Vei would be the next targets, all the students returned home as their parents prepared for evacuation across the Nam Khanh River to Phoukoum, again. The school was closed. The students from Phou Vieng had returned. They left at 3 a.m. Xao's sister, See, with whom we had stayed since the New Year celebration, stopped us from walking home for fear we might risk being captured by Communist soldiers patrolling along the trail between Bouam Loung and Phou Vieng.

Her husband, Lee Pao Vue, was the air logistic guide at the airstrip. She wanted us to wait for confirmation as to whether the people in Phou Vieng had moved to Phoukoum, and then we could be transported there by helicopter.

We waited for four days and watched American helicopter pilots standing and talking, although we did not understand their conversations. Finally, news confirmed our parents had evacuated to Phoukoum. We were boarded on a green chopper and flown over the deep Nam Khanh Valley on a nebulous day in March, leaving Bouam Loung behind to face heavy Communist attacks in the years that followed.

Phoukoum's upper village, which had been left empty since the establishment of the new airstrip down below, became once again crowded with refugees. The scene resembled what we had seen when the village was swarmed with refugees in 1964. The same people who had paid boat fares to cross the Nam Khanh River nearly five years earlier were back to their old camps where remnants of their temporary shelters remained visible under tall bushes, and they became airplane rice dependents, once again.

Among the people standing and walking in commotion at the airstrip were people from Phou Vieng who knew where Uncle Song Chai and my parents were. We were familiar with every part of the terrain in Phoukoum from those years as refugees and students. We easily followed the direction toward my parents' camp.

We walked past the old Phoukoum Village east of the airstrip, following the trail on which we used to travel to and from school every day, and down to the lower plateau where remnants of Neng and Lee Houa's houses were partially standing under tall bushes. The place we had left nearly two years ago was quiet, with only our voices and laughter during those years vividly resonating in our memory.

Continuing toward the settlement where we used to live for two years before my parents returned to Phou Vieng, we found the whole area covered with underbrush beyond recognition. After a half mile of walking through tall grass, we found my parents' camp where more than fifteen families from Phou Vieng had been staying for four days under fresh grass lean-tos. They had been restlessly waiting for Xao and me.

Many people had already started leaving Phoukoum a few days before we arrived. The people who had settled in Phoukoum since the late 1950s by the Christian missionaries and had been there before we became refugees had already left, leaving their houses empty. The swelling number of refugees had snowballed, reaching an unprecedented magnitude, and, this time, would move past Phoukoum.

"You boys have arrived!" Aunt Song Chai said loudly. "We've been talking about leaving without you!"

"We wanted to go to Phou Vieng with the other boys, but See did not want us to risk being captured by the Communists," Xao said.

It was nearly noon and some people in the camp had already started picking up their loads on their backs and moving up the hill. Our arrival was a relief for our restless families. Their loads had been strapped tightly, ready to move.

"If you boys have not eaten, there is rice and fried meat here," my mother said as she was busily getting the kids ready to move. "We have just eaten. We will start moving. You can follow as soon as you finish eating."

We were almost the last in the camp to leave. Having eight children—Teng, thirteen; Mee, ten; Kia, eight; Dang, six; Chao, three; Pai, a year and three months; Ker, only two months old; and me, fifteen and the oldest—it was extremely hard for our family. My mother wanted to start taking the young children on the trail.

My father, Uncle Song Chai, and the men from Phou Vieng looked solemnly sad for the men reported missing and presumed dead. They did not talk as much as they previously did.

"Glad you boys are here now," Uncle Song Chai said as he put his left hand on my right shoulder. "We only waited for you boys to arrive. If we had gone, we didn't know how you would find us."

I noticed my mother was walking barefoot. I wore a pair of flip-flops and had a pair of shoes in my backpack. I handed my flip-flops to her.

"Wear these, Mom."

"No, don't give them to me," Mom refused. "I have never worn those before."

"Take them, Mom!" I insisted. "The needle-grass sprouts are sharp."

She finally took them and wore them. She called everyone by name, making sure no child and no soul was left behind. They started moving on the trail, and their loads heavily sank on their backs.

As Xao and I were eating, some people—also from Phou Vieng, but camped at a distance away—came to talk to us.

"You came so late!" a woman said loudly. "Your parents were very worried about you!"

"See wouldn't let us walk home," Xao answered.

"Did you know that Na Khang had fallen and Chong Leng, Tong Pao, Ka Cheng, Lia, and Tou were reported missing?" she asked.

"Yes, we did," Xao answered again.

"Don't know what had happened to them," she continued. "We are really worried about them."

We picked up our heavy backpacks and started moving up the hill. The trail was narrow with coarse grass high up to our shoulders. We walked for about a half mile, and I noticed one side of someone's flip-flops was in the middle of the trail. It looked just like mine, which I had just given to my mother earlier. How could it have fallen off her foot and she didn't notice? I was wondering as I picked it up.

When we caught up with her, I asked, "Mom, did you lose this?"

She looked at her feet and found one foot without a sandal. She did not notice where she had lost it. She laughed.

"I told you not to give them to me. I have never had these on in my whole life."

I insisted that she keep them. It was the first time she wore sandals. To this day, when she talks about the sandal story, she cries and says how poor and how dumb she had been in her life as a woman, born poor and constantly displaced by war.

The journey was without a planned destination in our minds, except for escaping death. We just kept on moving until sundown, slept on coarse grass, and then started moving again before sunrise, hoping someone knew where we were going.

After a day and a half of walking on a rough, narrow trail, we arrived at a creek. It was partially dry in the hot slash-and-burn season, except for waist-deep puddles under giant boulders and dry leaves. Men, women, and children worked frantically scooping out water and catching frogs and stranded fish. Sounds of people talking and yelling echoed in low and high pitches in the jungle.

More than two thousand refugees came to settle on a bamboo grove plateau—in an undetermined distance west of Phoukoum. They cut down trees and cleared bamboos which they conveniently used for making temporary shelters. At the same time, they cleared bamboo and tree stumps to make a helicopter landing pad. We walked past the crowded camp to set up our own, not far away.

An old rice field owned by the people of a small Hmong village a mile away was used for a rice-airdrop field. Airplane rice had been dropped once or twice before our arrival—an indication that someone had communicated with Mr. Pop and that he had approved the camp site. Air America choppers made routine landings, delivering medical supplies and hundreds of cases of spicy canned meat.

While waiting for the refugee men to finish unloading the canned meat cases, the pilots talked under the shade of the aircraft. A black man who came along engaged in fun activities with the children in a distance. He had his pockets full of balloons with which he made different shapes and creatures to offer to the children, demonstrated a remote-controlled airplane, took a handful of wooden strips which he assembled to make airplanes, and threw them in the air, letting the children pick them up and keep them after they glided to a distance.

"Watch out for sharp stumps!" a parent shouted.

The children presented their own version of folded delta-winged paper planes that worked just as good. They did have fun, however, with the man they could only call "Mr. Black."

After he left on the same aircraft, the children talked

about him as they played with his toys and shared with other children who had missed the show.

"Today two Americans and a black man came," a boy said.

"No, he was an American, too," another boy said.

"He was the boss," still another said.

Three days later, Tong Pao, who was reported missing and presumed dead, arrived in tatters and with bruises and cuts all over his body. Everyone surrounded and hugged him in tears, thanking God and ancestors for protecting and bringing him home safely. He reported that Chong Leng, Ka Cheng, Lia, and Tou were not with him, and he presumed they were all killed. Everyone cried.

It was a big loss for the small community of Phou Vieng. The whole community mourned their fallen little heroes while continuing the endurance of hardship at hand as refugees fleeing death. They listened to Tong Pao's detailed account of what happened.

Their troops were overwhelmed by the heavy attacks on all sides; they were outnumbered and outgunned; explosives blew off barbed-wire fences; shouts of North Vietnamese soldiers came from all directions in their complex tonal language; and everyone ran out in the middle of darkness for his own life.

A woman, the wife of a soldier, ran with him; they were stranded in a muddy swamp and she lost her skirt, but still ran after him. Vietnamese soldiers shouted after them, shooting at them; bullets flew, whizzing over their heads and hitting branches above. He could not pull her with him nor could he defend her without a gun. Her cries for help became silent in the middle of darkness. Presuming she was killed, he pushed on all he could;

he called his ancestors to protect him and wished the sun would never come out and let darkness protect him until he passed the enemy zone.

Flares brightened the sky in a distance behind him, indicating the enemy had claimed victory.

"Would they just settle for a victory and would they not come after the fleeing Hmong soldiers?" he asked himself.

He was not out of the enemy zone yet. Vietnamese soldiers were everywhere. They had prepared for months to take the site and to make sure no one escaped alive.

He was alone and armed with only a short dagger. Had everyone been killed? Or captured? Had the Vietnamese soldiers been waiting on a rock or behind a tree to kill or capture fleeing soldiers? These questions went through his mind as he pulled himself up the hill. He had not had any sleep since the night before, but he did not fall asleep. Daylight arrived slowly, and the beauty of the world of nature returned, regardless of what happened in the world of men.

He walked slowly and stopped occasionally to listen to every noise, including the sound of a falling leaf. His eyes scanned every tree on the slope to see if someone was waiting there. It slowed him down significantly. He had no food or water. The sun rose brightly in the east, giving him the direction where he needed to go. He started going southwest, using the sun as a guide.

He walked past several hills and valleys, crawling under thick underbrush and bamboo vines woven like a blanket. He ate shoots and roots of anything he could get. It was 5 p.m. on his watch as he was approaching a hill on which the Communist Vietnamese soldiers had set up a post during the time they prepared to launch the attack on Na Khang. They heard noises of his approaching and started chasing him.

"Capture him! Capture him!" they shouted in Laotian language. "Don't let him get away!"

The sheet of thick bamboo vines slowed them down and prevented them from capturing him. They walked on top as he crawled underneath for about two miles before darkness came to save him.

He walked for seven days, surviving on wild banana blossoms and shoots and roots of anything edible before he made it to Phoukoum.

Uncle Song Chai cried and hugged him tightly.

"My son, you are my eldest son. You came back to lead us."

As a captain, the chief of Phou Vieng military post, his duty as a soldier reminded him every moment, despite the tears that lingered at the corners of his eyes and his bruises and cuts that had not healed, that his uncle and cousins still remained unaccounted for.

While his wife, parents, extended families, and other Hmong refugees had to move on, following the unfamiliar trail, going farther away from home, Tong Pao had to return to defend his homeland. He had to return to Phou Vieng—a village, now without residents.

Phou Vieng was a part of Bouam Loung, but more vulnerable in its isolation with a single post. His assistant, Lt. Za Houa Lee, who was also his brother in-law, and the small company of soldiers who were his comrades, friends, and relatives, were waiting in Phou Vieng for his return. Their families were gone. The village was empty and dominated by an eerie silence. Human voices only lingered as vivid memories, except occasional

A SOCIAL/POLITICAL CULTURE OF DESPAIR

dog barks at ghosts, wild animals, or approaching enemies. And their morale was low, feeling cold as they looked at the empty village down below.

Word came from Long Cheng ordering immediate evacuation because Phoukoum would be the next target of the Communists' attack. The line of walking humans began again, trudging wearily toward the south, crossing the Nam Khanh River once more. The trail led to another lowland Lao village by the riverbank where the villagers lived peacefully. The river was at its lowest level in early April. Men could walk across the thigh-high water, but the currents were too strong for the women and children. Wooden rowboats ferried them across the river—five or six at a time.

The long line of Hmong refugees started up the hill like a herd of migrating African antelopes toward Phou So, the home village of the Hmong of Phoukoum, where they would return to join their relatives who they had left when they moved to settle in Phoukoum. The Hmong from Phou Vieng and elsewhere would head toward Xiang Det—a village about twenty-five mile northwest of Long Chieng—where a new airstrip was constructed.

The trail curved and turned across hills and valleys toward Phou So—the village of Col. Xay Dang Xiong, a commander of the American-funded Hmong irregulars who was hardly home, for he was somewhere in the front line, fighting enemies. He was seriously wounded when he commanded an attack to retake Phoukoum a year later.

My sister, Pai, became very sick. She had severe diarrhea and became weaker and weaker. She stopped talking, she barely made noises in her throat, her eyes closed, and her head rolled from side to side. I carried her on my back, feeling her weakening breath. I feared she would stop breathing any time, but we pushed on without stopping. The weary refugees hardly talked to each other. The temperature in the early monsoon season was unbearably hot.

At one and three months, she was too young; she was deprived of milk and meat and nutrition needed for a young child, and she could not eat anything. We arrived at the Phou So village where the trail passed through barren ground between thatch-roofed houses. There were two women sitting behind their table full of merchandise next to their house. I stopped by to see what they had—maybe some medicines or something. Found among a dozen items were six dust-covered cans of sweetened concentrated milk.

"How much are these?" I asked.

"One hundred fifty kip a can," the woman said.

I turned around and saw my mother standing behind me. I told her we needed to buy the milk for Pai.

"It's too expensive," she said.

I insisted that Pai needed it or we wouldn't be able to save her.

"We need two cans," I said without further discussion.

We were so poor that three hundred kip (thirty cents) was too much to spend. But we bought two cans. We started making a fire and boiling water right away. My father punched two holes on the top of the can with his knife. He poured a spoonful of concentrated milk into a small bowl, filled it with boiling water, stirred until it was cool, and fed it to Pai's tired mouth with a spoon. We watched her swallow the sweet milk. She rested calmly.

We fed her every three or four hours, and she started opening her eyes and talking the next day. She was one of the hundreds of children who had suffered the common childhood illness caused by the lack of nutrition.

The long trail of refugees moved toward the plain of Muong Soui, a town situated on Route 7, west of Xieng Khouang. The weary refugees crossed Route 7, climbed up steep hills, and crossed mountain ridges before descending toward the Xiang Det Valley.

Located in a flat valley like a bowl surrounded by mountains, Xiang Det's weather was too hot for the Hmong who were accustomed to cooler mountain weather. Some of the refugees chose to settle in small Hmong villages on the surrounding hills, despite that airplane rice was only airdropped in Xiang Det, where they had to travel to receive their food.

We arrived in a small village on a mountain slope about five miles north of Xiang Det where Uncle Chai Houa, Uncle Song Chai's cousin, had lived for more than ten years. Uncle Song Chai, my parents, and five other families chose to settle there. They had to travel to Xiang Det once a week to get airplane rice. Those who settled in Xiang Det suffered from malaria fever and other illnesses. Those who suffered the most were children and pregnant women.

Although the school year had nearly come to an end and some students would have enjoyed the time off for the year, I was obsessed with the primary education certificate and secondary education entrance exams coming in June. Since Bouam Loung School was closed, I needed to go to Sam Thong to file my application for the exams.

As soon as we settled in Uncle Song Chai's cousin's

house, I started setting out on a grass-overgrown trail toward Sam Thong. Uncle and Aunt Boua See wanted to visit their brother, Capt. Sai, in Pha Khao, a village located about six miles southeast of Long Chieng, but they had never been there. A mutual support came at the right moment. They accompanied me to Sam Thong. After meeting with Mr. Ying Yang and consulting with him on my exam applications, I accompanied them to Long Chieng.

While in Long Chieng, I decided to visit Granduncle Chia Koua, who lived in a long corrugated-tin–roofed house near the Long Chieng marketplace. I had heard of him as a prominent member of our family on a few occasions from my father. Chia Koua was the eldest son of Youa Kao, who was one of Song Leng's younger twin brothers.

When Song Leng died, his younger twin brothers, Youa Kao and Yong Khue, were still single. Their older sister, who had married the son of a prominent member of the Vang clan, feared my great-grandmother would not be able to shoulder her younger brothers' wedding costs. She took them to live with her in Muang Cha, a village southeast of Long Chieng. She paid for their marriages. They moved to Phou Meun, not far from Muong Cha, where their families grew and they established a village, which in itself needed a leader.

Chia Koua, tall, with large cheekbones, became a young man suitable for a leader. Through the prominent connections of his uncle, he became the area military commander and district chief, although it did not come without the great sacrifice of people in his area, mostly members of his family. Commanders and district chiefs bore the responsibility for finding young men under their jurisdictions to serve as soldiers, putting their lives in harm's way. He moved to Long Chieng after Phou Meun fell.

I spent a night in his house without much interaction with his large number of guests, mostly dressed in green uniforms. It was after breakfast when I was ready to leave that he came out of his bedroom and sat down with me.

"What is your name, son?" he asked. "And who are your parents?"

"My name is Ge and my father's name is Cher Pao."

I expected he would know. He looked perplexed and unsure he knew who my father was.

"My father had a young name, Ber, and my grandpa was Chia Thong, I meant my step-grandpa."

"Oh, yes!"

His eyes flared as he slightly tilted his head.

"Now I know," he added. "I didn't realize Ber had a son already a young man like you. It's been long years since we were separated from our families in Namnya."

He paused and smiled.

"What are you up to, son? Why are you here in Long Chieng?"

"I came to Sam Thong to file my applications for the primary education certificate exam and the four-year teacher education entrance exam. Since I've heard my father talk frequently about you and I've learned that you live here, I just wanted to come by to visit while I am here."

His face lit up. I thought he was going to give me encouragement, support, a compliment, or some sort.

"Son, you come to help Grandpa. Come to be a soldier for Grandpa. I need your educational skill. You will receive money to help your parents."

My heart sank heavily, but I listened calmly as if in great interest as he continued.

"You know, son, in this land there are leaders and their descendants—seeds of leaders," he continued. "They all have held positions that will be passed on to their sons and grandsons. What are you going to do when you finish your education? There is no position of leader for you. You will end up coming back to work for them. Right?"

He paused and stared at me, waiting for an answer.

"I thank you for your advice, Grandpa," I replied in a manner not to further argue or continue a long discussion with him because our views were too far apart. "I'll think about it and I'll let you know."

"Very good! Think about it and let Grandpa know. And, by the way, tell your father that you have seen Grandpa."

I left the house, heading for Sam Thong. I never saw him again until years later, after the fall of Laos. He might have been disappointed in me for refusing to help him. To him, I was stubborn, arrogant, and rebellious. Perhaps he saw some potential in me working for him. But I was too young to simply stop school and become a soldier.

To me, he believed in the notion widely accepted in a social/political culture that has molded the minds of its people, including himself, for so long that they accepted their places as where they belonged.

Granduncle Chia Koua was right from his experience. In a system of oligarchy in which nepotism is accepted as part of the culture, there are only places for some people who are fortunate like trees in a fertile plain. Their seeds are born lucky and will always inherit their places as leaders and rulers. Those places must be permanently reserved for them. They don't have to be measured by their merits and characters. Many of them receive medals of honor and no one knows how they get them. They believe their descendants must have seats waiting for them. And if there are not enough, they must be created without functional and fiscal questions.

They believe there are people born to the lowest class of citizens and they belong to the places in which they are born. Hence, there are no places high in the pyramid of the hierarchy for them.

My father and millions of others like him happened to fall in infertile places, far from the periphery of the fertile circles. He was born in a poor place far remote from civilization, and he was alienated by big places like Sam Thong and Long Chieng.

He did not have the opportunity to learn how to walk the right way, salute the right way, and talk the right way. He was taught to be obedient, listen to his parents' advice, and follow their path of a natural way of life. He was taught to believe that the world had been made the way it was, and there was nothing he could do to change it. I, too, fell in a place not far from the place my father inherited—a place I was taught to see the world from the same angle.

In a culture that had molded our minds for too long, we would believe that it would be wrong not to repeat our fathers' paths and ways of life. In many cultures and societies, people in the lowest rings of the pyramid are discouraged from and deprived of the opportunity to discover lives in the world from different perspectives.

Granduncle Chia Koua did not speak of his false assumptions, but of what he had seen in a system which he had been a part of. He, too, had accepted the notion of leaders owning their places permanently—a notion embedded in the culture and frequently said in a Hmong ceremonial blessing phrase: *Tau nom tau tswv, tsis khwv los tau noj,* meaning, "Becoming a leader, blessed with fortune and wealth without having to work."

In a sphere of a static culture, there is a widely embraced belief in the notion that places of leaders are blessed by heaven or otherwise obtained by forces, not earned by efforts of good deeds and merits. Thus, those places of leaders are not transferable through fair contests with civility on the basis of merits, but through violent forces.

The power struggles, mostly in the poorest countries in the world, are the functions of a mob culture, as rightfully portrayed in the movies, which has been practiced for centuries. Still, to this day, leaders in those social political cultures only see the seats of power, not their services and responsibilities for the people that constitute the nations which they represent. Each leader of a group coerces or forces members to form a ring on the pyramid, hoping for something bigger for himself in the factious power-building scheme.

I could have taken Granduncle Chia Koua's advice, earned some money so I could carry my own weight, and paid Uncle Song Chai's money that my father had borrowed. But I saw a different path and rebelled against his advice. Had the country made a national draft that required all men, regardless of ethnic background and family status, who had reached eighteen years of age to serve in the military, I would have committed myself to my duly responsibility when I reached that age. But the

A SOCIAL/POLITICAL CULTURE OF DESPAIR

country was in a mob-fight mode.

I walked back to Sam Thong because I didn't have money for a taxi. I walked alone up the steep hill to the top of the north skyline mountain, where I stood and looked down at Long Chieng when I arrived from Sam Thong the day before. I would follow the zigzagging gravel road as it descended toward the valley below and elevated across low hills and wild banana-grove valleys towad Sam Thong.

Sam Thong was established in the early 1960s and had become a town swarmed with refugees. It became the place where Xieng Khouang province's administrative office, USAID headquarters, and an overcrowded hospital were located. Two years earlier, I had flown from Phou Vieng to Sam Thong with Grandma for a grenade-wound surgery and stayed only in the hospital. Back then, Sam Thong seemed far away, and it could only be reached by planes. Two years later, the Phou Vieng people were only a half-day's walking distance from Sam Thong. We had moved closer to the base, for worse.

To find a place for an overnight stay in Sam Thong or Long Chieng, one had to walk into someone's house. While walking along the gravel road, the only thing that dominated my mind was a place to stay for at least a month. The only person I knew in Sam Thong was Chue Ker Moua, Neng's wife's granduncle. But we were not closely related. I could show up on his doorstep and ask for a place to stay for a night, but not for a month or two during which I would depend on him for food.

Lee Houa and Bee Xiong, both my former teachers, were near the end of their first year as students at the Sam Thong Teacher Training Institute. Their wives stayed in Chue Ker Moua's small guest house. Each with a young child, they had been living there for nearly a year. Lee Houa and Bee Xiong were required to stay in the school dormitory. They only joined their wives on the weekends. They were without incomes, except for the monthly student allowances of six hundred kip (sixty cents), since they had left their teaching jobs as temporary teachers, paid by USAID.

I crowded in with them. We lived on a weekly distribution of airplane rice and salt. Every day we ate tiny bamboo shoots, young thistle plants, and clover leaves and tips picked from a freshly burned hill across a small creek—not far from where we lived. My two-month stay in Sam Thong was long and filled with hardship.

I ranked seventh out of 450 students who took the province-wide primary education certificate exam, a prerequisite for all the secondary education entrance exams. But the result of the more competitive Teacher Training Institute Entrance Exam (TTIEE) wouldn't be announced until August. I could not wait for its result, for I could no longer endure the hardship. I returned home after the TTIE exam, leaving early the next morning.

The trail from Sam Thong was crooked, curved, steep, rough, and muddy in the rainy season and seldom traveled. I traveled alone all the way from Sam Thong, crossing the Nam Nguem River toward Xiang Det, striding along the under-construction airstrip, and walking up the hill on a bush-overgrown trail across old rice fields. I arrived at home late in the afternoon.

A SOCIAL/POLITICAL CULTURE OF DESPAIR

My grandmother, who my childhood life had been hinged upon (from Vapao's collection).

My parents and young siblings posed for a picture shortly after arriving in the refugee camp in Thailand. From left to right: Ker, Pai, Kia, my mother, my father, Chao, Ger (who died in car accident in 1986), and Kou.

A WORLD WITHOUT BOUNDARIES

My parents looked physically great after less than a year in the US compared with their appearances upon arrival in Thailand.

Undated picture of Youa's parents with painting of Long Chieng's Phou Mok Mountain as a memory behind them.

A SOCIAL/POLITICAL CULTURE OF DESPAIR

Vapao Lee, my cousin and only childhood companion.

Chong Moua Lee, my cousin with whom I had spent all my childhood.

A WORLD WITHOUT BOUNDARIES

Youa's parents watched with tears as Neng and Nou departed to the US. Their hearts were torn between those who departed to an unknown world of final resettlement and those left behind. Youa's father died in the refugee camp.

Teng (with Saleng in left arm) and his crew of young Hmong men arrived in Thailand in tatters. The thirty hungry arrivals were given food by relatives from the refugee camp while they were held in a Thai border patrol police compound for entry processing. Some had long hair, reaching their waist.

A SOCIAL/POLITICAL CULTURE OF DESPAIR

Family members and guests posed for a memorial picture after a wishing well ceremony. Some had reunited and met after a brief or long separation. Others never met or saw each other again.

From left to right: Yang Xiong (Camp Center 2 Chief), a Thai friend, Ma Vang, and Ge Xiong posed for this picture after a farewell ceremony for Ge's family.

A WORLD WITHOUT BOUNDARIES

This picture is a vivid memory of those days of unsettled refugee issue in Thailand. Hundreds of people said "farewell" to family members and friends on departures to countries of final resettlement. Youa's father (front), Youa's mother (right behind her father), Uncle Song Chai (front left), Yaj (looking back), and many more gave us a farewell with teary eyes.

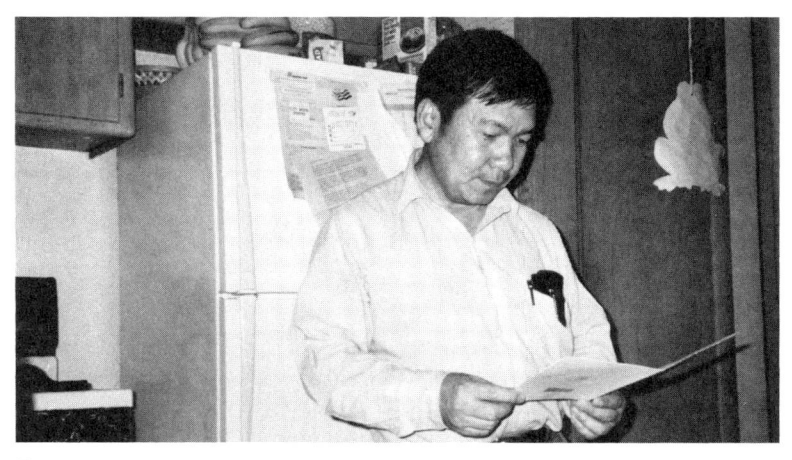

Father's Day has become a special family happy event as we became an integral part of American society and have begun to adopt the American culture. Cultural acquisition is a natural process of our changing world.

A SOCIAL/POLITICAL CULTURE OF DESPAIR

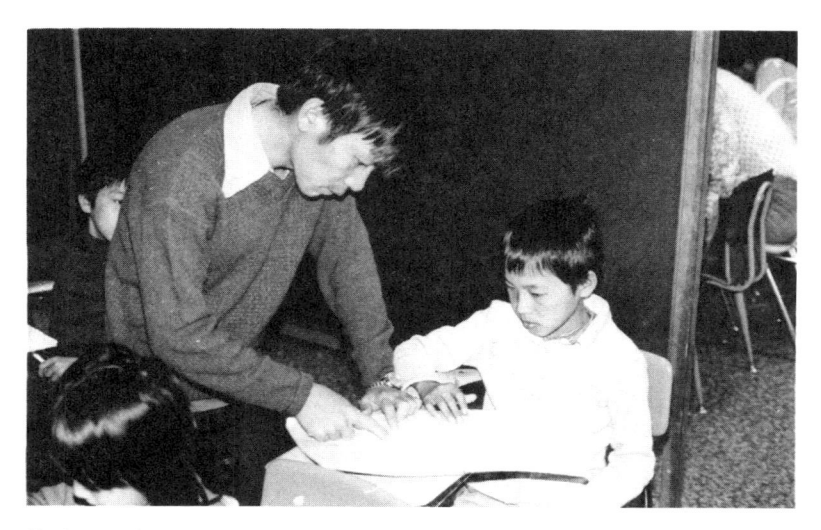

Ge helped newly arrived refugee children with math and reading in a refugee program during school break. The refugee program provided a variety of supporting services to the growing number of non-English speaking refugee parents and children in the Dekalb, Illinois, area in the 1980s.

As vice president of the Milwaukee Hmong American Women's Association, Youa actively advocated for gender equity and equality.

A WORLD WITHOUT BOUNDARIES

A memory of one of those days when I actively endeavored to help people overcome boundaries.

Ge and Youa at an educational conference dinner—a memory of our energetic days of active educational and social involvement.

A SOCIAL/POLITICAL CULTURE OF DESPAIR

A family picture at the 1993 Milwaukee County Annual Strong Family Award Luncheon. Our family was among the county's five award winners in 1993.

This photo was taken during class break. The English as a Second Language (ESL) class was filled with young refugees from Thailand. In 1977, the US began admitting (category two) mostly young refugees with the potential to quickly integrate into the American way of life and become self-sufficient. Ge (holding Saleng and sitting in the second row, third from right) and Youa (folding arms and standing behind him) were among those who were eligible for admission under this category.

CHAPTER 8

GOOD-BYE, SAM THONG

Outgunned and outnumbered by Communist forces, the Hmong ran out of men and boys. Sam Thong—a refugee sanctuary and a town where the regional hospital, USAID headquarters, Teacher Training Institute, Xieng Khouang's makeshift provincial office, and Xieng Khouang's educational headquarters were located—fell to the Communists.

In July 1969, Xiang Det Valley was filled with refugees living in temporary thatch huts. The construction of a new airstrip was underway in earnest. My parents had built a small thatch-roofed house in the remote village where I left them two months earlier.

Seven new families had added to the size of the small village, far from civilization but rich with natural resources: beautiful giant bamboos with arching tops, and clean creeks flowing toward the nearby Nam Chuk River. The refugees arrived there too late to start the slash-and-burn season, but hoped for a good season in the coming year.

Having been away from home for two months without a way to communicate how things were going back home and on my end, my mom was so happy to see me come home safely. She cooked some squash-vine tip soup the best she could for me. In a situation where there was no permanent home, my parents had always been my home regardless of the state of shelter. It was good to be home.

While anxiously waiting for the result of the TTIE exam, I was hopeful for an enjoyable time with my family, because I had spent most of my time away from them. Teng and I went fishing in the fish-abundant Nam Chuk River and caught a basketful of silvery fish. My seven-year-old brother, Dang, also enjoyed spending time with me and we had a good talk when he and I went to cut firewood.

"Ge, are there any ghosts here?" he asked.

"No, there are no ghosts here. Ghosts are not real, so don't be afraid. Did Mom tell you about ghosts?"

"No. I heard people tell ghost stories."

"I am not afraid of ghosts."

"Why not?"

"I said ghosts were not real!" I repeated as I gently pushed his head.

With Na Khang under the Communists' control, 1969 was a setback for Gen. Vang Pao. The Pathet Lao and North Vietnamese forces had made a significant gain in territorial control and moved closer to Long Chieng.

A message came from Long Chieng alerting that Communist forces might be catching up with the refugees in Xiang Det. The villagers who had been living there for over ten years and the seven families of new refugees decided to move to Sam Xan, a village on a narrow mountain ridge about eight miles south of Xiang Det. The new refugees did not have a chance to start a slash-and-burn season. They were back on the refugee trail, living in lean-to tents again.

Upon arrival in Sam Xan, Dang was sick, and his condition worsened. He breathed heavily, gasping for air. His eyes closed; his mouth opened; and his chest pumped heavily up and down, struggling for his life. He died in a thatched lean-to. We were extremely poor and did not have a pig or even a chicken for his funeral service. My good brother's body was buried the next morning.

While sorrows still dominated our minds, good news came. Neng and his wife came from Sam Thong with good news, saying I had passed the TTIE exam ranking number one out of 271 candidates. Out of 271 candidates, only thirty-five were taken for the two-year program.

I could have taken the four-year program, which only took four new students annually from Xieng Khouang province. But I was advised by Bee Xiong, my former teacher (who convinced my father to let me go to school in Phou Houa Xang) to choose the two-year program instead. He advised that I would have a better chance if I took the two-year program, and if I did well, I could apply to continue in the four-year program. His concern was that because of the competitive nature of the four-year entrance exam, coupled with potential briberies, I could be screened out despite my academic talents.

Passing the exam and ranking number one gave me a mixed feeling of delight and regret. In any case, I looked forward to the teacher training program which would begin in September. I would be away from home again, as I had always been. As refugees frequently displaced by the war, when I came home next time my parents would likely be living somewhere else, I thought.

As school time drew near, planning for the school

requirements was a big concern for my parents. Two uniforms, a pair of dress shoes, a cushioned sleeping mat, a water bucket, a pillow, and some notebooks would cost fifteen thousand kip. My dad had to borrow ten thousand kip from Uncle Song Chai.

Time had gone by quickly. On Friday, three days before school started, my mom handed me fifteen thousand kip (nineteen dollars in 1969 value).

"Son, this is all we can give you," my mom said with tears rolling down from her eyes, not mentioning ten thousand kip was borrowed from someone. "Please spend conservatively for what you need. We have been moving constantly from place to place for the last six years and have spent all the money we had earned and saved in our life. We have nothing left."

"Thanks, Mom," I said to her in a tone choked with emotion. "I will use this money conservatively. The school will pay for the place to stay and the food, so I'll be fine."

I set out early the next morning, walking alone on a trail under tall trees and thick wild banana groves, and arrived in Sam Thong on Saturday afternoon. The dorm had already been opened. All the faculty members and most students had arrived. Among some of the students I knew were Doua Lee (Lee Houa's younger brother), Ge Moua (Neng's brother-in-law), and Pao Vang, who sat with me during the TTIE exam.

I checked in and was given the school policies and other pertinent information. Arranged by rank, students slept on cushioned sleeping mats on a smooth, wax-polished wooden platform floor under an open-truss, corrugated-tin roof. I slept next to the last senior student (who was of lowland ethnicity—an unfriendly tall man—

and whose name I didn't recognize). Pao Vang who sat next to me during the exam and who ranked number four, was the only Hmong student sleeping close to me. He became my closest friend.

Fortunately, I had been in Sam Thong twice before. I was familiar with the marketplace and areas around Sam Thong.

Pao and I went to a couple of tailor shops in the marketplace, where he had already ordered his uniforms, to order two uniforms, consisting of simple black trousers and white shirts, for me. They would be ready the next day—the day before school would start. We also shopped for a sleeping mat and school supplies.

A pair of black trousers cost 3,500 kip and a cheap sleeping mat cost 2,500 kip. A pair of dress shoes cost 2,500 kip. I was very nervous, fearing I might not have enough money for what I needed. I still needed school supplies, a pillow, and a mosquito net. We were able to bargain a sleeping mat down to 1,500 kip. After everything was bargained and paid for, I had one thousand kip left.

At 8 a.m. on Monday morning, everyone, including fifty-six second-year and thirty-five first-year students, stood in three lines—forming a "U," facing the flag pole—and sang the national anthem. The opening ceremony featured welcoming remarks from the school director and student roll call.

Each student whose name was called would step forward toward the flag pole, slightly bow in salute, and retreat back in line. The faculty and students were curious to know who the number one student was. When the first student's name was called, I stepped forward. The crowd roared, in a combination of shouts, laughter, and hand applauds. I was the school's smallest and youngest student.

My first quarter in school was challenging, in part, because I was too young to be in an environment surrounded by adult students—many of whom had been teachers for many years. I ranked number twenty-one in the first quarter, causing many to question if I really had the academic talents.

The activities in Sam Thong seemed normal and like business as usual. While soccer matches between the Teacher Training Institute and the College Sam Thong were held nearly every evening, there were fierce battles between the Communist and Gen. Vang Pao's forces in the front lines. Bouam Loung was faced with numerous heavy attacks. According to eyewitnesses' accounts, dead bodies of enemy soldiers laid and rotted on the ground around the school buildings like logs for days. In a lawless world, there was no cease fire to allow time to cure the wounded and bury the dead. No one dared burying them for fear of snipers. Soldiers as well as residents fought for their lives.

Shockwaves of the intensifying heat of war were felt in Sam Thong, where everything seemed peaceful, as gruesome scenes of wounded soldiers filled the hospital. Men as young as thirteen, who walked without uniforms in the marketplace, would be forcibly picked up and sent to battlefields. We were advised to wear our uniforms and badges at all times or risk being sent to battlefields. Students without uniforms were warned not to go to the marketplace or walk on the roads around town.

Situated in a flat valley surrounded by low plateaus and grassy hills, Sam Thong was a beautiful town—a town with great potential for development. The large spaces between buildings and structures provided a beautiful view. It would be more beautiful if a proactive urban development was on the minds and priority list of those in the leadership positions. Unfortunately, more than 90 percent of its inhabitants were dependents of airplane rice, and the high-ranking leaders of one of the poorest nations on earth were intoxicated with indulging in their personal power.

The early dry season preceding the Hmong New Year celebration provided an unmatchable weather condition, with a clear sky and a fresh and cool breeze. The air was crisply fresh as I sat in the open school cafeteria on a Saturday afternoon with a cup of freshly boiled green tea, drawing a beautiful rose as part of my art class project.

After the two-hour nightly study, I walked from the school building to the dormitory on the neatly clean grass as the fluorescent lights shone brightly from the school corridor. I felt the mighty modern civilization imaginably paralleled to a heavenly world. The schools, the hospital, and the lights that shone brightly and illuminated the school at night were attributed to the dedicated work of Mr. Pop with the soft humanitarian side of the American involvement in Laos.

The second quarter of school began in earnest after we returned from the first-quarter break and the Hmong New Year celebration. I realized a sense of growing up that enabled me to better cope with the adult social environment. I scored the highest in every subject, except handwriting. All the students and teachers shifted their opinion about me and projected that I would, no doubt, rank number one.

As the year drew closer toward the monsoon season with muggier air, the North Vietnamese took advantage of the dry season to stage heavy attacks against Gen. Vang Pao's forces before the monsoon rains arrived. Four or five days before the attack of Sam Thong, Gen. Vang Pao's intelligence was informed that Communist forces were spotted several miles from Sam Thong and there would be an imminent attack on both Sam Thong and Long Chieng within a few days. Despite the warning, Gen. Vang Pao did not have enough men to defend the town, because all forces had to be used to defend Long Chieng, which was also a target.

Despite the warning, the schools remained open. Mr. Pop and the hospital staff, on the other hand, had begun evacuating all patients to the town of Vang Vieng, located on Colonial Route 13 about thirty miles to the southwest, and to Vientiane, the capital city, three days earlier. Some of Sam Thong's residents, including the teachers and the school superintendent, Mr. Moua Lia, did not want to leave the town.

On March 18, the day before the night of the attack, some people started moving to Long Chieng despite intelligence indicating that both Long Chieng and Sam Thong would be attacked. Looking from the dormitory toward the only gravel road that linked the two towns, there was a long line of people walking past the checkpoint toward Long Chieng since sunrise. The marketplace was closed.

Half of the students of Sam Thong Teacher Training Institute had gone home to join their families. The rest remained on campus; most of them came from villages in areas which had been ordered to evacuate. Others came from villages outside Xieng Khouang province.

The cafeteria was open as usual, preparing too much food for the students that remained on campus.

After lunch, Professor Chanthala, who was in charge of food service, had a meeting with all the remaining students.

"Most of the teachers were sent here from Vientiane by the Division of Teacher Training Education and we are still here," he informed us. "We will evacuate with you if an attack should occur. We are hopeful that nothing will happen. But, please go together if there is an attack tonight. We are not sure which way we will go. We will have a meeting with some of the leaders this evening on the escape plan."

At 3 p.m., I decided to go to Long Chieng to join my uncle's family. My parents were in Sam Xan, which had already been ordered to evacuate. Uncle Tou was the grandson of Pa Ger, who was my great-grandfather's uncle. He is actually my granduncle (more distant in the family lineage), but I call him uncle because of his closeness to me—he's more than a granduncle. About thirteen years older than I, Uncle Tou was an officer in the accounting bureau in Long Chieng Headquarters.

I put my clothes, mosquito net, school supplies, and personal items in my green military backpack; strapped my green blanket on top; rolled up my sleeping mat against the wall; and put my water bucket on top as if I would return. I said good-bye to everyone, not mentioning where and when we would meet again.

The dusty school playground and soccer field were quiet and empty as I walked past all the school buildings toward the dusty gravel road and up the hill toward the empty police checkpoint. I looked back from the hill toward the brown wooden-walled and bright corrugated-tin–roofed school buildings, the airfield and USAID building, the towering blue karst, the hospital, and the vast empty space toward the provincial administrative building.

"Good-bye, Sam Thong," the phrase ran through my mind, wondering if the lights would still be on at nightfall.

Without anyone I knew, I felt alone among the people walking along the rough and poorly maintained road. I walked past the slow-moving refugees—old men, women, and children trudging along the edge of the narrow and rough gravel road—each with a load on his or her back, steadily being sunk by its weight. Some might not make it to Long Chieng and might spend the night somewhere along the road.

I arrived in Long Chieng at 6 p.m. The noisy town was quiet, for most airplanes had left to Vientiane or Oudorn, Thailand, except for the T-28s, whose pilots lived in Long Chieng and were ready to protect their hometown at any moment if they were needed. The town seemingly showed no sign of panic, although some people might have left to Phou Kang Noy, across the Nam Nguem River.

Uncle Tou had not returned home from work. Waiting anxiously at home were Aunt Tou, the baby girl, and Uncle Tou's older brother and his wife. They all lived in a large thatched-grass, T-roofed house on a slope below the king's palace. They all welcomed me warmly.

At 7 p.m., supper was ready; we were waiting for Uncle Tou, but he had not come home. Aunt Tou started worrying, because news about possible Communist attacks on Long Chieng and Sam Thong had spread like shockwaves.

Uncle Tou arrived at the door.

"Hey, you are here!" he said.

"Yes, I don't know where to go. I don't know what I would do if you're not here."

He laughed as he took off his green cap.

"Did you hear any news about your parents?"

"No, I thought you would be the one who knew."

He turned to Aunt Tou and asked, "Honey, is supper ready?"

"Supper had been ready, waiting for you since seven o'clock."

The fear of a possible Communist attack on either Long Chieng or Sam Thong was on everyone's mind, but was not confirmed until Uncle Tou rushed everyone to eat quickly and move out of the house that night.

"Do we have to move out this late?" Aunt Tou asked in resentment. "Why didn't you come home earlier?"

"We had a meeting with the commanding officers," Uncle Tou explained. "Pathet Lao's radio conversations were picked up on our intelligence radio, saying they wanted to make sure the bottom of the cauldron is shattered tonight. We don't know if they meant Long Chieng or Sam Thong. It was very likely they meant Long Chieng."

We panicked and ate in a hurry, then packed some clothes, baby wraps, blankets, and straw mats. Each with a flashlight, we walked on a foot trail up the hill—turning and curving around banana and bamboo bushes, chaotic patterned houses, and stick fences of private gardens—toward a thick white-flower brush field just below the king's palace.

We crawled under the thick brushes; we felt cushions of dirty and dry leaves cracking under our feet.

There was no time to check, clean, or reject the spot. Some people were already there, whispering. We quietly unrolled our straw mats on top of whatever was underneath and lay down like a flock of fowls among others who were already there before us.

The night was quiet, except for brief cracks of baby cries here and there. Someone sneezed from a distance followed by whispers and then silence. Cock crows from nearby houses indicated daylight was approaching. Nothing happened as frighteningly anticipated.

Daylight came with fresh morning air at dawn. Frightened humans came out of thick brushes like waking zombies and drowsily walked with armfuls of what they could carry with them toward their houses down below to be informed that Sam Thong had been attacked before dawn and fallen into the hands of Communists. Long Chieng braced for its defense as families fled in disbelief that the headquarters of the mighty American CIA would be just another vulnerable place.

Uncle Tou and his older brother, Uncle Hnia Vue, who stayed in the house, were awake and up before dawn. The morning meal was prepared in a hurry, enough for breakfast and lunch in anticipation of an unknown journey.

The line of refugees had already started up the hill on a foot path partially ditched by rainwater erosion, trudging past the king's palace at a distance, toward the top of the mountain on the west of Long Chieng. The path, which led down on the other side of the mountain, was only traveled by foot-traveling farmers, mostly family members of soldiers, who had rice fields across the lower elevation of the mountain slopes. The steep and freshly burned slopes were black, scorched, barren, and smooth, making it difficult to walk on.

Granduncle and Grandaunt Xai Teng, Uncle Tou's father and stepmother, had been staying in their thatch hut in their freshly burned field, halfway down the slope, for several days. The seventy-year-old couple was shocked by the news brought by people passing by and anticipating that their family members would be there any time to decide what to do.

We arrived there before noon and did not plan to stay overnight because the hut was too small for all of us. The surrounding terrains were steep and the scorched black dirt-barren field was filled with charcoal-black stumps. The closest few trees with leaves were a quarter of a mile away. Our skin became sticky and covered with a mixture of black dust and sweat after crowding in the small hut for fewer than four hours under the scorching sun.

They only had half a dozen chickens, including two hens with little chicks. We killed them all, except the mommas with chicks, which they knew would be stolen by passersby or killed by wild cats later, anyway.

At about 2 p.m., after lunch, we began merging with the line of walking humans and continued down toward the Nam Nguem River. The river was at its lowest level in March, but could only be crossed by bamboo rafts. Both sides of the river were noisy with human voices—a mixture of shouts and calls.

The trail was filled with walking humans trudging wearily up the steep slope—each with a load on his or her back. Even Uncle Tou, a military officer, had a load on his back. Three rolls of blankets were strapped securely on top. The scene was more than déjà vu for me because I had been a refugee, moving on similar trail from place to place, since 1963.

We walked past the Phou Kang Noy village and settled on a ridge shaded by giant oaks where we built a lean-to covered with green military tarps. There was a nebulous, but spectacular, view of the mountains surrounding Long Chieng over the horizon. There were more than ten lean-to tents on the ridge along the trail which led down toward a crystal clear spring about five hundred feet away.

That night, one of the posts on the north misty skyline mountain was attacked. Explosions of hand grenades were heard across the Nam Nguem Valley, and flares brightened the mountainside, north of Long Chieng. The refugees watched nervously from the mountain ridge of Phou Kang Noy and prayed to their ancestors for the safety and victory of their fellow soldiers defending their homes behind. The post survived the attack for the night and had just another day to plan for defense of Long Chieng—the Hmong's last stronghold.

In the subsequent days and nights, Gen. Vang Pao, Hmong T-28 pilots, and soldiers had virtually no time to sleep. They were constantly on the move in defense of Long Chieng while sons and daughters of high-ranking government officials in Vientiane crammed into movie theaters to watch their best Chinese Kung Fu action or Indian love movies. Life in Vientiane and surrounding lowland Lao villages was peaceful, and it seemed as if there was no war in Laos.

I stayed with Uncle Tou for five days; walked on the same trail on the ridge to receive distribution of airplane rice; carried the same bamboo pipe to bring water from the same spring source more than six times a day; and listened to the same old men talking about the war.

There had not been any good news about the situation in Long Chieng. Nor did I hear any news about where my parents had moved.

In the afternoon of the sixth day, the wife of one of Uncle Song Chai's nephews arrived on the hill with a baby girl on her back. I called her Aunt Ge. She broke into tears when she saw Uncle Tou and me, for it was the first day she saw the people she knew since she left Long Chieng five days earlier. She had spent nights in different places among people who she did not know. Her husband, whose name was the same as mine, was a military radioman on duty in his home village of Phou Vieng where she went back to visit. She was sent to Long Chieng and traveled from there to look for her husband's family who lived with my parents in Sam Xan. There were rumors indicating the people in Sam Xan and surrounding villages would move to Muong Phoun, a village about six miles northwest of Phou Kang Noy.

She asked me to go with her to Muong Phoun to look for our families. Uncle Tou hesitated to let me go, especially in a situation of great uncertainty where we might not find our families. But, I agreed to go with her. I took my military backpack and blanket. That's all I had. It was nearly 5 p.m. We walked past the spring from which I brought our water supply every day and followed on a grass-overgrown trail along the ridge.

By nightfall, we arrived at a village whose residents were of the Khmou ethnic tribe who liked to live close to Hmong villages. It was believed the Khmou were natives of Laos who had been in Laos since the Khmer Empire, which occupied the entire Southeast Asian region, and were left behind when the empire retreated to what is now Cambodia. They lived in above-ground platform houses, similar to those of the lowland Lao, but spoke a unique language, different from Hmong and Lao. The adults, however, were fluent in Lao. Like the Hmong, they practiced animism, a spiritual worshiping in their private homes, and a belief of spiritual guardians of mountains, rivers, valleys, and major objects such as large rocks and trees.

We climbed up on the bamboo-mat platform of a small thatch hut by the trail. A young woman in her twenties came out. She stared at us and did not say anything or greet us.

"Good evening, sister," I said to her in Laotian language.

"Yes, good evening," she said with a smile.

"We are traveling to Muong Phoun, but it's now too late for us to travel on. Can we sleep in your house tonight?" I asked.

"Yes, come on in," she said in a friendly manner.

We entered the house and the floor squeaked under our feet. The young couple had only a baby girl. The young man, with no shirt on, walked in and out of the house bringing firewood and did not talk much. The woman set a round bamboo-woven table by the faintly burning fireplace and offered us supper. There was nothing special, only warm sticky rice and sour bamboo shoot mashed with chili pepper and garlic. It was an appreciated meal.

We spent the quiet night in the forever remembered house, although they had no blanket. That did not surprise me. They were a newly married couple who had just established their family life in a country where the vast majority had no source of cash income. I gave Aunt Ge and the baby my blanket. I suffered only a few mosquito bites.

The young woman was up before dawn and steamed warm sticky rice. She wrapped it in a fresh banana leaf and delightfully presented it to us. We wholeheartedly thanked the young couple for their special hospitality, and then set out on the trail early in the morning toward an unknown destination.

The trail was widened and more frequently traveled, an indication that a village was not far ahead. Soon we approached a clearance—an airstrip with a thatch hut on the side crowded with people walking, standing, and sitting in and around it.

We walked toward the open thatch hut and found a man sitting among weary men and women. He was from Phou Vieng and he had known my parents and all the people from Phou Vieng all his life.

"Oh, you are here!" I said to him, assuming my parents had arrived there. "Do you know where my parents are?"

"No, I haven't seen your parents or any of the Phou Vieng people. I heard they were coming here, but haven't seen them yet."

While we were talking and had not given Aunt Ge time to ask questions, a helicopter approached like a dragonfly over the treetops and landed. An announcement came on the loudspeaker.

"Are there any Sam Thong teacher training students here? The helicopter is taking them to Ban Xorn right now."

I grabbed my green backpack and ran toward the green chopper. I was the only one. I climbed on board and turned back to wave good-bye at Aunt Ge, but found her sitting with her legs flat on the ground, sobbing with both hands on her face. She did not see me. I was sad. The helicopter lifted off with its door open and hovered over the treetops and steep hills toward Ban Xorn, where twenty-nine other classmates had camped for several days waiting for other classmates who fled Sam Thong the night of the attack.

USAID provided them food and green tarps for shelter. They had lunch ready—plenty of rice and canned meat burgers.

After eating, we walked to the busy new USAID building, waiting to be transported to Vientiane. We never returned to Sam Thong. My last look at the town from the police checkpoint on the hill is still vividly retained in my memory to this day. Sam Thong was truly a beautiful town.

Approaching Long Chieng from the southeast. The misty Phou Mok Skyline Mountain is seen in the backgroud. From the collection of and courtesy of Peter Alan Lloyd (peteralanlloyd.com).

CHAPTER 9

LONG CHIENG, THE LEGENDARY HMONG CITY

To the Hmong, Long Chieng was a Hmong city of progress where the Hmong had transformed culturally, educationally, and economically. But, to the Americans, it was simply a base of American secret military operation in support of the Vietnam War, without an urban development plan.

Arriving from Sam Thong on the top of Phou Mok, the misty north skyline mountain, Long Chieng was seen in a spectacular view down below like the city of Oz, with bright tin rooftops among green banana trees. The poorly maintained gravel road that linked Sam Thong and Long Chieng was visible on both ends, zigzagging like a resting snake.

A cluster of several lean-to tent shops—with steaming hot noodle soup pots, bags of colorful candies, and half-filled clear plastic bags of green and red syrup water hung from wooden bars—served as a life-saving place for the hungry and thirsty foot travelers.

Walking down toward Long Chieng, foot travelers would find themselves thirty feet below where they were minutes earlier as they walked on the zigzagging dirt road from curve to curve, unless they took the shortcut trail straight down through the grassy steep slope.

Jeep-converted taxis ran by at a creeping speed, stirring dust into the air and onto brownish dust-covered vegetation on both sides of the road. Frequently, military ten-wheeler cargo trucks roared up the hill and moaned as they exhausted their mighty power, blowing clouds of dust to a distance. The trembling sounds of the ground were heard from the flat valley below.

The road zigzagged past foot bases of towering limestone karsts at the bottom of the mountains. There were corrugated tin-roofed houses among thatch ones along the roadsides, partially obscured by dust-covered bushes and fenced-in banana gardens.

Continuing on further, on the right, tall steel radio towers were erected and secured in place by steel cables like spiderwebs, stretching tightly over nontraditional buildings. On the left, ice cream carts lined up in front of the ice cream factory, waiting to be loaded with a variety of popsicles whose flavors were marked by red, green, yellow, and orange colors to be sold to residents walking under the one hundred degree sun blaze. Among the seemingly unhurried pedestrians, young men and girls—holding red, blue, and green umbrellas to shield the scorching sunrays—chatted eye to eye along the gravel road.

Walking toward the airfield, the center of Long Chieng, the road curved slightly to the left, and elevated slightly as it curved around the base of the towering karst where the American Advisors' compound was located. In some quiet evenings, as they rested from the long day of work, the Americans played throw-and-catch football in the middle of the town's only paved road—a boring game to the Hmong, who were volleyball and soccer fans.

Proceeding on past the American compound, the road descended slightly as it passed the Military Regional II Command Center. It intersected with a road which ran by Gen. Vang Pao's compound on the right, and ran around the airfield toward the new marketplace, the dusty soccer field, the noisy school, and the police station on the northeast side of the runway.

The airfield was busy. Helicopters, small Air America Helio and porter planes, T-28 bombers, and C-46, C-47, C-123, and C-130 cargo planes hovered above or approached from the southeast to land. At the head of the runway, logistic office staff received orders and planned daily flights to deliver supplies and transport soldiers or residents to military sites, identified by the code "LIMA site #," throughout northern Laos—locations that would take days to reach by foot. Some planes would move to the head runway preparing for takeoff.

The mighty power of the United States was felt as if it was the heart of the world measured by its unmatchable technology that made everything possible.

Military jeeps, pickup-converted taxis, and army cargo trucks stirred dust on gravel roads as they ran errands or delivered passengers and supplies around town. The environment was far worse than the colonial gravel road that sickened my mother in the 1950s, when she first encountered the car emission fumes.

About a mile from the end of the airfield to the southeast there were sporadic explosions of dynamite, busting limestone for road gravel. The rock-crushing complex was just a short distance away from the end of the runway, on the right, sending crushing sounds and dust to the clustered neighborhood nearby.

Clusters of corrugated tin-roofed houses and

buildings connected by as-needed constructed gravel roads—without names or signs—made Long Chieng a poorly designed town, consisting of clustered public service and residential elite complexes. They were more distinguishable at night when more than 85 percent of the town's residential areas were dark, for they had no electricity. Commanding officers in US-funded irregulars—nearly all of whom were ethnic Hmong—had gained ranks and increased in numbers, holding positions of dangerous responsibilities while feeling proud of their privileges.

Long Chieng resembled an urban town by noise, population density, a busy airfield, a marketplace, and pollution. Long Chieng was larger and noisier than Sam Thong and was a town in which its residents proudly lived. They were proud of their city-dweller status—especially in a country vastly dominated by poor rural farming residents.

The marketplace was crowded as people walked elbow to elbow or bumped into each other, shoulder to shoulder in narrow dirt-packed aisles without saying "hi" or "sorry." Vendors, standing in their booths cluttered with merchandise, aggressively invited shoppers to stop in their 10-by-12 rooms as if they would be willing to sell for any price. Shoppers would politely walk backward, refusing and pulling themselves away. These business manners seemed unnatural to the Hmong. Perhaps they had learned from the more successful and aggressive Indian salesmen, in the Vientiane's marketplace, whom I hesitated to walk near.

Nearby, there was a less crowded area where butchers busily fought armies of flies to keep them away from freshly cut meat on wooden benches painted with layers of brown and red blood as they waited for customers. Sales seemed slow, for few could afford the eight hundred kip per kilogram beef or pork. Occasionally, a woman or two would walk by, holding their noses as they haggled, and buy less than a half kilo of beef or pork.

Among the seemingly prestigious shoppers, based on the bulk of their purchases, were vendors from remote villages who would buy large quantities, measured by boxes, of a variety of merchandise, such as candles, matches, candies, school supplies, sandals, and fabrics. They would be loaded up on Air America porter and Helio transport planes and flown back to their small and isolated villages deep inside enemy territories—a mutual-interest service that kept remote residents supplied with what they needed. They would go back to get some more when their inventories ran low.

These business practices were previously perceived as a non-folk tradition only practiced by the Chinese. It became a prestigious status proudly attained by many Hmong, although it was only a very small scale of trade with virtually no overhead cost and management skills, and might not be sustainable without the support of airplane rice.

The truth was that the Hmong —both the vendors and the consumers—had not really transformed mentally into a business-oriented society in which people felt a sense of interdependency in exchanges of cash, products, and labor. Self-sufficiency was not seen in self-sustainability with specialized products and skills for exchanges with others, but rather in the notion that a family should produce everything for itself without exchanging or trading with others. If a family would engage in frequent exchanges of either products or cash purchases, it would be considered lacking self-sufficiency.

Therefore, the motive for innovation and specialization aimed at market success and competitiveness did not come to the picture of economic sustainability. Trade remained largely in the form of passive retail such as bulk purchases of goods from larger non-Hmong merchants at discount prices to be resold at higher prices for profits. There was no profit-markup standard. Consumers would haggle for the lowest prices.

Food service was the least successful business in Long Chieng. Vendors only served non-Hmong cooking, such as rice noodle soup, called *fawm*—a Laotian term acquired from the Vietnamese word *pho.* Pho was a Vietnamese food dish which became popular in Laos and was largely served by Long Chieng roadside food vendors, without the full knowledge of where it originated.

The exchange of labor for cash in the private sector was lowly valued as a shameful status; in Hmong, it was called *Ua zog noj*, meaning "living on pay as a hired hand."

The large collection of people in Long Chieng could not be sustained by food and vegetables produced by local residents through the slash-and-burn farming tradition. Thus the culture of a barter system was replaced by cash and product exchanges. Families with men serving in the military depended largely on the marketplace for everyday food, providing new business opportunities.

Animals and vegetables were among few locally produced commodities brought for sale in the marketplace from as far as twenty miles away. The tradition of always preparing extra food for unexpected guests and serving three large meals a day had been changed due to limited monthly budgets. People in remote villages who visited Long Chieng complained and criticized their Long Chieng folks, saying "they had transformed from a friendly tradition to a culture of arrogance and snobs."

The reality was that the Hmong in Long Chieng were brought from different places and regions by the war in large numbers, too many to greet in every turn and every corner. This had changed from the culture in which they used to greet anyone who came by, invite them into the house, and offer them water or a humble meal.

At first, the Hmong frowned upon the American co-workers who each paid for his/her own bottle of Coke, but later accepted the same practice as a norms, realizing the changes in societies over which they had no control. The urban culture in Long Chieng was not only a subject of gossip, but a real concern for residents in rural villages. "Long Chieng people are snobbish," a woman had said. The concerns of changes in values, culture, and attitudes of the Hmong in Long Chieng had been brought up in numerous intermarriage negotiations because of fears that differences in values and culture might affect marriage relations.

Hmong was the dominant ethnicity among the multiethnic population in the town, thereby making the Hmong proudly believe that Long Chieng was the Hmong city in modern time. Each ethnic group lived in segregated neighborhoods distinguishable by house styles and spoken languages.

The second largest ethnic group was the lowland Lao, mostly from the town of Xieng Khouang, who settled at the end of the airfield on the northeast, surrounding the Buddhist temple. Interethnic marriages were infrequent. Each ethnicity had its own culture and religious practices, but all shared one thing in common—airplane rice dependency. The lowlanders were Buddhists, whereas the Hmong and Mien (the highlanders) were animists. Animism is a spiritual worship privately practiced in individual homes. There were small communities of Khmou and Thai Dam who also practiced animism. Although Christianity was introduced to the Hmong in the early 1950s, church membership had been small.

To the Hmong, Long Chieng was a new establishment of a town—a development of progress, trade, education, and technology—with the king's palace shining on the hill. To the Americans, Long Chieng was just an American secret military base whose purpose was to support the American fight against the Communists' expansion in Southeast Asia—no urban development plan was in mind, no street names and signs, and no address numbers. To achieve the Americans' national-interest goal, the Hmong, frequently called "Meo" by non-Hmong people, were used to rescue downed American fighter pilots, cut off North Vietnamese ammunition supply routes, and prevent North Vietnamese from using Laos as a backdoor ramp and troop-moving route toward Thailand and South Vietnam at the lowest cost possible.

Long Chieng was only a collection of refugees with more than 95 percent depending on airplane rice. More than 95 percent had no running water and electricity. Long Chieng did not have a sewer system. There was no sanitation management system nor was there a future plan in mind. Every family was on its own. There were no flushable toilets and septic systems.

Of course, the Americans had the urban engineering and technology, but they were there for only one thing—the Vietnam War, not the development of a city or town. Long Chieng was viewed from the rooftops as a forever remembered beauty by many Hmong who had seen it. It was the place where many had the opportunity to be exposed to technology and meet many good American friends. It was the airplane rice that kept them alive together in the bathtub-shaped town. Without it, Long Chieng would collapse on its own weight.

All Long Chieng's residents used firewood for heating and cooking. Trees around Long Chieng and on nearby mountain hills and valleys for as far as a ten-mile radius had been cut down for firewood. Thick jungles on mountains around Long Chieng were depleted and replaced by coarse grass. It would take decades for trees to grow. In some areas, it would be irreversible to the original natural state. But everyone worried about the war, and there was no time to think about what the ecological impacts would be.

Firewood had become increasingly scarce and could only be brought into Long Chieng by the mighty military ten-wheelers from farther and farther away. When the Americans were gone, everything would be gone, including the airplanes, airplane rice, the mighty ten-wheelers, the soldiers' salaries, and the plentiful amount of fuel that kept everything going.

Gen. Vang Pao and other Hmong leaders' main concern was to win the war and protect the North Vietnamese and Pathet Lao from taking over their homeland in northern Laos and to defend what the Hmong loved the most—peace and freedom.

For the Americans, the goal was to win the Vietnam War, which many Americans back home viewed not worthy of money and American lives. They had no time to discuss Long Chieng's long-term development plan, nor did anyone pay attention to its natural resources such as water supply, firewood, farmlands, and its long-term economic sustainability.

Located at 3,200 feet above sea level, the roads that connected Long Chieng to other towns and villages, such as Sam Thong to the north, Muong Cha and Pha Khao to the southeast, and most importantly Na Sou to the southwest, were rough and steep. There had been frequent incidents where trucks, jeeps, and taxis rolled back and turned over, resulting in fatalities. The roads, which were largely eroded by rainwater and frequently blocked and damaged by mudslides, were costly to maintain. Construction of a good paved road would be expensive and could not be paid for by the Lao government, whose entire national budget came from foreign aid.

Long Chieng was selected by Gen. Vang Pao and supported by the CIA to be the headquarters of the United States secret military operation in support of the Vietnam War because of its natural fortress. Its flat valley was long enough for an airfield, sufficient for C-46, C-47, C-123, C-130, and T-28 planes to land and take off. It was protected by a wall of mountain ridges surrounding the base and limestone karsts towering over the head runway of the airfield. Its remoteness and rough terrains made it inaccessible for the enemy's ground transportation, which worked in favor of the Americans, who used air transportation—a perfect place for a secretive operation.

Long Chieng's population grew rapidly as more and more men served in the CIA-funded irregular forces and more territories fell under the Communists' control, which resulted in waves of refugee influxes from as far as villages in Sam Neua province seeking sanctuary in the already crowded town. This unprecedented phenomenon had changed the Hmong from a society of small communities in which they maintained a close relationship and cared for each other—even though they lived in different villages—to one in which people living in the same cluster did not know each other.

Although it was a place many were deeply proud of, Long Chieng could not be a long-term, economically sustainable town for many reasons. First, the steep coarse grass hills outside the bowl could not be used for long-term sustainable rice fields. Second, hauling everything uphill on a dangerously zigzagging road was not economically feasible. Third, without sustainable employment and economic interconnections with the outside world, Long Chieng's population would diminish and the airfield would become economically meaningless. And last, Long Chieng could not continue to exist, unless affordable energy could be obtained to replace firewood for heating and cooking.

In 1970, while Long Chieng continued to be perceived by the vast majority of Hmong as the power base of the Hmong in Laos, the war in northern Laos was spreading like blazing fire, burning closer and closer to its buffer zone. Gen. Vang Pao felt he was battling an enormous fire with very little resources and manpower. While the Communist forces advanced in offense, Gen. Vang Pao's forces retreated in defense.

LONG CHIENG, THE LEGENDARY HMONG CITY

The Americans knew the situation and the fate of Long Chieng well. They knew when they were going to pull the plug of the life-support machine and stop sending equipment to battle the fire as their leaders in Washington secretly negotiated with China and the Soviet Union, the superpowers who were behind the fire.

After the Communists' attack on Long Chieng and takeover of Sam Thong in March 1970, the Hmong realized Long Chieng was just as vulnerable as other places from which they had run away. Thousands of refugees, including families of some senior officers like Col. Youa Pao Xiong, Lt. Col. Vang Foung, and others, had moved to settle in villages outside Long Chieng, especially closer to Ban Xorn. Some had residences in Vientiane, where their families lived more than half of the time.

In 1971, the Communist Vietnamese and Red Lao forces had pushed hard against Gen. Vang Pao's forces. Their goal was to gain control of Long Chieng, hoping when it was shattered and under their control, the Hmong would be baseless and the Americans would give up. When Long Chieng fell, the rest of Laos would fall, and the Royalist regime would collapse.

Long Chieng endured another Communist attack, which put it under siege for several months in 1972, causing a large number of Hmong refugees to move toward villages in the southwest. A virgin jungle on the Phou Xang Mountain—about eight miles north of Ban Xorn—became a refugee settlement, large enough for a full elementary group school. Mr. Ying Yang, my former principal and sixth-grade teacher, who became the principal of the Elementary Group School of North Long Chieng, was assigned to head the makeshift school, which still carried the same name as the one he headed in Long Chieng. Most of the refugees never returned to Long Chieng after the siege was over. Although the refugees tried to live in a normal life, their lives were hinged upon airplane rice, and their concerns about the Communists' gaining control of nearly all of Xieng Khouang were throbbing in their heads.

Gen. Vang Pao had seen the benefits of the Hmong seeking settlements outside of Long Chieng for economic self-support if the war ended. If that had been the case, he would have thought of what Long Chieng would become. However, as the war continued, Long Chieng still provided a good business opportunity for many vendors, particularly because it was the place where thousands of soldiers were dropped off and picked up to and from the front lines every month. In addition, thousands of Thai troops were deployed to Long Chieng to help defend Laos against the Communists' takeover. Vendors were essential for providing food and supplies for the soldiers who were there, far away from home.

In 1973, Gen. Vang Pao had envisioned a few economic development projects which included the poultry farm experiment project in Nam Ngua, the agricultural development project in Muang Cha, the saving and loan project, and most importantly, the adult education program in partnership with the Ministry of Education, Division of Primary and Adult Education. However, these projects and programs were in their developmental stages and had not been fully implemented to benefit the people.

Long Chieng might serve as the headquarters, administering all the economic programs, but the projects themselves would need to be located outside of Long Chieng. The landscape around Long Chieng and in areas where the Hmong became heavily concentrated since the start of the war were rough. Building an economically sustainable mechanism that connected Long Chieng with surrounding villages would be very costly.

I visited Long Chieng in March 1974, as part of the adult education teacher training program, and found the town was still very busy, but many parts of the residential areas had become empty. The change in Long Chieng had visibly taken place because, after the cease-fire agreement, the Americans had left Laos, taking their airplanes with them. And all their support, including airplane rice, had stopped. Hence, the Hmong in Long Chieng who once depended on airplane rice had to support themselves by farming outside of Long Chieng. In addition, thousands of soldiers were discharged from military duty and sent home outside of Long Chieng, back to civilian life.

Had the peace agreement turned out the way all the citizens of Laos wanted, Long Chieng still would have been reduced in size, leaving many areas empty, but not in the present state of complete brush-covered ruin.

In the minds of many Hmong, had the war not ended the way it did, Long Chieng would still be a shiny city of the Hmong on the hill. And, Gen. Vang Pao would lead the Hmong to prosperity with educational and technological advancements.

Although Long Chieng has turned into a brush-overgrown ghost town after the Communists' takeover, many Hmong have named their businesses after the legendary town. Today posters of the town are widely distributed and proudly displayed on the walls in their houses. Long Chieng will vividly be remembered by thousands as a Hmong city, and its stories will become legends and will be told for many generations to come. At the same time, the pictures will continue to be a reminder of the legacy of the United States' secret war in Laos.

CHAPTER 10

HMONG STUDENTS STRIVING FOR SUCCESS

During the Vietnam War era, Hmong children, nearly all boys, were sent to makeshift schools in refugee camps and to Sam Thong for post primary schooling. After the fall of Sam Thong, more Hmong students were sent to Vientiane, where they became exposed to a life completely different from that of the Hmong in their war-ridden region in northern Laos.

Thirty people—all students in white-shirt and black-pant uniforms who escaped the Communists' attack on Sam Thong—were lined up in a single column, marching to board an Air America Caribou cargo plane. After a forty-five–minute flight, we landed in Wat Tai National Airport in Vientiane at 5 p.m. on March 25, 1970.

Of the thirty students, seventeen were ethnic Hmong, all from Xiengkhouang province. The rest were ethnic lowland Lao. None of the Hmong students had any relatives in Vientiane while some of the Lao students had relatives who lived on the outskirts of Vientiane.

On arrival at the airport, the Hmong students stood in bewilderment—not far from the aircraft—for about five minutes, discussing where to go. The Lao students, on the other hand, had made up their minds while on the plane. One of the Hmong students came up with a suggestion.

"The only place we can go tonight is Tou Yia Lee's house, our provincial representative," he said.

"Yes, how come . . . Never thought of that! But, we don't know where he lives," another student said.

The Lao students had taken taxis and left the scene. They would spend the night in their relatives' house before looking for the place where we all needed to go. A taxi rolled toward us and the driver asked if we knew where we were going.

"Do you know where Representative Tou Yia Lee lives?" a student asked.

"Yes, he lives not far from the National Parliament Building, across the street from the morning marketplace," the cab driver responded.

There were too many of us for one cab which could, at the most, take five. And it was late. It was our first time in the capital city, and everyone feared that after nightfall approaching someone for a place to stay would be difficult. But, we felt relieved when two more empty cabs rolled by and the first cab driver gestured at them. We all squeezed into the three cabs. The cabs rolled past the capital's business district. Five-story buildings resembled skyscrapers, towering over narrow streets. We busily competed for better views from the crowded cabs to see the civilization we had never seen. The place that looked confusing and complex to the rural dwellers was the center of Laos. It was the home of the people who had very little or no clue about the war in Laos.

It was a place whose streets were dominated by taxi cabs and foot-pedaled three-wheelers competing for passengers. Frequently, young men in disco-era clothes would roar by on their motorcycles. The 36-inch bottom and tight-fitting forelegs of their bell-bottom pants made them look completely out of traditional fashion, causing the schools to issue policies against such outfits.

Each of those spoiled brats would compete with each other for images of celebrity. They would spend a fortune of their parents' assets to buy motorcycles and a great portion of their father's salaries which they had no idea how to earn. The high-spending punks would impress their girlfriends by taking them to elitist restaurants and would not miss a single good movie. To meet the costs of a lifestyle they could not afford, corruption occurred.

The cabs stopped in front of a nice fenced-in white house on Lane Xang Avenue. Two students went to knock on the door and introduced us while the rest of us stayed in the cabs, watching and feeling uncertain of the outcome.

A nice lady, Mrs. Lee, came to the door and they talked for about two minutes. She came out and greeted us quite warmly. We paid the cabs—one hundred kip per person—and Mrs. Lee led us inside the house. An unexpected crowd of people crammed in a large tile-floored living room with beautiful furniture—completely different from a traditional Hmong home—a place located in the heart of the country.

They lived close to the parliament building, the place where parliament members, ministers, the prime minister, and frequently the king came together in their princely garments decorated with shiny medals of honor to hold their meetings. In those meetings, which were frequently broadcast live on the national radio, they contended mostly about not getting what they thought they deserved and not much about what the country was facing.

The country was ruled by a system of government without checks and balances of power, where briberies were a common practice. Many positions were created at the top without objective reasoning and fiscal analysis, while those critically needed in the bottom were disregarded.

Lane Xang Avenue, with the Anousavary National Memorial Monument towering in the middle of the beautifully landscaped island, not far from the parliament building, was Laos's public square where parades of every major national event took place. The citizens in remote villages only saw those events and this place in US-funded documentary films shown every now and then in remote villages.

Representative Lee's residence fit in well with the high-profile environment. There were some young men and young girls in the house, helping to prepare supper. We were unsure if they were family members, relatives, visitors, or servants. Our presence was a complete surprise and undoubtedly a burden. The living room became overcrowded. Family members were driven to the kitchen.

Supper was served on a long table—with multiple bowls of rice and Chinese cabbage and pork soup—just for us. The family ate in the kitchen, except for occasional checks to make sure dishes were not empty.

After supper, they unrolled straw mats on the tiled floor for us to sleep. It was about 10 p.m., and, perhaps, unusually late for the family.

We had our own blankets and used our backpacks as pillows. Waking up before members of the host family, we put our blankets away and rolled up the straw mats. Awakened by our talk and noises, everyone in the family got up. The unusually large number of people competing for the single toilet and water faucet to wash faces made the morning quite unpleasant.

This might seem a bit burdensome. But, it happened all the time to families of Hmong leaders of the remote villages in northern Laos.

Hmong elders had an old saying: "To be a Hmong leader, one must have an oversized rice steamer." This was the only service expected of leaders by their constituents in a culture where they had nothing else to hold them accountable or by which to measure their performances.

By 8 a.m., we were served football-shaped French sandwiches and tea, presumably purchased from the morning marketplace. This seemed different from the Hmong's traditional hospitality, in which they would serve rice and vegetable soups—even for breakfast. Perhaps preparing a traditional Hmong meal was labor intensive and buying French sandwiches from the marketplace was a more convenient choice. Maybe Representative Lee had adopted the Western modern culture—a way of life which my grandmother had feared.

Just as we finished eating, some people came, knocking on the door. There were two of our fellow students from the Sam Thong Teacher Training Institute sent by Professor Chanthala. He was informed of our location by the lowland Lao students who came with us aboard the Caribou plane.

The two students gave us the location of and directions to the professor's house. They hopped on a motorcycle, owned by the professor, and drove away, roaring on Lane Xang Avenue back to the professor's house, where they had been staying for almost a week.

Representative Lee was not home, obviously. He was either in Long Chieng or on a meeting trip somewhere. As young students in a culture where the young and the ordinary citizens didn't ask many questions of their leaders, we simply thanked Mrs. Lee for the hospitality and carried our belongings out onto the street in front of the residence.

A taxi pulled up and the driver asked in Laotian language, "Where are you guys going?"

"We are going to Professor Chanthala's house," a student said. "Here is the direction."

"Yes, I know where it is," the driver said after a quick glance. "It's four or five houses away from the Thath Luang Temple."

The driver talked as if we were familiar with the capital, and that was a good thing. In that part of the world, you would not want to be known as newcomers to the city because you could be subject to exploitation. That's why my parents and other rural dwellers feared going to Vientiane.

Two more cabs came by and he gestured at them. They turned around and pulled behind his cab. He talked to the other cab drivers while six of us crammed into the first one. Led by the first cab, they turned around on Lane Xang Avenue and headed toward the Thath Luang Temple.

After passing the giant memorial monument, the cabs bore right onto Thath Luang Road, then drove toward the temple. Thath Luang Temple is, to this day, the largest Buddhist temple and a historic national monument in Laos.

At the end of the paved road, there was a wide-open and clean dirt and grass court, preserved for the Thath Luang Festival, which was held on the fifteenth day of the twelfth lunar month every year. The statue of Phrachao Xaysethatthirath, the king who reigned during the golden era of Laos, was erected in front of the golden temple. The cabs turned to the left before the empty court, then followed a dirt road for about a quarter of a mile into the residential area where houses were overshadowed and obscured by dense fruit trees and banana groves.

Professor Chanthala's house—an old-style, high-above-ground-platform tin-roofed house—was on a half-acre lot, well shaded by fruit trees. It was an indication he had lived in the capital for generations, especially in a culture where houses rarely went up for sale. A new corrugated tin-roofed house was being built next to the old one. The roof and the hardwood platform were finished, except for the walls. Our arrival had put the work on hold, leaving a pile of hardwood lumber underneath the platform for the unfinished walls. Manual wood planers and handsaws were neatly kept on a bench.

Almost all of the students were there. Some slept in the old house, on the wax-polished living-room platform floor. Others slept on the platform floor of the new house, in green and white mosquito nets tightly stretched like spider webs. Professor Chanthala's residence served as temporary dormitory for the thirty-five first-year students, waiting for arrangement to be made at the Dong Dok Teacher Training Institute—the four-year program campus. His wife, two beautiful daughters whom we frequently teased, and some relatives became cooks, preparing three meals a day for us for nearly a month—perhaps a rare job opportunity for his family members.

A cafeteria had been vacated to be used as a temporary dormitory for the fifty-six senior students where they slept on cushioned mats lined up on a concrete floor for the rest of the school year, awaiting their graduation, coming in June. At the same time an entrance exam would be held in Ban Xorn. A new class of thirty-five freshmen from Xieng Khouang province would join the institute in the next school year. The institute had sharply decreased its student enrollment in the subsequent years despite the fact that certified teachers remained far from meeting the needs of the country's growing school-age children population, not even counting female children who had traditionally been kept from attending schools.

The air in the days preceding the monsoon season was hot and humid. Men and women in peaceful residential areas in Vientiane relaxingly sat under well-shaded house platforms. Back home, in northern Laos, the situation was critical. Nearly all Xieng Khouang residents had become refugees and crowded in safe-haven camps south of Long Chieng under temporary shelters. I was concerned about my parents and their living condition. I had not seen them since I left them before the fall of Sam Thong. They, too, had not heard from me, nor had anyone told them my whereabouts since Sam Thong was attacked.

We stayed idly in Professor Chanthala's house, doing nothing but sleeping, telling stories at night, and helping plane his lumber underneath the new house platform when bored.

It was the season when fruits were abundant—

many of which we did not have names for in the Hmong language. He supplied us with fish sauce and sugar, and we picked and ate all the fruits in his garden.

Finally, classroom and dormitory arrangements were complete, and we were sent to the Dong Dok campus. The first-year students were assigned to sleep in the cafeteria of the English Session School, about a quarter of a mile down the slope toward the southeast corner of the campus.

The neck-high–walled cafeteria only had two ceiling fans and two fluorescent lights hung from the ceiling—one at each end. The weather preceding the monsoon season was unbearably hot and humid. Bugs and flies were bad at night. The wooden screens on the upper parts of the walls did not prevent them from coming in toward the lights. They dropped and landed on the floor and on the beds.

Each student was given a green stretcher arranged by rank, coincidentally putting the Hmong students on one end and the Lao students on the other, on the open concrete floor. My bed was the first against the wall—next to the kitchen. Khamphay, the student president, a twenty-eight-year-old former teacher who was ethnic Lao, was across the aisle, not far from me. Pao Vang and I were the only Hmong students among the Lao majority on one end of the floor.

I became sick two days earlier and slept quietly in my green mosquito net without interacting with anyone. Although being the youngest, my academic talents earned high respect from my peers of both ethnicities.

Khamphanh, a short and stocky twenty-six-year-old Lao student next to Khamphay, also a former teacher, turned off the light on our end. All the bugs went to the other end. Moua Kai, a short and stocky Hmong student—also a former volunteer teacher—turned off the light on their end. The room went dark, except for sporadic lightning in the distance, which indicated a storm was approaching.

Khamphanh went to the other end and turned on their light. Moua Kai came to our end and turned on our light, then turned off their light. The two traded light-switching on and off several times. Khamphanh started a racial curse: "You stupid Meo savages."

And eighteen Lao students stood up behind him. Nine Hmong students stood up. Both sides were ready to engage in a fight. Four Lao students kicked and knocked down a section of the plywood wall on the side facing the dorm building that was being vacated.

I stood up and yelled at Khamphay.

"Shame on you, Mr. President! How could you let this happen? What are you going to do about this? Are these the kind of men who will be teachers to teach children? Shame on you—all of you!"

"Stop! Stop!" Khamphay shouted at both sides.

"I am disappointed and disgusted," I added. "Are these whom we call teachers? You need to fix the wall tonight. Otherwise, I will not be shy to report tomorrow on what happened."

Everyone apologized and put the painted-white plywood wall back on. Two hours later the storm arrived with gusty wind over sixty miles per hour, blowing rain and tree leaves inside the room. Everything and everyone was wet.

The next day some older Lao students came to talk to me and thank me for preventing the fight—an indication of social competency and tentative professionalism, on their part. The incident was never reported to the school officials. The Hmong students acted as if nothing had happened. None had said anything to me about the near-disastrous incident. Although the school officials tried to make racial slurs a punishable offense, racial tensions among some of the students were not subtle. Hmong students in other schools, including the Dong Dok campus, who represented only tiny percentages of their school populations, reported similar ethnic tensions.

The rest of the school year had not been going well for me. I had been sick and had not been able to attend classes. While everyone was in class, I was in bed. The cooks brought me food every day. But fried fish and sticky rice on plates were left untouched. I was brought to the campus hospital and stayed there for nine days, feeling better just before the school year ended.

Because all the test scores were lost in Sam Thong, the first-year students were required to take a test of passage to be promoted to the second year, for accountability purpose, we were told. The second-year students, however, satisfied the graduation requirement with their student teaching scores.

Despite not having completely recovered from illness, I was not exempted from taking the test. The reason was that, ranking number twenty-one in the quarter prior to the fall of Sam Thong, I had not proven that I had met the required academic skills, a requirement I could not argue with. I would either take the test or repeat first-year classes in the coming year, thereby delaying my graduation by a year. Most of the professors felt assured and confident that I would minimally pass the test. I took the test, despite not having attended classes.

I passed it, ranking number four, and surprised everyone.

The school year ended in the middle of June. I was able to get out of the bed and walk around, although still weak.

The monsoon rains had started and it rained nearly every day. The gravel road between Colonial Route 13 and Ban Xorn was damaged by rains and in bad condition. In addition, there had been no passenger buses traveling to Ban Xorn for nearly two months, because there had been several incidents of robberies and ambushes on the buses in the jungle areas of the road between Hoy Mo Village and Ban Xorn. The students, mostly Hmong from villages around Long Chieng, would be stranded in Vientiane, unless air transportation was provided.

The school and the Division of Teacher Training Education had been able to work with the Royal Lao Military Region Five to provide two military cargo trucks to send us home, accompanied by an armored vehicle. Because of my health condition, I sat with the driver and a soldier in the cabin. All the other students sat in the back of the trucks, covered with green tarps. The seven-hour trip was frightening and greatly unpleasant.

Upon arrival in Ban Xorn late Friday afternoon, I was informed by Chue Ker Moua that Uncle Song Chai and my parents had been relocated from Muang Phoun to Phou Xang Noy by helicopter. Phou Xang Noy was a small village with an airstrip, about six miles north of Ban Xorn. Mr. Pop and Chue Ker Moua wanted the refugees to be inside the safe zone and away from the enemy line for USAID relief program.

In 1970, thousands of refugees, including Lao,

Khmou, and a vast majority of Hmong, swarmed the entire area south, southeast, and southwest of Long Chieng, forming the largest concentrations of refugees ever, in villages which included Phou Xang Noy, Namveh, Namkob, Phak Kheh, Phou Kang, Nam Luang, Hoykham Tai, Nam Phah, Pha Khao, Muang Cha, Na Luang, Na Xou, Phoun Xay, and Na Luang. Lao and Khmou refugees, all from Xieng Khouang and Sam Neua provinces, settled along river valleys and in the lower elevations. They all depended on Mr. Pop for airplane rice.

The trail from Ban Xorn to Phou Xang Noy was muddy and dangerous, especially crossing the Nam Nguem River, which had turned into a muddy color and risen up to the drop edges with strong currents in the monsoon season. The other students went to their villages in separate directions. I was still weak and frail. Chue Ker Moua put me on a helicopter on a regular supply delivery flight to Phou Xang Noy.

The refugees from Phou Vieng settled in freshly built lean-tos on the east side of the airstrip, just below an old military outpost. The swelling of refugees crowded the area in unprecedented numbers. They settled in temporary shelters, on the south, southwest, and west sides of the airstrip.

Refugees from Bouam Loung and Phou Vei areas settled in large concentrations in the Nam Veh Valleys, where another airstrip was built. A concentration of Khmou, distinguishable by their above-ground platform houses, was in the flat bottom of the valley by the creek. They all depended on airplane rice, which was airdropped once a week.

My three-month school break was fleeting and short, especially because it was inundated with helping the refugees calculate rice distributions. Teng and I had a few days enjoying fishing trips down the Nam Lao Creek on the slope of Phou Xang Noy Mountain, where we caught baskets full of stripe fish.

The slopes and hills on the Phou Xang Mountain were filled with human voices—all Hmong. Most men were soldiers, serving in the front lines and leaving their families among the refugees. The war in northern Laos in 1970 resembled a raging fire burning out of control. The Hmong were taking the brunt of stopping the advances of the fire.

Most young Hmong boys and men were bearing guns, sacrificing their lives to fight for freedom for the rest of Laos, instead of being in schools and learning what was best for themselves, for the Hmong, and for the country as a whole.

The beginning of the school year was drawing near as September approached. It was time for me to return to Vientiane to resume the final year in the teacher training program. My goal was to be the best teacher I could to provide Hmong children with the best education they needed to move out of an unsustainable slash-and-burn farming tradition.

Life in Vientiane was as if it were in a different world. There were hundreds or even thousands of young students, disproportionately Chinese and Vietnamese and about 90 percent male, in black and white uniforms, walking on school campuses—a complete contrast to the young men in green military uniforms, walking on Long Chieng's dusty gravel roads. I traveled between these two worlds at least twice a year, witnessing their great disparities.

A new class of thirty-five freshmen arrived to join

the institute. The fifty-six seniors had graduated and become teachers, teaching students in different communities across Laos. The thirty-five students who were freshmen the previous year had been promoted to the second year, waiting to graduate and become teachers.

My final year of school was filled with hope and confidence that I would have a full year of school without interruptions, and that my academic achievement would allow me to continue to the third year in the four-year program. I earned high scores on every subject, ranking number one every quarter.

While others looked forward to becoming teachers, I prepared to continue into the four-year program. After the third quarter at the end of March, fourteen of us were assigned to do student teaching in Elai School District, about eleven miles north of the campus. Elai was a large village on Route 13 which linked Vientiane and the Royal capital of Luang Phrabang. Elai consisted of two villages—the old village of the native residents and the new village of the refugees from Xieng Khouang.

Five female students, none of whom was ethnic Hmong, remained on campus and were assigned to do student teaching in a nearby school. They were supervised by the school's only female staff—a nonteaching position.

The main part of the school was in the new village where the principal spent most of his time. We were rotated weekly between the new and the old schools, experiencing the different social cultures between the natives of Xieng Khouang and Vientiane provinces. The two groups spoke slightly different dialects, but both were ethnic lowlanders with similar cultures and ways of life.

The native residents lived in clay-shingle or corrugated-tin roofed and hardwood platform-floored houses shaded by mature coconut and other fruit trees. They practiced wet rice paddy cultivation for generations. The refugees, on the other hand, lived in small thatch-roofed and chopped-bamboo-platform-floored houses. They practiced slash-and-burn cultivation since they had left their rice paddy fields in the fertile Xieng Khouang plateaus. It would take years before they could establish wet rice paddy fields in the vast plains around Elai.

Sixteen other students were assigned to a school district five miles farther north on the same road. We visited them occasionally on the weekends, enjoying the colorful sour lychee fruits, which did not grow in Elai but were abundant around the other village, enough for us to use for decorating our graduation-welcome gate.

The graduation ceremony was held in the other village and filled with fulfillment and joy in a culture that could not have been better. We danced until midnight around the fire on which we roasted a whole cow. Dr. Somphou Oudomvilay, director of the National Division of Teacher Training, and his wife, who was director of the National Division of Radio and Communication, were special guests of the event.

We concluded the student teaching program and returned to campus to wait for the announcement of our final scores for graduation. This time we felt more grown up and better than when we started two years ago. There would be a newly graduated class of teachers going out to fill the holes of teacher shortages in remote communities—a triumph over the century-old shadow of illiteracy.

The three-month student teaching experience was

wonderful. The relationships between the student teachers and the students were great. And the relationships with the parents and the community were learning experiences appreciated for a lifetime.

The final moment of the two-year training program for which everyone had been waiting eventually arrived. And the time to file applications for teaching certification with the Ministry of Education had come. It was the happiest moment for everyone, especially those who had left wives and children at home without incomes. While I planned on submitting my application for continuing to the four-year program, everyone would look forward to becoming a teacher in the coming school year.

I spoke with Professor Chanthala about my interest and he proudly brought my request to Professor Outhapoun, director of Sam Thong Teacher Training Institute, who immediately contacted the director of the Dong Dok Teacher Training Institute. After reviewing my transcripts, I was accepted, except for one thing. I did not meet the four-year math requirement, which had to be satisfied prior to entering the third year, because the two-year program did not offer college algebra.

I would be accepted if I was willing to take the course, which would be offered during the school break, free of charge for students who had failed the requirement. Students would be provided room and board free of charge, but they would have to pay for their own food and meals, which would cost around twenty thousand kip for the three months—an equivalence of fifteen dollars (1971 value). It would be impossible for my parents to come up with that amount of money. They still owed Uncle Song Chai ten thousand kip when I started the program and had not had any idea how to pay it back.

My heart sank heavily in disappointment and worry. But that had not stopped me from trying.

In Ban Xorn, I talked to Chue Ker Moua about my situation. He was willing to give me fifty pounds of airplane rice, which would help reduce the cost. But, I was told no rice was allowed to pass the checkpoint in Hin Heub because there had been large cases of rice smuggling to the Vientiane black markets. In any case, I went home, preparing to do whatever I could without creating any more concerns for my parents. My parents were not unique in the situation where the cost of education presented fears and concerns and shadowed over the pride of their children's achievements, especially for those whose lives were dominated by poverty.

My only hope was Uncle Tou, who had been supporting me all along, but I had never asked for that much money from him. I only had ten days to report to the class. Upon arriving at home in the wet and soggy monsoon season, I asked Yaj, who went to school with me in Phoukoum and Bouam Loung and whom I had helped with homework every night, to go with me to see Uncle Tou. I wanted to borrow twenty thousand kip, exactly the amount I was told was needed. I had saved four thouand kip from the student-teaching food allowances—enough for the taxi fares.

We set out early in the morning, on a muddy trail crossing the jungle of Phou Xang Mountain, the deep Nam Pha Valley, and the Nam Pha Creek, toward Phak Keh—a refugee sanctuary seven miles northeast of Phou Xang Noy or ten miles south of Long Chieng. We arrived in Phak Kheh, a yellow, dirt-barren village which became muddy by sporadic rains, in late afternoon.

As we walked past the muddy marketplace, a woman in Hmong dress walked up on the muddy dirt path with a bamboo basket on her back.

"Excuse me," I said to the woman. "Do you know where Tou Xiong lives?"

"Yes, in that big house by the dry creek there," the woman said, pointing to a large thatched house, where there were flowers around the dirt porch.

We went to the wide-open front door, which indicated someone was at home. Aunt Tou came to the door and greeted us.

"Ge, you've come to visit us! We haven't seen you for nearly two years!"

"Yes, the last time we got together was when Sam Thong was attacked by the Pathet Lao. Uncle Tou did come to see me in Vientiane in the beginning of this year, but I didn't see you. He gave me 1,500 kip. I thank you both for your support."

Aunt Tou laughed and invited us inside.

Before we sat down, I asked, "Is Uncle Tou home?"

"Yes, he just came home from Long Chieng a few days ago. But, today he went out to join a ceremony somewhere in the village. Don't know how late he'll be back."

"When did you move here?" I asked. "Uncle Tou told me you had moved here, but didn't say when."

"Not long after we evacuated to Phou Kang Noy and you left us there, we came back to Long Chieng and decided to move here," she said.

"How is school?"

"Actually, I have graduated, but I wanted to continue to the four-year program. I would like to borrow some money to take some courses during the school break to meet the four-year program requirement."

"For that, you have to talk to your uncle."

It was already dark outside and started raining. We spent the night there after supper. Uncle Tou did not come home until after midnight. It continued raining hard all night.

We got up in the morning and it was still raining outside. Uncle Tou got up and took a big bowl of warm water that Aunt Tou had prepared. He went out to the front porch to wash his face and brush his teeth. He came back and sat by the fireplace.

I wasted no time. I moved my wooden stool and sat close by him. I told him that I wanted to borrow twenty thousand kip to continue to the four-year program.

"I have been so proud of you and I am happy that you want to continue further on your education. But, I will not receive my salary until next month. I cannot give you any money right now. If you can wait until next month, I may be able to help you."

"I only have ten days to report and decide what I will do. It's okay if you don't have any money to let me borrow now. I'll talk to my parents to see if there is any other way. Thank you for the support you have given me."

After breakfast, Aunt Tou wrapped some rice in fresh banana leaf, and we returned home in the rain. They asked that we wait until it stopped raining, but I couldn't wait.

We set out on the same muddy trail in the direction we came from while light rain continued and we carried our plastic rain shield over our heads. While walking down the hill toward the Nam Pha Noy Creek, a middle-aged woman walked up the hill with her six- or seven-year-old boy. The rain had stopped intermittently, but rainwater still rushed down on the dirt trail like a creek. The barefooted woman with an umbrella paused and talked to us.

"We just returned from down there. The bridge is gone and the creek has swelled up over the edge. You won't be able to cross it. I think it would be better to come back tomorrow."

"It has been raining all night," I said to her. "We should have thought about the creek before coming. We just want to go down to see if we can cross. If not, we will have to come back tomorrow."

We walked past them and continued down the trail. The boy, also barefooted and with his plastic rain shield over his head, paused and briefly looked back at us, then continued on up the trail.

We arrived at the creek and saw the muddy water had risen over the drop-edges and flooded the corn fields on both sides. The bridge, actually just two wooden planks, was nowhere to be found. In a society where people lived in temporary shelters, not certain where they would live next month or next year, no one was thinking about investing in any permanent structure.

We followed along a flooded bamboo fence downstream for about four hundred feet, where the fence ended at a giant bamboo bush. The bamboo leaves were swarmed and blackened with blue flies. What lay dead and rotted under the waist-deep water was not known.

There were bunches of giant bamboos falling across the water to the other side, with some right above the water, making a perfect bridge, and some at a perfect height to hang on to. We waded through the swarm of flies and thick bushes of bamboos. I crossed first. I made it to the other side and felt relief. Then it was Yaj's turn to cross. He wore a pair of heavy military boots and a heavy military suit, and carried our lunch and his older brother's .38 caliber revolver.

He walked clumsily on the bunch of four or five bamboos, which paralleled loosely. I held my breath deeply as I watched him cross. All of a sudden, he slipped, broke one of the bamboos, and fell into the water. He disappeared. The currents were strong and flowed in a swirl toward the side where I was standing, and then into a swirling pool at the curve of the creek before it flowed down toward a rapid where water rushed down, splashing on giant boulders.

He appeared again, trying to swim, but he couldn't. He was about fifteen feet from me, drifting closer to the swirling pool about fifty feet away. I pulled a ten-foot bamboo from the fence and handed the other end to him. He was too far away. The water was already up to my waist. I walked five more feet toward him. Water was up to my armpits, but I felt grass and corn stalks under my feet. He grabbed the bamboo and pulled me in. I let go of the bamboo and he lost it. As I turned around, trying to get another bamboo, one of my feet tripped on an old stump. I pulled another bamboo. I gave him one end, with my foot on the stump, I pulled him out.

We went up to the wet cornfield. I sat down, crying and angry. My best friend nearly drowned and lost his life for my cause.

We went home without money; we had barely survived. Our lunch was gone. Yaj had swallowed a lot of dirty water and vomited everything he ate in the morning.

I decided to withdraw my application to continue to the four-year program. I went back to Vientiane and submitted my application to the Ministry of Education to become a teacher—the job and profession I accepted passionately.

PART THREE
THE AFTERMATH

CHAPTER 11

BECOMING A TEACHER

In a society where the purpose and quality of education were widely misunderstood, we had faced the war that always worked against our efforts to educate the educationally deprived children.

The transition from the world of childhood to the world of adulthood, from the world of a student to the world of a teacher, and from the world of a receiver to the world of a giver and contributor presented new perspectives and challenges.

Starting September 1, 1971, as students looked for another year of learning and accomplishment, I began my new responsibility and accountability, which would be measured by my students' accomplishments. The students would come with different strengths, talents, and weaknesses. Despite the fact that students and teachers had a mutual goal and interest, the war was always against us.

In my two years of training in the Sam Thong Teacher Training Institute, I had the opportunity to learn different teaching approaches documented in textbooks and had accepted the teaching styles of good professors while being a critic of the teaching styles of others from whom I did not benefit much as a student.

In my application, where I was asked to choose

three locations to which I wished to be assigned, I chose Bouam Loung—the least-wanted place—as my first choice. I was assigned to Bouam Loung, my old school—the most dangerous and isolated village deep in enemy territory—where many children did not have a choice. It could only be reached by Air America transport planes. It was a choice I had selected out of other places I would have preferred.

The young and newly appointed school principal, Ko Xiong, was a former sixth-grade teacher from Pha Khao School. He had a reputation of being an excellent teacher with a good sense of humor, and he was good in mathematics. His older brother, Kou Xiong, was a T-28 and Raven pilot who died in a plane crash in Long Chieng.

The beginning of school was an extremely busy time for him as a new principal. All the certified teachers assigned to Bouam Long were new graduates, many of whom graduated from Sam Thong Teacher Training Institute just a year before I did. All were young and energetic and committed to providing quality education for Hmong children who had been deprived of educational opportunities in their remote villages—the places where they wished they were born elsewhere.

A week before September, a young team of teachers was boarded up on an Air America Porter cargo plane—four at a time—for a forty-five-minute flight toward Bouam Loung. The coordinating process, in a society where no one received notice in the mail, required individuals to be responsible for obtaining their information, even if it would take one or two days of walking.

Moua Lia had done a phenomenal job. But, without USAID's little fishtail helicopter or Air America planes, which took him to Bouam Loung once a month or more, it would take walking messengers days or weeks to reach.

I walked from Phou Xang Noy to meet with Ko Xiong in Phak Kheh, where we flew to Ban Xorn, and from there we flew to Bouam Loung. The Porter plane flew high above the clouds over the Plain of Jars of Xieng Khouang—a dangerous area controlled by Communist Vietnamese and Pathet Lao forces.

Arriving in Bouam Loung was like coming home. I met with people with familiar faces—many whom I had known and lived with since childhood. I was surrounded by so many people who came to ask how my family had been. I should have asked them how they had survived. But I did not.

Bouam Loung, in just more than two years, had changed from a smooth and barren ground village to one in which dirt mounds and sandbag bunkers were built among houses. It made me wonder how much suffering the people of Bouam Loung had endured from waves of bombardments of enemy attacks since I had left.

After two months into the school year, Ko Xiong was given an additional assignment as principal of the newly built Nam Veh School. He talked to Col. Cher Pao Moua and arranged monthly designated plane flights for us to get food supplies in Ban Xorn or Luang Phrabang. Col. Moua was furious and said the demand was too much and, if we were not happy, we should all be fired and replaced.

Ko Xiong had a heated discussion with Col. Moua.

"Because of teacher shortages, while other villages receive temporary volunteer teachers, you receive teachers trained and licensed by the Ministry of Education," he said. "They cannot be easily fired and replaced just based on this request."

Col. Moua insisted he needed to talk to Moua Lia, the provincial school superintendent. Moua Lia was called and he arrived the next day to meet with Col. Moua.

"This is a dangerous and confined community, deep in enemy territory," Moua Lia said. "No other teachers want to come here. These teachers care about the children and they volunteer to be here and are willing to risk danger. They have no place to find food and other supplies. Everything available in the marketplace here is too expensive for them. I will work with Mr. Pop and Gen. Vang Pao to make sure you have teachers for your children."

Col. Moua agreed. Moua Lia assured the teachers he would assess the situation closely. The school would only be open if the situation would not put the lives of teachers and students in danger.

Ko Xiong returned to Nam Veh to assume the additional assignment as the principal of the Nam Veh Group School—a new fifteen-room school, built for the children in a settlement of refugees, mostly fled from Bouam Loung long before it became isolated. He flew on Air America planes to Bouam Loung once a month to visit the school, deliver teachers' salaries, and collect reports.

The school still looked the same and was in the same condition as it was two and a half years earlier when I was still a student there, except for visible broken sections of the barbed-wire fences. There were green turfs of bushes around the school fences. As I was looking around from the dirt-barren ground in front of my classroom facing the gardens below the airstrip, some of my students walked up to me.

"Teacher, do you know there are dead bodies of Vietnamese soldiers in those bushes?" one of the students asked.

"Really?" I said. "No, I didn't know. I was just thinking we needed to clear them because they looked bad around the school."

"My dad said we should not go near them because there are ghosts in there," another student said.

I talked to some teachers, and we went to see them with our own eyes. What we saw was something tragic. Human remains were still inside their green uniforms. Although the act they had committed was vicious, they carried out someone's orders, which they could not resist. Someone's son, husband, or father never returned home. The vicious human acts, if looked at deeper from the surface, were preventable.

The acts were contrary to what we were committed to achieving as teachers. It is sad, to this day, that humans, who are intelligent and capable of teaching each other, cannot resolve their differences and avoid conflicts. Human viciousness is far more dangerous and destructive than the most ferocious and far less intelligent beasts in the wild. Human violence happens across continents and across the globe, resulting in atrocities and death.

The beginning of school was filled with excitement, which reminded me of the early days of my school life. I had always enjoyed learning.

My twenty-seven second graders were respectful and eager to learn. When I told them I had been a student in Bouam Loung and had lived there for many years, they asked me more questions than I asked them.

"How old were you when you were student here?" one student asked.

"Why did you leave Bouam Long?" another student

asked.

"How did you become a teacher?" still another student asked.

"I want to be a teacher when I grow up," another student said.

I laid out my goals and what we would learn. I also told them up front what I expected from them and how we would achieve what we wanted. In addition, I told them to tell their parents who I was and that they were welcome to come see me anytime.

My way of teaching surprised many parents. They said they had never heard a teacher talking this way. Most teachers only controlled students with a stick, not vigorous and interesting teaching. Controlling students with a stick was the way teachers taught in the days when I was a student. Those days, some parents even used scare tactics to frighten their children, saying if they didn't listen, they would tell their teacher to whip them at school.

In a society where more than 90 percent of adults had no literacy skill, teachers were highly respected. Students had zero disciplinary problems. They took teachers' words seriously. I often heard children talking to each other. "You shouldn't do that. Do you remember what our teacher said to us?" they would say.

Unfortunately, the percentage of abusive teachers was high. I had been forced to walk on my knees around a long school building three times for being five minutes late as the teacher stood watching and laughing. I had hit so many students on the head when they could not read, and had been hit back hard by those whom I did not hit hard enough.

I wanted students to feel that school was a fun and desirable place to be. My first month as a teacher was filled with enthusiasm, joy, and vigor. The students were great. I was full of energy and ideas for the job of teaching for which I felt personally and independently responsible. The progress of the students, to whom I felt personally connected, fueled my everyday lesson planning. When students showed no eagerness to learn, I felt they needed help to see the world from the perspectives that would guide them in the right way.

Three months of school had gone by quickly, and December arrived, seemingly sooner than expected. All the teachers, none of whom was from Bouam Loung, looked forward to returning home for a full week of New Year celebration. The students also looked forward to a week of school break, although Bouam Loung did not plan to have an enjoyable celebration.

Young girls and young men, who had been confined in Bouam Loung—a dangerous world whose safe boundaries did not extend beyond the horizons—felt great pain seeing the teachers fly away to a different world beyond the horizons.

On December 13, 1971, the day before our scheduled flight to Long Chieng, some girls planned to sneak away with some of the teachers, pretending to be their wives. Otherwise, if they tried to get on the plane, they would be pulled away from it. They came to sleep at our residence overnight, nervously hoping that when the plane arrived they would deceptively get on board and fly away with us.

At 3 a.m., Communist Vietnamese and Pathet Lao pounded Bouam Long with long-range artillery from Ban Ban. Mortar hit and exploded at various parts of the village. We got up and crammed into the bunker nearby. Col. Moua could not respond in retaliation with his shorter-range 105mm and 106mm guns. The Communists' shelling lasted for two hours. They stopped as daylight came, for fear that Col. Moua would retaliate by calling air strikes.

At 8 a.m., we were already at the airfield waiting excitedly for the plane to arrive. The girls were nervous because the artillery shelling in the early morning had caused fear and panic and there were many people at the airfield, trying to board the plane as well.

A two-engine Air America plane arrived and became swarmed by people fighting to board. Four teachers were able to get on with two girls, and two or three residents also got on board. The overwhelmed plane closed the door and took off. There were four teachers left, including me, unable to get on board. We went to talk to Col. Moua about what had happened. He was furious.

"No resident should go near the airfield, except for the teachers!" he declared.

He called Long Chieng for another plane. Four hours later, a single-engine Porter cargo plane arrived and the four of us got on board without competition. We arrived in Long Chieng too late for the transportation arrangements. We had to find our own way to go home in separate directions. I was sent to the USAID office where I was boarded on a helicopter to Ban Xorn late in the afternoon. I walked to Phou Xang Noy the next morning and was two days late for the New Year celebration.

Communist Vietnamese and Pathet Lao had continued pounding Bouam Loung with heavy artillery and followed with overwhelming ground attacks throughout the dry season. The situation became critically dangerous and the school was permanently closed. Bouam Loung residents never had their New Year celebration, except hiding for their lives in bunkers.

We never returned to the school again after the New Year celebration. I never saw those twenty-seven eager-to-learn students again. The three months for which I was their teacher, when I started my teaching career, was short, like a dream.

After the New Year celebration, all the teachers from Bouam Loung were assigned to teach in Nam Veh Group School, where student population increased rapidly by the influx of refugees into the Phou Xang Mountain region. Instead of teaching a class, I was assisting Ko Xiong and serving as a floating teacher, teaching any class when a teacher was absent.

In March, the Communists' attack on Long Chieng caused a large number of Hmong refugees to move southward toward Nam Veh and Phou Xang areas. The third- and fourth-grade classes became too crowded. A new building was added. The large fourth-grade class was divided and I taught half of the fourth graders for the remainder of the school year. The school year ended without a solid sense of accomplishment on my part, but with much to look forward to in the coming year.

When the next school year started, I was assigned to teach one of the two fifth-grade classes—a highly motivated group of students, some of whom were from my fourth-grade class in the previous school year. In a society where children were expected to assume adult responsibilities at an early age, the fifth-grade students were socially mature and willing to learn responsibly. As a teacher, it was my responsibility for making learning a purposeful endeavor.

Schooling had traditionally been perceived only as learning the basic literacy skills of reading, writing, and morality. Math and science were new subjects taught in formal education settings. However, their purposes and objectives remained widely misunderstood.

The vast majority of teachers, including those who had been trained and licensed, failed to expand education beyond the traditional perception of a primary educational goal. They failed to make learning relevant to the reality in the modern world. In effect, the lack of effort to create or promote good teaching models through standardized accountability measures had perpetuated poor-quality education and was passed on to the next generations of teachers.

I had acquired some excellent teaching styles from a few good professors, but not much from the books from which they taught. I had put them into uses that made education both practical and exploratory. My students enjoyed the discussions of the functions of living things in nature, how historical events affected human races, cultures, discoveries, and societies, and how everything was interrelated. And the discussions of the practical implication of education made learning a meaningful experience.

My teaching throughout the first year and the subsequent ones received praises from parents and appreciation from students, many of whom became productive and successful individuals, to this day. My rewards as a teacher were not the value of the salaries I received, but the contributions of relevant skills that I gave to my students who needed them.

In 1973, there was an increased number of Hmong refugees moving south, past Ban Xorn, in search of new farmlands and, in part, in anticipation of the end of the long war. My parents and the refugees from Phou Vieng and Phou So were among them. As a result, teachers were assigned to go with the flow of refugees.

In response to my request to Moua Lia that I wished to be closer to home, I was transferred to teach in a newly built school in a refugee village; it was only called Kilometer 22 (Km 22) and was located by the gravel road that linked Ban Xorn and Vang Vieng, where I taught first grade. I wished to have the experience of teaching different grade levels.

In May 1974, just before the school year ended, I was transferred again to replace Pa Lee Yang, a senior teacher who taught in a school on the summit of Phou Kho Mountain—a refugee village about five miles northwest of Km 22 and one mile from where my parents lived. He was promoted to become the principal of Km 22 School. The transfer not only served me well, but also met the needs of the school system. I inherited his classroom of eighty-three students in first through third grades.

The school was expanded for the growing refugee population, and two more teachers came to teach first and second grades when the new school year started in September. I taught third grade and served as head teacher of the school of 108 students.

In 1974, the war-torn country hoped for a long-overdue reconciliation among the three political factions as they negotiated a coalition government. The National Division of Primary and Adult Education of the Royal Lao Ministry of Education launched an adult education program with an emphasis on adult literacy and community economic development. I was among the teachers selected to take part in the program.

In collaboration with Gen. Vang Pao's economic development program (still in a developmental stage),

USAID, and Xieng Khouang Provincial School System, a week-long training session was held in July 1974, in the Provincial Superintendent Headquarters in Na Luang, about three miles east of Ban Xorn. The training focused on key issues, such as adult literacy skill development, health, family planning, and economic development through sustainable farming. Books, fuel, and kerosene lamps were provided for adult night classes.

The program started in the beginning of the 1974–75 school year. Enrollment was overwhelming. The two-hour night classes three nights a week in addition to my full-time job as a third grade teacher was quite overwhelming. It was, however, filled with enthusiasm and joy.

After supper, people—young and old, men and women—started coming to class. By 7 p.m., the third grade classroom was full with adult students, willing to learn. Among the most excited students were young teenage girls who had been kept from attending school. Everyone called me "teacher." They had never gone to school and sat in a classroom with a book in front of them. The opportunity to learn was what they had only dreamed of, but never thought would become a reality.

We laid out our goals and different components of the program, and most importantly, we would measure the outcomes that each would achieve. We had planned the milestone measure of achievement to be held by June 30, 1975. A collection of writing and math samples had been planned for an achievement ceremony at the end of the school year.

Hmong communities throughout northern Laos had suffered from a multiplicity of problems that included displacement by war; unsustainable slash-and-burn agricultural tradition; and child malnutrition and mortality.

Lack of sanitation and clean drinking water, adequate health care, quality education, gender equity and equality, and knowledge of livestock production and disease control had never been discussed among leaders of different levels.

The top-down system of social and political culture did not support grassroots initiatives and empowerment. It maintained a system of corrupt and self-serving political culture in which leaders saw their positions as privileges and not responsibilities. Top leaders expected welcome ceremonies with food and gifts when they made visits to remote villages, which did not serve the purpose of need assessments and living condition assessments.

Leadership positions were only reserved for members and descendants of those in the elite circle. Bright and capable children of the poor, and especially girls, were not given the opportunity to test their potential. Resources and support were kept high at the top and within the elite—nothing trickled down to those in the bottom. Citizens only bowed to their leaders and no one had the right to either question their performance or demand accountability and transparency. In fact, challenging the authorities by the bottom rank of citizens was considered a punishable act.

There were people like my grandmother who deeply believed in and took for granted the way of life in their centuries-old tradition. They accepted their world and their status as the way it should be. There were people like my mother who had no choice, because all decisions were made by men. There were too many people who simply had no way and no resources to elevate themselves out of the holes in which they did not choose to be. Some had been in the holes for so long that other places alienated them.

The program, which might alienate many, had to start at the very basic stages to address the problems, which had been deeply rooted in the lives of the remote village residents and had been widely accepted as the way it was in their world.

The participants would learn basic reading and writing, starting from learning Lao alphabets and slowly progressing toward words that had farming, health, and educational focuses. Numbers and simple math problems were also learned as part of the basic literacy component. For the first time in their lives, the participants learned how to put characters into words and use numbers to represent counts.

We engaged in lively discussions about the home environment that was a preventable cause of health problems, such as contaminated water, improper water drainage, and poor sanitation, which were integral parts of the program. Child diseases and mortality were discussed as part of family planning. Family planning was a difficult issue in a culture that embraced large families. Therefore, it was carefully discussed so that it would not offend cultural and traditional values.

The residents were more interested in economic development and sustainable farming. We discussed two aspects of traditional farming. 1. We examined the unsustainable slash-and-burn farming tradition, which caused constant displacement in search of new farmland and a lifestyle deeply rooted in the minds of many who believed that "they might not live in one place long enough to see the fruits of a banana tree." 2. We discussed the devastating animal diseases that had wiped out pigs and chickens in many villages and how to prevent them. Disease tracking from village to village without proper containment would continue to devastate production.

The last component of the program was quality education, which was widely misunderstood and had presented some fear factors. The program itself had presented self-evidence of educational values. We discussed these fears, giving myself and my story as an example of how those fear factors could have prevented me from obtaining an education and how I had overcome them. There had been a strong belief among members of the remote communities that education would change lifestyle, values, and beliefs, and would be in conflict with their culture. We discussed these fears.

We also discussed the importance of parents' understanding the values of education and of what constituted quality education. Our goal was also to see gender equity in education.

As part of the program, we committed the entire National Labor Week in early May to engaging students and community members by fixing shallow wells to prevent them from being contaminated by rainwater runoff. We also fixed foot trails and picked up trash around the village. This was an effort to practically demonstrate some basic improvements which could enhance the quality of life and help avoid preventable diseases.

As a teacher who had become exposed to the broader understanding of the world, I was so happy to do everything I could to help them—the people, including many young ones, who had been deprived of the opportunity to learn what is best for them. The hope and the goal were filled with enthusiastic spirit as we falsely looked forward to the coming peace after a long war.

A WORLD WITHOUT BOUNDARIES

We reviewed our traditional way of life, the traditional slash-and-burn cultivation, and the centuries-long illiteracy. We hoped for a new way of life, although the prospect of becoming self-dependent as airplane rice would no longer be available had presented a new phase of challenges. Despite the fact that their families would produce their own food as they had always done before the war, they needed cash for purchases of goods they could not produce with their own hands.

In early May 1975, the Communists' takeover of Laos suddenly changed everything. The village, the school, the adult education program, and my career as a teacher were abandoned altogether. I left the people, who called me "teacher" and who hoped to see something different in their lives, without an opportunity to say good-bye.

As a woman deprived of educational opportunity in her young age, Youa had made persistent efforts, forging to achieve adult literacy skills, which enabled her to help other Hmong women establish family daycare and gain knowledge of family nutrition.

CHAPTER 12

YOUA'S STORY: "SAVING THE SUN"

A girl tells a story describing her life in a secret world and a culture with many mysteries in which girls frequently froze, dreaming of equal opportunities, as they watched boys attend school from a distance.

Youa and I had met briefly as we crossed each other's path occasionally, but I never paid much attention to her, and she did not have any interest in me.

When I asked my mother about the people across the airstrip and the talented girl who was surrounded by a large crowd during the New Year celebration, my mother talked a little about Youa.

"They were from Thamheub and San Luang villages, located on the hills around Xieng Det, but we had never known them before," she told me. "We share the same water source down the slope with them. They are very nice people. That's all I know."

"How long have they been living across the airstrip?" I asked.

"They were already there when we came. There were already a lot of people down the slope, mostly people of the Lee clan. They had already opened the airdrop field below the airstrip by the time we arrived."

"There were a lot of girls during the New Year ball

tossing, but Youa's talent seemed to draw people's attention, and you seemed to enjoy her songs, too. Do you know her?"

"I don't know much about her because, unlike some other girls who frequently walk across the airstrip to buy candies and papaya salads, she is hardly seen coming around. The only place I frequently meet her is at the water source, and she seems very friendly."

"You seem to be interested in her?" Mom asked with a big smile.

"No, not really. I am just curious because her talents seem to stand out among the girls in the crowd."

Hearing me ask questions about Youa, my mother would think that, after graduating from school and becoming a teacher, I would be thinking about getting married. Actually, the inquiry did not lead me to engage any relationship with Youa at all. I still had not given up my wish to continue beyond the two-year teacher training program. I wanted to at least finish a four-year training, although the system made it difficult if you were not a member of the elites.

After an unsuccessful attempt to borrow money from Uncle Tou, I decided to take my teaching assignment, hoping that after completing two years of successful teaching, I could take the window of opportunity to continue toward completing the four-year program. Engaging in a relationship with any girl, including Youa, whom I wished I had more time to know, was a low priority.

My time spent at home was short and inundated with many critically important issues. Traveling to borrow money from Uncle Tou, returning to Vientiane to submit my application for becoming a teacher, and finding out my teaching assignment were all done in the manner of physical traveling. Two months had gone by like two days.

There was no postal service delivering mail. And there were no mailing addresses in a nomadic society. District and village chiefs were the only guardians of handwritten lists of people, which were updated yearly by fourth- and fifth-grade students during school breaks to add newborns and delete names of those who had moved away or died.

Finding out my assignment took a half-day walk, one way. Moua Lia, by himself, was both the school superintendent and mailman, administering school performances and delivering salaries and supplies to remote schools across mountains and hills. I gave thanks to Air America—the only transportation provider that made everything possible.

The foot trails on the hills were muddy and slippery and were difficult to travel during the monsoon season, which lasted from June to September. I had made a few trips past the airstrip and across the old Phou Xang Noy village to visit my grandmother in a new settlement on a slope, overlooking the newly built Christian church and the shiny tin-roofed school across the Nam Veh Valley. As far as I could remember, those trips I had made to visit my grandmother were the best thing I had done before leaving home again for months before returning to see her.

At the New Year celebration in December 1971, for which I was two days late, I had the opportunity to visit different villages, seeing young girls and young men dressed in their finest traditional costumes for the once-a-year celebration. I only had one week to enjoy the annual festival before being flown back to Bouam Loung, isolated deep inside enemy territory.

The dusty head end of the airstrip in Phou Xang Noy was filled with people in their occasional costumes. Like the previous year, Youa, who was locally known for her folksong talents, did not waste the limited opportunity to express her poetic songs in her young and beautiful voice. She drew a crowd of young and older men, standing nearly a half circle around her, to whom she would toss her ball in an orderly manner as she sang her songs in poetic rhymes, expressing her vulnerability and limited liberty as a Hmong girl. Standing nearly in a half circle behind her were older women—many from Phou Vieng—who occasionally praised her for her talents.

I approached the crowd to make sure I did not miss any special feature of the celebration. She did not miss my presence among the crowd and tossed her ball at me.

"Would you like to toss the ball?" she asked.

"Do I know how?" I asked teasingly as I caught her ball—a baseball-size tightly sewn cloth ball she made by herself.

"Here you may not know how, but elsewhere, I am sure you do," she joked.

I approached and stood in between two young men in the long half-circle line. She busily distributed her ball among the people in line as they waited patiently for their turn. She asked me to sing a song.

"I have never sung Hmong folk songs. I am afraid I would freak everyone out if I sang. I was just about to ask you to sing for us."

She accepted without hesitation and started singing a song about refugees displaced by war to an unfamiliar land where vegetation might look similar in appearance, but might not be edible as in another land. The crowd grew larger and everyone competed for conversation with her. After twenty-five minutes of enjoyable ball tossing, pleasant conversations, and listening to a beautiful folk song, I thanked her and left to join the volleyball game in the school playground nearby.

The New Year celebration was over—too quick and too soon for young people who could not wait for the event to come around next year. I reported to Ko Xiong in Nam Veh to check on the situation in Bouam Loung, and in anticipation that all the teachers would return to duty as planned. I was told we would not immediately return to Bouam Loung because the situation had not been fully assessed. All the teachers reported to work in Nam Veh, awaiting word from Moua Lia. We were told a week later Bouam Loung was too dangerous for us to return. Communication was extremely difficult to convey. Some teachers had to walk for a full day to report and get their assignments.

Nam Veh was only a forty-five minute walk from Phou Xang Noy, where I lived. I left home at 7 a.m. every day to arrive at school at least fifteen minutes before it started. I looked at Youa's house across the airstrip every day as I walked along the four-hundred-meter dirt airfield toward the end where my path was joined with the path from her house. She tried to avoid meeting me at the joint of the path. She would either leave her house thirty minutes early or wait for me to walk past the airfield and the cross-path before she left home for her rice field about a half mile down the slope.

We had unexpectedly crossed each other's path a

few times. She had tried to avoid engaging in conversation with me by walking away at an increased pace. I tried not to pursue and force conversation with her. The reason she tried to avoid me was, perhaps, the way I interacted with her during the New Year ball tossing, which made her believe I had no interest in her.

In my mind, I was obsessed with the false hope of going back to school, although Uncle and Aunt Song Chai encouraged me to get married because I had established a stable career. I refused and consistently maintained I would not seriously engage in a relationship with a girl until I fulfilled my goal.

In reality, the system had no budget for a continuing education program. By setting enrollment caps, the system had purposely kept the number within its annual budget, funded by foreign aid. Higher education opportunities had been kept away from regular citizens, especially the poor and women. Higher educational institutions were all located in Vientiane, which was not an affordable place to be and had been out of reach for the poor.

The Phou Xang refugees were informed that airplane rice would be cut off effective December 1971, as soon as they harvested their rice. Traditionally, many farmers would celebrate their early crop in October with thanksgiving meals of the first harvested rice. They would invite friends and relatives to join them in their homes for a thankful meal. That had not happened for many years for thousands of Hmong since they had become refugees and airplane rice dependents.

I taught a class during school break. The three-month school break went by very quickly. Long Chieng was under Communist attack, sending another wave of refugees to the Phou Xang and Nam Veh areas. Two teachers had requested transfers to be closer to their families in their villages. Four more teachers came to join us. The Nam Veh student population had increased, reaching 550.

Chue Yang, a teacher who went to Bouam Loung with me, and I became close friends. He liked to come to Phou Xang Noy to hang out with me on the weekends, and we visited some girls in the evenings. In Hmong culture, young men only visited girls late in the evening and would avoid being seen by their parents.

One late evening, we were outside of the house of one of Youa's friends, Xia, who lived only two hundred feet down the slope from her house. Youa's father, a tall man in dark Hmong clothes, came out of her friend's house. He saw us and, suddenly, came to grab our hands.

"Hi, teacher, it's you!" he said to me loudly. "Who is this young man? A teacher, too . . . ?"

"Yes, he is a teacher, too," I answered in a very low voice, trying not to let Xia's parents hear our voices.

"Come! Come to join dinner with me," he invited, holding tight on our hands.

"No, sir. Thank you very much," we both said, almost at the same time.

"No, no, no, I am not going to let you refuse!" he insisted loudly.

We wanted to follow him farther away from Xia's house, so we could decline loudly and respectfully. But, before we had the chance to say anything, we were almost in front of his door.

We went inside and saw Youa, a slim Hmong girl in a casual Laotian outfit, working frantically to get dinner ready. Her younger sister, Mee, helped under her direction and put food on the round table. There was newly harvested steamed rice and different dishes of chicken meat, cooked in different ways.

It was 9 p.m., too late for some people. As always in Hmong culture, the men ate first. There were only three of us, sitting at the table: Youa's father, Chue, and me. We tried to invite Youa's mother and everyone to join together. They refused.

Youa was busy adding more food to the dishes. She was virtually responsible for the meal. Her older brothers were not present at the special meal. If they were living somewhere nearby, there would be no reason for them not to join such a special family occasion. Their absence was not uncommon for families in a war-ridden part of Laos, where men who served in the front lines would miss many special family events.

A few days later, I went back to talk to Youa after supper. She greeted me warmly.

"What a pleasant surprise to see you come to visit after all these times," she said jokingly. "I have a feeling that we will have too much sunshine this year, because I will be very happy."

"I fear it would be the opposite because someone's boyfriend would be very mad."

"That is incorrect."

I complemented her for the good food. She asked what had I been doing and where I had been. I told her about my itinerant life just like her brothers'. I also learned more about her and her family.

I went back to visit her again and found she was sick and coughing. The next day I bought some aspirin and cough medicine and brought them to her. I went back the following day, and she was still not too well. We talked for a little while.

"You know, I was concerned about you," I said. "Yesterday I gave you the medicines and I forgot to tell you that a pregnant woman could have a miscarriage from taking those medicines."

She laughed.

"What are you talking about? I am not pregnant. Where did you hear that from?"

"Sorry, I was just kidding and did not mean to offend you."

Our relationship grew. We decided to get married on February 8, 1973, after having a good time together at the New Year celebration. We engaged in ball tossing after school for four more days after the New Year celebration was over. Yaj and some girls and young men joined us. We talked, joked, and laughed, and she sang Hmong folk songs.

In a society where we had no restaurants, night parties, or movie theaters to go to, our way of life was simple. And we took it as the best in the world. We tried to keep it civil and meaningful. There were plenty of good things to enjoy in our own way. Yet, there were also plenty of sad and horrible stories that we shared; most of them were about things beyond our control.

After we married, Youa told me about her situation as a refugee in Phou Xang Noy. She said she had met my mother a few times and knew she had a son who came home briefly and was gone for a few months, but she tried not to ask any questions. She shared stories about her family's hardship and her trip to Long Chieng. She had stayed with a relative there, taking the opportunity to sell food and soda to soldiers at an open roadside market on the northwest side of the airfield, not far from the radio station.

She returned home, after staying in Long Chieng for more than two months, when her parents sent her a letter informing that Granduncle Chong Toua, who lived with her parents, was very ill. He died shortly after she arrived.

Her two older brothers, Toua and Ma, were serving in the front lines and did not return for his funeral. She gave all the money she earned from Long Chieng to her father, plus the start-up money he gave her, for her granduncle's funeral.

"It was a tragic moment for us," she said. "We were very poor as refugees, fleeing war and losing everything."

She never returned to Long Chieng again. As the enemy forces moved closer, the situation in Long Chieng became increasingly dangerous.

Youa shared with me more about her childhood life, which helped me understand more about Hmong girls and women in a society where girls and women were deprived of equal opportunities.

As a man, I had taken for granted the culture in which a girl was perceived as an asset loss in her family and an asset gain in the family of her husband. She told me how much it hurt seeing students standing around the flagpole and singing the national anthem. Every time she would freeze for a few minutes after the song had ended or even after the students had been dismissed into the classrooms.

Although she didn't know exactly what education would entail, she had always wondered if education was a secret path to a different world. She had seen the inequality between her world of girls and the world of boys. She did not completely understand the reason. She could not prevent herself from being carried away by thousands of thoughts going through her mind that had frequently caused her to be a daydreamer. Her mother had often yelled at her when she did not hear her talk.

"Hello!" her mother would yell and throw her a small rock. "What are you thinking? Dummy! Your head is not with you?"

"Sorry, Mom, I didn't hear you," she would say as she turned around.

Youa had wondered why boys and girls, and men and women, were treated differently as if they lived in different worlds. She helplessly felt engulfed by those thoughts for a few moments and was only awaken by her mother's loud calls.

Born in the remote Phoukeu village on the hill of a mountain, located northwest of the Royal capital of Luang Phrabang in northern Laos, she had the luxury of mountain views, clean air, and surrounding green vegetation—the world that many had believed was better than every other place on the planet. She vaguely remembered the dirt-barren village where her grandmother brought her some baked sweet yams every day. Her grandmother cried and told sad stories of her bitter life as a woman being forced to marry someone, even to become a second wife. Her grandmother's stories echoed in her mind nearly every moment and reminded her of how vulnerable she was. She told me how scared she had been listening to her grandmother's stories in a society where decisions were mercilessly made by men.

Her grandfather, Yia Vang, died when her father was

two years old and her grandmother had just given birth to a girl, named Xee. She was forced to become the second wife of her grandfather's cousin. She had two children with the new husband—a boy and a girl. Yia had an older brother, Pao, who also died very young, before having any children. His young wife adopted his half-brother, who was young. She never remarried.

"I agreed to marry your grandpa's cousin as his second wife because if I didn't and I married someone outside the family," she said with tears rolling down from her eyes, "they would keep your dad. I had no choice. The only choice I made was that, at least, I was with him, so he could have a mother."

Youa's grandmother sent her father to school in a nearby lowland Lao village located a half-day walking distance in the valley to the southwest, leaving her working in the rice field alone. He stayed with a lowland Lao couple, whom he called "Mom and Dad," where he attended school, and he only returned home every two or three months to visit his poor mother and to get some more rice. He traveled alone, on a dangerous and seldom traveled trail that cut through thick jungles, because none of the boys in the village went to school.

He only finished third grade but earned a title to his name, "Cha the Letterman," because he was the only man who could read and write letters. He later married Yamee, his mother's niece, the youngest daughter of Yong Yia Thao.

Hmong cultural system permits marriages of brothers and sisters' children while prohibiting marriages of children in the same clan, even not closely related—a tradition still practiced today. The Hmong believe people who share the same last name (clan name) derived from the same paternal lineage. Hence, they are considered internal relatives—a notion believed in their small world in which they believe centuries might have passed, but the roots and branches of a tree are not far apart.

In 1950, Cha's uncle, Da Xeng Vang, was appointed district chief and Cha became his secretary. The French lost control of Indochina and the North Vietnamese gained power in the Viet Minh movement. Prince Souphanouvong took his Pathet Lao faction to ally with Communist North Vietnam and took control of Phong Saly and Samneua provinces, which bordered Luang Phrabang province to the north.

The Phoukeu village's residents took position to ally with the Pathet Lao and became in favor with their nightly conferences and dances around the campfire. Cha criticized and opposed the activities. The Communist undercover agents and cadres planned to kill him, but his relatives informed him his life was in danger. He told his relatives he wanted to visit his other relatives in Xieng Khouang province for two weeks. He told his wife and children—Toua, eight; Ma, five; Youa, three; and Mee, two months old—to go to the farmhouse for a few days.

Youa's father, Cha, took his family on a trail across the Nam Khanh River to Thamheub, a village southwest of the town of Muang Soui where his Uncle Wang Xeng had been living for three years. After moving to the new village, leaving their extended families behind, Cha and his wife were very homesick and Cha became seriously ill. His young wife became concerned. She took Cha to Xai Lue of the Yang clan, an extended relative of Cha's Uncle Pao's wife, for help. Uncle and Aunt Xai Lue adopted Cha as their godson and performed numerous healing ceremonies, including a soul-calling and name-changing ceremony. They gave Cha an adult name, *Watou*, or "son of hope." Since then, Watou became his adult name.

At eight, Youa already took adult responsibilities. At first cock's crow in the morning, Youa illuminated her house with firewood as everyone in the village illuminated theirs. She would get up before everyone in the family to prepare breakfast for the family to eat before sunrise. Toua was recruited to serve in the CIA-funded Special Guerrilla Unit (SGU) in the front line. Ma was sent to school in Ban Na—a village about ten miles to the south. Youa was expected to do everything while her mother took care of her younger siblings. Sometimes, she would be asked to deliver food to Ma in Ban Na, taking a long day walk on a muddy foot trail and crossing dangerous jungle hills accompanied by only a horse behind her.

Since moving to Thamheub, Youa's parents had three more children—two boys, Neng and Thai, and one girl, Nou. Her family had nearly doubled in size and her responsibilities increased. Youa was smaller than Mee, who was two years younger.

Youa's father was a musical instrument maker, making flutes, Jew's harps, and six-tube instruments (*queej*)—all were in high demand. He battled between short-timeline agreements and the slash-and-burn seasons. His unique talents gave him the only cash-earning job. Some people worked for him in the rice field in exchange for one or two instruments.

Youa's mother shouldered the child rearing and everything her husband was not available to do. There were plenty of those jobs—feeding the animals, cutting firewood, bringing water from the bottom corner of the village about a quarter of a mile away, sewing and washing clothes, and anything in the field that did not absolutely require a man.

At age ten, with her head shaved around the lower part, leaving only the top for easy care, Youa, energetic and never seeming to have enough to do, would offer to help with everything and function as an adult. With such a maturity, her parents forgot to realize how young she was.

Under the cool breeze of November, rice fields turned from green to gold color, ready to be harvested. Nature gave only a short time frame for each season without explanation and regardless of what else might come to interfere.

Having a rice field an hour walking distance away from home was not uncommon in a slash-and-burn society. The best way to save time and maximize work for Youa's parents was to move to where work was, leaving only Youa to commute daily between the house and the field to feed the pigs and chickens, and deliver needed supplies.

One day, while she was walking alone, innocently humming and hopping along the trail—a short distance before her parents' small farm hut—an old man of the Lee clan, who worked frantically harvesting rice by the trail, asked her in a teasing tone, "Where are you going, young lady?"

Spooked by his voice, Youa screamed; she ran, fell, and rolled toward her parents' stay—a distance down the slope. She did not remember seeing how many logs she had crossed. Her dad shouted at her, but she did not hear; he ran toward her and comforted her. She finally calmed down, and her pale face regained color.

Mee, much bigger and taller than Youa, could not be left to stay home with her. Mee seldom talked, but laughed loudly. She could help when given specific jobs and directions. She could carry Nou on her back, better than strapping her on a stump. But most of the time she would get yelled at for teasing her bothers.

Despite what happened on that day, Youa returned home alone with a load of sweet yam leaves on her back for the pigs. She would return the next day on the same trail. But that night she did not feel well. She did not want to get up as she had always done when morning arrived. She did not feel she wanted to go back to the rice field. She decided to stay home to get some firewood instead.

Trying to maximize what she needed to get done for that day, she carried a firewood carrier on her back—usually for adult use only—and a slashing sickle in her hand. She walked alone into the woods, feeling a little dizzy. She cut and collected a full load of firewood, strapped it on the laid-flat carrier, then raised it up. It was too heavy. She tried again. Finally, she put her back against it, trying to carry it. It fell on her, and she fell on her face on a slope, kicking, turning, and struggling to free herself and get up.

Finally, she freed herself. She reduced the load in half, carried it home, and then returned with a bamboo back-basket for the other half.

It was about noon, measured by the sun in the sky. She had not eaten anything in the morning. She felt cold and went outside to be warmed by the sun.

Suddenly, the sun turned dimmer and dimmer despite it being a sunny day with no clouds.

"Is it something wrong with me or something wrong with the sun?" she asked herself.

Some men and women came out, shouting.

"Demon is eating the sun! Demon is eating the sun!"

They ran inside the house. The women and children did not come out. The men came out with guns and crossbows. They shot at the sun and shouted.

"Help save the sun! Everyone! Help save the sun!"

They pounded empty rice foot mills; they ground empty corn mills and banged pots and pans to scare the demon away.

Granduncle Wa Xeng walked toward her with a basket on his back and an old flintlock in his right hand.

"Why are you out here?" he shouted. "You should be inside! You are a girl! Go! Go inside! Girls cannot be out here!"

"I am cold, Grandpa."

"Go inside and get warmed by the fire. Go!"

"Why are people shooting guns, Grandpa?"

"The demon is eating the sun. We are saving the sun from the demon. Go inside, right now!"

The solar eclipse was over. The sun was saved.

In remote Hmong villages, for centuries, the Hmong always must do something to save the sun or the moon when there is a solar or lunar eclipse.

Youa went inside. She felt colder. She felt very tired. She went to bed and put a blanket over her; she still felt cold and was shivering as if she did not have enough blanket. She felt asleep, and then woke up with dizziness and saw it was dark outside.

The mother pig was hungry; it cried around the house, expecting to be fed. Youa heard it and knew it had passed feeding time, but she was too tired to get up. It knocked the door open, fed itself in the cauldron on the fireplace where she had cooked some feed early in the morning, and went back out.

Grandaunt Pao walked by and saw the door open and the house without light. She went to check it out. Standing at the door and peeking in the dark house, she called, "Yajpov, are you home?" Yajpov was the name Youa's mother called her.

"Yes, I am here," Youa answered from the bedroom.

Her tired voice was barely heard. Grandaunt Pao went inside and touched Youa's forehead.

"You are having a fever," she said.

She made a fire, closed the door, and left.

In a society where moral expectation was high, but conscience and commonsense deficits were not uncommon, some people did everything to save the sun, but did something inexplicably hard to understand. Perhaps, Grandaunt Pao just did what her mind told her.

Grandaunt Pao went to the rice field early in the morning without checking how the young girl was doing—the young girl who had accompanied her often to get pig feed and made her cry when she sang her beautiful songs. She walked near Youa's parents, but did not go over to tell them that their daughter was sick, not until the sun had gone down and she walked home. She told them what had happened the previous night.

Youa's father was angry and he scolded her for not telling them earlier. Youa's parents grabbed whatever they could and walked home, pulling and pushing the young children with them. They ran half of the time on the dark trail. They arrived at the door and the house was quiet and dark. The mother pig was coming toward them, demanding food; the villagers did what they routinely did in their faintly illuminated houses, not knowing what had happened. Youa's mother cried and called loudly; Youa's voice was too weak to be heard on her lips. They pushed the door open, rushed to the bedroom, and found her barely alive.

Youa's father made a fire, then came to grab her wrist, measured her pulses, listened to her heartbeats, and put his hand on her forehead.

"You have been frightened by something," he said assuredly. "Don't worry. Your mom and I are here, taking care of you."

Youa's mother cleaned her face and her dry lips and gave her water. She cooked some soft rice gruel for her. Youa had not eaten for two days.

The next morning, before dawn, Youa's father went to the house of the old man (in a different village, but not very far away) who teased and frightened her, for he was a shaman. The man came to greet him at the door.

"I knew you were going to come," the old man said. "Otherwise, I have prepared to come to your house. I have already prepared a little pig and two chickens and planned to come to see you today."

"I am coming today to ask you to perform a ritual for my daughter. She is sick."

"I knew something had happened since I have not seen the beautiful girl come by for the last two days. I knew I had frightened her and her soul. I am sorry. I shouldn't have done that to her."

"You did not mean anything malevolent. You just teased her. It was completely understood."

Youa's father kneeled down with both thumbs on the floor, begging the man and his shaman spirits—a cultural practice to show sincerity, honor, and respect. They gathered his shaman tools and brought the pig and the chickens to Youa's house. The man performed the shamanic ritual and called her frightened soul that might have been lost to return to her body. Youa soon recovered.

Youa was always busy. She served food and refilled dishes on the table at meal times. When everyone was finished, she would eat whatever was left. Sometimes there was nothing left but plain rice. Her father observed what happened. Sometimes he would take extra amounts of the good food and reserve it in front of him for her, causing complaints and resentment among other siblings.

"Dad reserves extra food for his favorite daughter," Mee said.

"Your sister cooks, serves food, and does everything," Youa's father said. "She does not have time to eat. By the time we finish eating, there is nothing left for her. You should see that and start being more responsible."

In 1968, Youa's mother gave birth to the youngest child—a girl. Everyone in the family competed to submit their best name for the youngest sister. A consensus was reached and she was named *Vaj*, meaning "beautiful garden."

In June, Ma took and passed the Sam Thong TTIE exam. A student in the village who took the exam with him and failed returned home and lied to Ma's father that Ma had failed and was afraid to return home.

Ma returned home after helping to get some work done for his father's cousin, Phia Lee, with whom he had stayed to attend school. As Ma arrived at the door, his father was furious about what he was told. Ma tried to explain, but his father maintained he lied and hit him on the head with a tool that he used for making musical instruments, causing an inch-long cut; blood ran down on his neck and shoulders. He ran out of the house and went straight to Long Chieng to join the SGU and volunteered to serve in the forward intelligence unit, the most clandestine and dangerous assignment. When his name was posted on the exam result, showing he was among those who had passed it, his father went to Long Chieng to look for him, but was informed that Ma was somewhere far in the front line.

Three months later, some relatives—also soldiers—visited home. Ma sent his father fifteen thousand kip, a green blanket, a green fatigue parachute, a half roll of black fabric, and a small note, saying: "Dad, I am sending you fifteen thousand kip to help you and Mom with any expenses you have. I am doing well. Thank you for your concerns and expectation of me. I have disappointed you, but I love you. I may not be home very soon. You and Mom take care. Love, Ma."

Ma's father received the money and the items and read the letter. Tears rolled down from his eyes, acknowledging he was wrong. He had irrationally let his emotions take over his mind and felt sorry for what he did.

In the early monsoon season of 1969, the North Vietnamese and Pathet Lao forces advanced toward Muong Soui. Word spread like shockwaves that the flip-flopping neutralist Kong Le had changed his position to join the Communists again. The Hmong in villages on the surrounding hills, including Thamheub, had to evacuate and move closer to Long Chieng.

In April 1969, the people in Thamheub, including Youa's family, had to move across the Nam Nguem River to Nam Tow, a small village with an airstrip. They arrived on the airstrip just before dark, not having enough time to cut wood to build a tent. Youa's father went to knock on the door of a family living by the airstrip who had a pile of long wooden poles. He borrowed one of the poles to build the parachute tent. The people were kind to give him some firewood and wood sticks for tent stakes.

Youa's mother was busy taking care of her young brothers and sisters because they were tired and hungry. After erecting the parachute, Youa's father started making a fire before dark, leaving Youa to finish setting up the tent. Ma arrived while she was driving the stakes into the ground and fighting with the weight and tension of the parachute. Ma tiptoed toward her and stood behind her. He covered her eyes with both hands, not saying a word that would provide a hint for her to recognize who he was. Youa put her hands over Ma's and over his head, thinking it had to be one of her brothers or a close relative. She recognized Ma's hands. She was so happy. She started crying and she screamed.

"Ma is here!"

Everyone inside the tent came out. They hugged each other and spoke, in voices choked with emotion, of how happy they were to have him come to help in a time of family crisis. Ma told Youa to go inside and prepare food for supper because everyone was hungry and tired. Ma finished the tent setup. He brought three green tarps, and they used them for sleeping mats.

"I apologize for what I did to you," Ma's father said. "I was wrong and irrational."

"Dad, you don't have to apologize. Let's forget about what has happened in the past. Right now I need to take care of our family and find you a safe place before I go back on duty."

Supper was served by the dimly burned fire. They only had freshly cooked rice and pickled mustard greens. The poor family ate quietly before they rested for the night, while light rain continued outside. The evacuation orders were sudden and immediate, giving no time for preparation and killing their animals for food.

After midnight, the village of Hoy Sathout, across the Nam Nguem River in which Youa's parents nearly spent the night after attending a young girl's funeral service and burial, was attacked by Communists, killing some people and wounding some others. Ma and a small company of soldiers went to assess the situation. Among the people who were attacked were Granduncle Wa Xeng and Granduncle Chong Toua, who chose to spend the night there.

Ma found Granduncle Chong Toua alone in the empty village. His young wife and nephew, Wa Xeng, escaped unharmed, leaving him behind. The Communist Pathet Lao and North Vietnamese soldiers had left the village in the morning, leaving the crippled old man with a leftover cooked chicken and a pot of rice.

Ma took Chong Toua with him to reunite with his wife and Wa Xeng, who fled in the early morning and arrived in the Pas Qav or "Frogspond Village," located two miles north of the airstrip where Ma's parents camped. He brought them together and helped them build temporary shelters before returning to duty in the front line. It was the first time the residents of Thamheub became refugees, depending on airplane rice.

A month later, Toua went to bring his parents, Chong Toua and Wa Xeng, to Phou Xang Noy near the airstrip and outpost to which he was assigned as a soldier and where there had already been a large concentration of refugees. Wa Xeng refused to go with him. Chong Toua chose to stay with Wa Xeng.

In April 1970, after Sam Thong fell, all refugee settlements in the area were ordered to evacuate. Chong Toua was once again abandoned by his wife and nephew. The abandoned old man was found by Gen. Vang Pao's soldiers and was taken by helicopter to Phou Mee outpost, west of Long Chieng, where he spent two months, crying and not knowing where his family was. He had been calling his grandnephew's name every day, asking if anyone knew Watou.

Eventually, one of Mr. Pop's assistants, Xeng Lee, was able to find out who and where Watou was. Chong Toua was brought by helicopter to reunite with Watou in Phou Xang Noy, where he became sick and died shortly thereafter. His wife never attended his funeral. She remarried shortly after his death. Watou adopted three of his children—two boys, Yee, ten, and Dang, six; and one girl, Bee, eight—leaving with the mother the youngest girl, who was only two and believed to have been conceived in an extramarital affair.

The Communists' increased control of northern Laos, including the regions north of Sam Thong and Long Chieng, which served as the buffer zone between Gen. Vang Pao's headquarters and the Communists' strongholds, resulted in large concentrations of refugees south of Sam Thong and Long Chieng. This pattern of large concentrations of populations whose way of life was hinged upon the slash-and-burn farming tradition had caused great consequences on natural resources in the area, particularly in the eve of the cease-fire process when airplane rice was no longer available. But it was the war that brought us together.

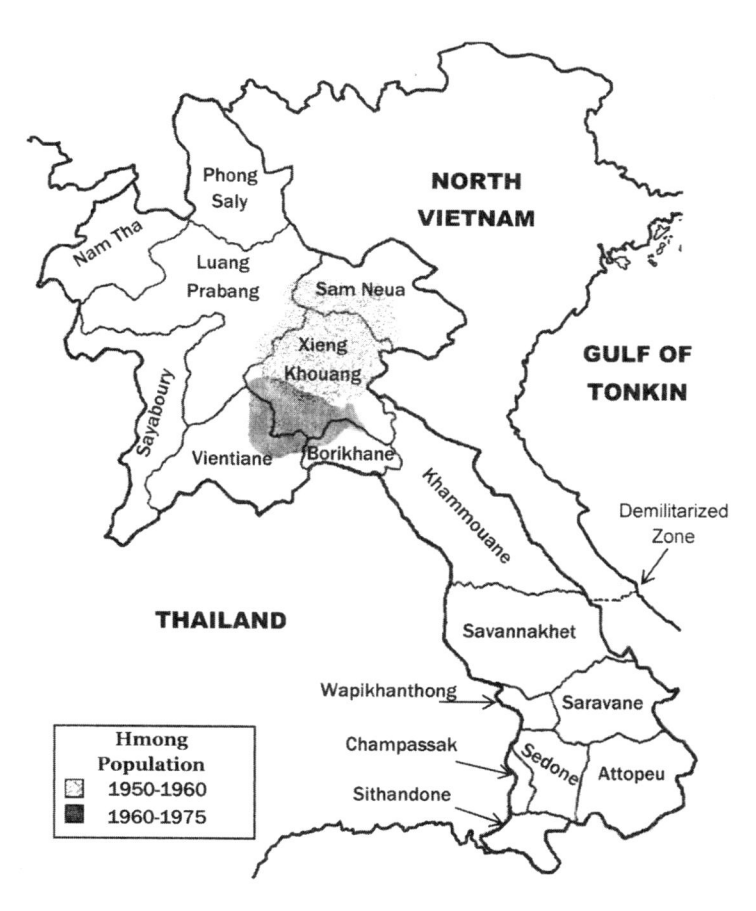

A darker shade indicates areas in which there were massive concentrations of refugees.

CHAPTER 13

THE CEASE-FIRE AND THE FALSE PEACE

The war-weary Hmong hoped for peace, although they felt uncertain about what life would be like when peace came, because then airplane rice and the soldiers' salaries would be gone. In reality, the cease-fire only served as a secretly planned lull for the Communists to stage their final takeover, which the Vientiane government was either unaware of or felt helpless about.

In early 1973, a major change had taken place in the highly populated regions south and southwest of Long Chieng as gossip about peace and the end of airplane rice spread across Hmong villages. The refugees from Phou Vieng moved past Ban Xorn to start new slash-and-burn farming in the virgin jungles of Phou Kho Mountain, five miles north of Km 22. My parents were among them, leaving Teng with Youa and me in Nam Veh, where he attended fifth grade. USAID continued dropping airplane rice until they harvested their first crops.

Youa's parents and the people from Thamheub and San Luang remained in Phou Xang Noy, but had planned to move out as well because jungles in the area had been depleted into a coarse-grass mountain since the refugees settled there in 1970. Toua would be among the CIA-funded irregulars to be released of duty

THE CEASE-FIRE AND THE FALSE PEACE

and sent back to civilian life. His family lived in a farm hut down the slope of Phou Xang Noy Mountain, not far from Youa's parents. Ma was transferred from Gen. Vang Pao's farm in Nahai Deo, in the outskirts of Vientiane, to oversee the poultry farm project in Nam Ngua, north of Long Chieng.

The cease-fire came as a hope for peace for the weary Hmong in Laos who had fled atrocities and wars in China and whose lives had been dominated by wars since the beginning of the French colonial era.

First, it was the Hmong uprising against the French's unfair taxation, known as the Meo War by the lowlanders or the Pachai War by the Hmong. The French called it *Guerre du Fou*, meaning the madman war. Later, they became an ally with the French, shouldering the responsibility for hiding French soldiers from the Japanese and feeding them in thick jungles until Japan was defeated and its troops retreated in 1945.

Second, the Hmong were recruited to help the French fight against the Viet Minh revolution and continued fighting the Viet Minh even after the fall of the French northern headquarters at Dien Bien Phu.

And third, the Hmong became involved in Laos's civil war, fighting the Communists' forces, and became solely responsible for blocking the Communists' expansion in northern Laos when the United States became involved in the Vietnam War.

Although skeptical about the cease-fire and the peace pre-agreement and agreement signed by leaders of Laos's political factions, Gen. Vang Pao kept his lips tight like a good soldier and let the political leaders in Vientiane work with the Communist Pathet Lao on the negotiation process. The Americans, including Jerry

Daniels, Vang Pao's closest advisor, kept their lips tight as they took orders from Washington on a timeline plan to withdraw American equipment and military advisors out of Laos. The United States also had a planned timeline to pull out of South Vietnam. It was all arranged in the same deal.

Explosions of artillery shelling and hand grenades and sounds of rolling machine guns had stopped in the front lines for the first time in Laos since the French had left Indochina. Troops on both sides were on standby along territorial lines they had gained or retreated to before the cease-fire, waiting for fighting to resume on orders, in case the negotiation failed.

But, the Americans were leaving as planned on their timeline, regardless of the outcome of the negotiation. Air America planes were gone. The number of airplanes flying over and landing in Long Chieng were reduced. The voices of men and women wailing for their dead, that echoed through the nearby karsts at the head-runway of Long Chieng's airfield as dead soldiers' bodies were unloaded, had stopped.

The Royal capital of Luang Phrabang was quiet, except for sporadic sounds of motorcycles roaring along the town's largely dirt roads. Merchants and roadside vendors were doing business as usual. The royal family (the symbolic head of state) had been aware of the situation, but waited helplessly and nervously for the unfolding situation of the peace negotiation drama in Vientiane.

Gen. Vang Pao knew the United States would pull out its military support. But he believed within his conscience the international community would help facilitate a fair and peaceful solution that would transition

THE CEASE-FIRE AND THE FALSE PEACE

Laos toward a long-lasting peace and that would guarantee citizens and leaders of all parties against persecution. In reality, the international community was just biased, helpless, and divided like a monkey court that could not rule out a fair decision on any wrong cause.

Between 1973 and 1974, Gen. Vang Pao had made frequent visits to refugee villages and spoken of the prospect of peace and his plan for the Hmong-Lao residents of Xieng Khouang.

"There are nothing our people love more than peace and freedom," Vang Pao had said in his visit to Km22 village during a New Year celebration in December 1973. "It's time for us to heal our wounds and build our lives again."

Among the programs included in his plan were the community adult literacy program with a community economic development focus, developed in collaboration with the National Division of Primary and Adult Education of the Ministry of Education. The program also stressed family self-sufficiency through sustainable family farming. The initial implementation of the program heavily hinged upon the adult education component and relied upon teachers to introduce the program concept, goals, and objectives.

The entire provinces of Phong Saly and Sam Neua, and over 75 percent of Xieng Khouang province, the areas where the majority of the Hmong lived, were under Communists' control. The Hmong and Lao in these three provinces had been drawn into the war, fighting against the Communists and each other. All those who followed Gen. Vang Pao and formed an alliance with the United States were displaced from one camp to another, surviving on airplane rice.

Consequently, they ended up in a small area south of Long Chieng and along the borders of Vientiane and Xieng Khouang provinces. The population density in the area, which consisted of high mountain ridges, steep hills, and deep valleys along the Nam Nguem Valley, had reached an unprecedented phenomenon.

The limited irrigable farmland along creeks and rivers had been occupied by ethnic lowland Lao. To help the refugees achieve self-sufficiency through sustainable farming in a highly concentrated population and limited farmland was a great challenge for Gen. Vang Pao who was a military leader, but had become a humanitarian problem solver. With the assistance of the USAID program, a few ideas, such as a small fish pond and pig and chicken farming, were considered practical options, should peace become a reality. There had not been any discussions among the leaders about the prospect of the refugees returning to the plains and plateaus of Xieng Khouang.

The Nam Nguem Dam was built north of Vientiane and was completed, providing a large reservoir where fishing would become a source of business and food supplies. However, it would be years (or never) before the residents of Laos could see any electrical benefit from the dam's hydropower plant, depending on whether or not foreign aid could make it happen.

A few sites of farming experiments had been established. But unlike the opium demands during the French colonial era, there had not been outlets planned for any massive production that would need cash exchanges. Laos is a land-locked country without a seaway to the outside world. It would require an economically savvy government to pull Laos out of poverty. That did not exist in the minds of the corrupt government officials who, themselves, had preyed on foreign aids.

Lao leaders only worried about their own status and had not established trade relations with neighboring countries. As a regional military commander, Vang Pao could not do it. He could not bypass the Lao government to sign international trade agreements.

When the Americans were gone, the money was also gone. A large number of Hmong irregulars had been discharged from military service and sent back to civilian life. Each was given a small lump sum of cash, a cow, and corn and rice seeds to start their new lives. The small monthly cash salary and the airplane rice that their families depended on were suddenly stopped. All the Hmong refugees, particularly the newly discharged soldiers, were trying to figure out what to do next should peace come, but they were confined in the geographically rugged and crowded area.

Ignorant of how the economic system worked, Lao leaders never gave any thoughts to how this would have ripple effects on the nation's economy. Who should get which position in the new coalition government was the only focus on their minds.

Some of the irregular soldiers would be integrated into the Royal Lao Army. Complaints among lowland Lao officers about the irregulars' inflated ranks and lack of qualifications were heard, loud and clear. Their ranks needed to be reduced significantly and commensurately with their educational qualifications. More than 70 percent of the Hmong irregulars, young and old, were forced to join the fight against the Communists' expansion, and more than 80 percent of them, including some senior officers, had no formal education.

While this would be an enormous endeavor, leaders of the Lao political factions focused on their self-serving interest—who would get which seat in government. The most important issue affecting the citizens of Laos was not on the agenda and had never been on the agenda of any kind. Self-serving interest, corruptions, top-down social-political culture, a rubber-stamp parliament, and largely illiterate and uninformed citizens had made Laos one of the poorest nations on earth.

The cease-fire and peace agreements did not describe specific plans on how the new coalition government would address the problem of refugees displaced by war and how Laos would address economic sustainability for its citizens. Their conflicts were not about whose ideas were better for Laos, but about who should have the control of the resources harvested from its citizens.

The cease-fire and the peace agreements reflected the political culture the Lao leaders shallowly and traditionally envisioned. The Viet Minh leaders, on the other hand, saw something bigger for Vietnam—the vast and untapped natural resources in Laos which could be used as a payback for their support. In fact, the Communists' expansion was on course and target.

Here were some of the elements of conflicts in Laos. Laos had a long history of power struggles among princes of different Lao kingdoms of the past that formed different political factions and always involved alliances with foreign forces to bring down each other's power. The last fight for power among the factions in Laos's most recent history started near the end of the French colonial rule. The grudging Prince Souphanouvong formed an alliance with the Viet Minh and seized

THE CEASE-FIRE AND THE FALSE PEACE

control of Sam Neua and Phongsaly provinces, coercing and forcing residents, including the Hmong therein, to join his Pathet Lao faction and fight on his side. His half-brother, Prince Souvanna Phouma, took a different path, allying himself with King Sisavangvathana, the Luang Prabang royal family.

The royal Lao government led by Prince Souvanna Phouma as prime minister of a coalition government, maintained its allegiance with the French and later the United States. Each claimed to embrace the lofty, but meaningless, national slogans, "Peace, independence, democracy, unity, and prosperity." Hmong leaders had their own problems as well, all about power—a stem of the same corrupt social/political system. The rift between the Ly and the Lo clansmen had separated the Hmong right in the middle.

Touby Lyfoung led some Hmong to side with the Royalists and the French while Nhia Vue, Lo Foung, and Fay Dang Lo Bliayao chose to side with the Communist Souphanouvong, drawing some Hmong on their side. Each aimed at a victory over the other by force and something for himself, capitalizing on the country's uninformed and uneducated citizens. The Viet Minh leaders had their aims, bigger than what the Lao-Hmong leaders could envision. The Communist Viet Minh took advantage of the situation and continued to intensify their attacks on the Royalists' forces in Xieng Kouang. They faced Hmong resistance there, led by Vang Pao—then a low-rank commander in the Royal army—far from the political center, but well known to the Hmong as Maj. Vang Pao.

The conflicts among the faction leaders intensified after a coup in Vientiane in 1960 that everyone called the Kong Le Coup. Although far from the center of politics, the Hmong had learned what happened through words carried by mouths across villages, and had been familiar with these events. Kong Le's coup released the Communist Pathet Lao's leaders, Prince Souphanouvong, and others from prison in Vientiane. The Viet Minh retaliated with heavy attacks on the Royalist forces in Sam Neua and Xieng Khouang provinces. Kong Le, only a low-rank officer, proclaimed he was a Neutralist and that he wanted to clean up corruption and form a Neutralist government, banning all foreign forces from interfering in Laos's internal affairs.

Prince Souvanna Phouma, who lost his job as his coalition government collapsed, was reinstated prime minister of the new Neutralist government. The Pathet Lao applauded his action because its goal was to ban foreign forces from entering Laos. The Americans and the French who looked physically different would not be able to deploy ground troops there—an advantage for the Vietnamese who could play mute and intermingle with Pathet Lao soldiers.

Top Laotian leaders, in their titles of lords and princes, were fighting and staging coups against each other, as they frequently said, "Using secret plans against secret plans," and put Laos in a state of chaos and confusion. Each leader always had a secret plan against the other, but nothing for the country.

The Vietnamese, who had served in most administrative positions in Laos during French colonial times and who had taken victory in the Viet Minh revolution against the French, knew they were smarter than the princely Lao leaders who did not have any ideas on how to build anything better for Laos. The Viet Minh's

THE CEASE-FIRE AND THE FALSE PEACE

plan was to use the Pathet Lao to bundle their civil war with the war against the US-supported South Vietnam because the Ho Chi Minh trail system was an important backdoor ramp for the north's troops and an ammunition delivery route to the south.

The North Vietnamese were willing to put forty thousand to sixty thousand of their troops in Laos instead of putting them in the fight in South Vietnam. The plan was to bundle the old French Indochina together to form greater forces against their foreign enemies—the French and the United States—riding on the tide of the Communists' expansion at the height of the Cold War. The goals were to not only unite Vietnam, but to also take the Indochinese peninsula out of foreign control—a tactical ploy that worked well. Souphanouvong naively got his feet caught in the powerful jaw of the Viet Minh—a pact to which he had agreed and could not get out. Not knowing the Viet Minh's secret plan, Souvanna Phouma naively believed that he could work out a deal with his half-brother Souphanouvong on a peaceful solution.

Souvanna Phouma flipped his position and tried to turn his face toward the Soviet Union, asking for military assistance. Maybe he thought the Soviet Union was better than the US or he wanted both. The Soviet Union responded to Souvanna's request in-kind by sending ammunition, artillery, and heavy armor to Vientiane. A fleet of black cargo airplanes flew daily over Hmong and Lao villages to Vientiane, delivering munitions.

The United States noticed something wrong and threatened to cut the funding that largely funded the Lao government. The United States' goal was to stop Communists' expansion, which the Soviet Union was behind.

There was a leader called Gen. Phoumi Nosavan who everyone talked about all the time. Some would call him leader of the Rightists. Later in the same year, there was another coup taken by Gen. Nosavan—a countercoup against Kong Le in Vientiane. After heavy fighting and three-day exchanges of artillery pounding on each other in the capital, Kong Le's forces moved north toward Vang Vieng and toward the Plain of Jars where they joined forces with the Communist Pathet Lao and Vietnamese, leaving behind a large quantity of Soviet-supplied ammunition and heavy armor. The war began in smoke and flames.

The Hmong were caught in the fire, became the sole load bearers, and faced the consequences of the conflicts. Lt. Col. Vang Pao, then a low-rank officer in the Royal Lao military, prepared the Hmong for the unavoidable conflicts, allying the freedom-loving Hmong with the Rightist Gen. Phoumi, who was also referred to as the Royalist.

Vang Pao became the military commander of Xieng Khouang after he took a successful coup against Gen. Amkha Soukhavong, who was a Neutralist and chief of Xieng Khouang Military Command. Hmong men who witnessed the situation talk about these events all the time in community events.

In a funeral service, former Maj. Neng Thong Thao was surrounded by a large crowd as he spoke of Vang Pao, the courageous young officer who disarmed and arrested the Lao general. He said he and the Hmong soldiers who accompanied Vang Pao in that event were scared, but Vang Pao took command and did what he had to do.

THE CEASE-FIRE AND THE FALSE PEACE

Although outgunned and outnumbered by the well-equipped Communist Vietnamese forces, the Hmong who were called the Meo mountain tribe formed resistance against the advances of the enemies who invaded their homeland. They bore the responsibility for holding against the floodgate of the Communists' expansion toward the rest of Laos—facing more than a decade of war, suffering great losses of lives, and earning threats of retribution for their actions.

Hmong villages in and around the town of Xieng Khouang were attacked, sending growing numbers of Hmong into refugee safe havens throughout northern Laos. Noticing the Hmong's freedom loving nature, which fit in the anti-Communist description, a prerequisite for an ally to help win the war in South Vietnam, the United States came to contact Vang Pao on an agreement to employ the Hmong to help with the fight against the North Vietnamese and to prevent the Communists' control of Laos, where American ground troops could not be deployed.

Nearly all able Hmong men, including teenage boys, were recruited not only to fight the advancing tides of the Communists' invasion of Laos, but also to help save American fighter pilots shot down along the North Vietnam-Lao border. The agreement was a mutual engagement of friendship which the Hmong took seriously.

For the fourteen years that followed, the Hmong engaged in guerrilla warfare against the Communists. They set up outposts on mountaintops, serving as barricades against Communists' advances, and they pushed back Communist forces to regain lost territories. These actions in partnership with the United States had angered the Pathet Lao and the North Vietnamese. They called the Hmong "the American hunting dogs" on their daily radio broadcast, implying the Hmong were loyal servants of the Americans who must be punished.

Weary of the war, the Hmong wished that it would end soon, but not in the manner in which it ended. The cease-fire they had long been waiting for did not come in the manner of good gesture for peace from the Pathet Lao, but a hostile demand of agreement conditions in their favor.

Actually, the Pathet Lao faction did not have the liberty to speak for itself or act on its own interest. It was under a pact controlled by the North Vietnamese and must act under the direction of North Vietnam. The land grabbing and boundary flagging and territorial disputes preceding the cease-fire and peace negotiation clearly signaled the bold, hostile intent of the North Vietnamese—the prime agent of Communist expansion purported and supported by Communist China and the Soviet Union. It was not the gesture of Lao Reunification or "Lao-Reunite-Lao" for peace, as some Lao leaders had falsely hoped.

Ignorant of the Communist North Vietnamese and the Pathet Lao's goal, Souvanna Phouma hoped for a reunited Laos at the end, thereby giving in everything in the negotiation process.

There are lawless cultures that do not believe in rules and honesty in the game of war. The Communist Pathet Lao and North Vietnamese used deceptive tactics that worked to their advantage in the negotiation process. Cease-fire agreements were used as a lull to gather forces and supplies to win the fight and not as a genuine step toward a peaceful solution. Hence, the negotiated conditions, stipulations, words, and language

THE CEASE-FIRE AND THE FALSE PEACE

printed in the agreements that were aimed at achieving a solution for peace in Laos and Vietnam were meaningless.

Souvanna Phouma falsely hoped that, as a Neutralist who had supported the Pathet Lao and had formed an alliance with the Soviet Union when the Rightists were weakened by the departure of the United States, he would maintain his position as a Neutralist prime minister of the coalition government and that Laos would remain as a neutral state after the reunification.

In a larger scope of the war, the United States' concern was the Communists' expansion in Southeast Asia, including Thailand and countries in the South Pacific, as it was heightened during the Cold War. An agreement that the Communists' expansion would not go beyond the borders of Thailand would be acceptable to the United States.

For the North Vietnamese, a united Vietnam was their goal. After taking victory in the fight against the French at Dien Bien Phu and driving France out of their northern control, the next objective, by which the Vietnamese felt motivated, was to take victory over the Americans by any means that would bring Vietnam out of foreign control.

For the Communist Pathet Lao and Khmer Rouge, bundling their conflicts with their bigger brother North Vietnam was a strategy that worked to their advantage. When the Americans pulled out and South Vietnam fell, Laos and Cambodia surrendered without resistance.

The growing American POWs, the loss of American lives, and the mounting cost of the war had put political pressure on the United States at home. The North Vietnamese had detected the growing American public sentiments toward the war, and the Communist Pathet Lao had been informed of how the war would end. They had been informed victory was near while the people on the side of the Royal government believed the factions would end the war on an equal basis, giving each of the faction leaders their shares of the pie that would satisfy their hunger for power.

Ho Chi Minh's idea had progressed as planned. The Communist cadres had been trained to be smooth and powerful public speakers advocating for a citizens' bottom-up revolution against corrupt top-down establishments. Ho's idea had worked well in the Viet Minh revolution against the old French-supported regime and had been the burning fuel that motivated the Vietnamese fight against the United States throughout the Vietnam War.

The cease-fire had given the North Vietnamese time to focus on planning for the final assault on South Vietnam and the Pathet Lao the opportunity to build relationships with college and university students and teachers for staging the final showdown of the Communists' takeover. The Communists' strategy had been working effectively in political revolutions around the world. The same strategy was used in the situation in Laos, and that was to take over the country from the corrupt elitists—the wealthy right-wing establishment.

Fooled by the Communists' rhetoric and fed up with the control under the same wealthy corrupt leaders for decades, thousands of students and union government workers marched on the streets of Vientiane, protesting unfair pay and shouting "CIA go home." Some Hmong parents were angry at their sons and daughters who participated in the protest.

THE CEASE-FIRE AND THE FALSE PEACE

Tou Lee—a student at Sisavangvong University, whose father, Pa Thong Lee, lived in a small village nearby Phou Kho village where I was a teacher—received an angry lecture from his uncle, Qhoua Pao Lee, when he returned home.

"You have betrayed me and the Hmong," Uncle Qhoua Pao said with teary eyes. "What you have done was wrong. You have just supported the Communists whom I have been running away from for over ten years. I want you to know, son, your father is a district leader who talks loud. But, do you know how much money I have given you for all these years for your education? You have disappointed me greatly."

Tou Lee later crossed the Mekong River to Thailand without his parents and uncle. He stayed in Nong Khai refugee camp with his cousin whose husband was my first teacher in Phou Houa Xang in 1964. The Hmong refugees in the camp called him a traitor and a Communists' spy. He went to France and returned to Laos a few years later.

Hmong students were closely watched for their behavior because they were Hmong and they were pressured to join the demonstration. They just shouted with the crowd to avoid being suspicious and they were scared, some of them had said.

After the New Year celebration, the beginning of 1975 began with cool and dry air, and with a soft breeze in January. Young men and girls, who engaged in courtship during the New Year celebration, had to go in different ways as the slash-and-burn season began and Hmong parents were in search of farmlands. That had been the way of life of the Hmong for centuries until it was interrupted by the war.

It was the first time in a long time that Laos was in a period of eerie silence, except for the noisy schools where students and teachers engaged loudly in subject matters. It was the happiest moment for Youa and me. Our long-expected first child was born on February 10—a girl! We named her Blia, a name we had long prepared for a girl.

In April 1975, the Hmong farmers worked frantically to have their rice planted before the monsoon rains arrived. The southwest wind blew storm clouds rolling across the sky like dirty giant cotton balls. Sounds of Hmong mothers echoed in the nearby hills and valleys, yelling at their children and telling them to be careful to avoid falling on sharp stumps. The scene represented hope and optimism in remote villages of farmers.

Over the horizon, a series of events was sporadically announced on Vientiane Radio news: Cambodia had fallen to the hands of Communists on April 17; the Lao leaders were working on the peace agreement; North Vietnamese troops advanced closer toward Saigon with Soviet tanks, heavy armor vehicles, and artillery; and the United States Congress denied further funding to support South Vietnamese military.

Later in the day, there was an announcement in the news stating South Vietnam had fallen and North Vietnamese troops had marched on Saigon streets, shouting victory over the South Vietnamese regime and the United States. The Vietnam War was over. The United States was defeated and gone.

Hmong farmers had feared that Laos would follow in the same path. But they continued working, assuming Laos would be different.

In Laos, the teachers' strike still continued in Vien-

THE CEASE-FIRE AND THE FALSE PEACE

tiane and remained one of the issues dominating the news on Vientiane Radio. But there were no school shutdowns in other parts of the country. With summer break just around the corner, students who attended schools away from home looked forward to returning home and spending time with their families.

Teachers were helping third graders with the symbolic application process for the transitional exam. Students who could not pass the exam would be retained for as long as they kept on failing without regard to age. However, there was no data collection nationwide for accountability purpose. Everything was just traditional.

In a country where life was dominated by war for so long, peace time alienated its citizens. Everyone in Phou Kho and the entire region wondered what life would be like when peace came.

I invited District Chief Pa Kao Vang for a sit-down meeting about formulating parent and community support of teachers so they could commit to their full-time job, because airplane rice was no longer available. A one-hundred-pound bag of rice would cost more than a third of my monthly salary. My other fellow teacher, Chou Ly, received seven thousand kip (less than five dollars) a month as a USAID volunteer teacher. His entire salary did not cover a bag of rice.

To impose this measure on parents in a poor slash-and-burn agricultural society would not be possible; the burden would be too hard for them to bear. We asked the community to contribute rice to Chou Ly's family, leaving the two licensed teachers, myself and the other teacher, Yang Sue, to buy our own rice from the farmers.

The end of war would change the way of life in every sector in Laos. None of these economic aspects was on the minds of incompetent and shallow-minded leaders, including Representative Tou Yia Lee.

Teachers across Laos looked forward to an agreement that would close the salary gaps between the primary and secondary school teachers. We did not know if the intensified teachers' strike was orchestrated by the Communist Pathet Lao or was a coincidental event that took place at the dawn of the Communists' takeover of the country. But, the domino falls were near the end.

On May 10, the Long Chieng Radio station was silent. I thought it was a technical problem, which occurred from time to time. I tried again fifteen minutes later. It was silent. I, then, tuned to the Vientiane station. There was only soft music playing continuously. It was an unusual situation. Up to that moment, no one in the entire Phou Kho area had any information about what had taken place in the country, other than the latest news on the situation in South Vietnam and the teachers' strike.

Later in the afternoon, during lunchtime, I tuned again to the Vientiane National Radio station. There was an announcement about changing and transferring positions of some regional military commanders and high-ranking government officials. Among them, Gen. Vang Pao was transferred to Vientiane.

In my mind, on the one hand, I thought it was a shuffling of government officials as part of the progress of the Lao peace agreement. On the other hand, I thought this could be a tactic aimed at trapping Gen. Vang Pao and removing him from his protection in Long Chieng. I knew Gen. Vang Pao would not accept the transfer, but if he refused, he would be subject to contempt of orders. Either way, it was a trap. It became obvious that it was a tactic played by the Pathet Lao, especially in a country where there were plenty of tricks, traps, and deadly surprises. This might be the end, I thought.

On May 11, an announcement on the Vientiane Radio stated that some government officials, including Gen. Vang Pao, had resigned and fled the country. Later, Prime Minister Souvanna Phouma addressed the nation, confirming members of the Rightists had fled the country and conceding the Leftists had taken over the government. He assured everyone: "The new government will make every effort to make sure the transition is peaceful."

The Communists had taken over Laos, violating the peace agreement signed in Paris. Laos fell exactly the way South Vietnam and Cambodia did. In some cultures, there is no rule for wars. The Hmong, who had been called "the American hunting dogs" and publicly targeted to be eradicated down to the roots, panicked and reacted in fear and chaos.

Everyone feared their lives would be in danger, but only the top military officers and their families, top civilian officials and families, and Hmong assistants who worked for CIA (SKY) agents and their families were on the list to be evacuated by planes to Thailand. The rest of the Hmong were left behind to flee on foot or by taxis and face opportunists and crooks who preyed on fleeing Hmong along the Mekong River. Others faced persecution, mass massacres, starvation, and death by the thousands.

CHAPTER 14

AT THE MERCY OF THE TIGER

As their lowland Lao counterpart traveled freely, the Hmong were confined with travel restrictions, which subjected them to become the prey of crooks and opportunists, like mice at the mercy of the tiger.

South Vietnam had fallen after Cambodia. The situation in Laos was not unanticipated. General Vang Pao's American advisors might have told him months earlier that the end was coming in a matter of months. They might have feared Laos would be the first to fall, instead of the last. That could have been the case without the Hmong's stubborn resistance. General Vang Pao refused to agree with their advice and did not want to tell his people anything other than assuring them he would do everything he could to help them.

The Hmong residents in the Phou Kho region, who had just stopped receiving airplane rice at the end of 1973, hoped for another good year of rice harvest as the smell of freshly burned rice fields entered their nostrils. Up to May 11, 1975, the villagers were working in their rice and corn fields from dawn to dust, leaving their villages quiet during the seemingly peaceful summer days.

On the late afternoon of May 12, some local people

arrived from Long Chieng, gasping for breath and telling everyone Laos had been taken by the Communists and Gen. Vang Pao was leaving the country. They said Vang Pao would send helicopters to transport all the Hmong to Thailand.

They gave specific instructions that said: "All the people in Phou Kho need to gather on the school ground in Hoy Sangai village," a village located three miles from the school where I was teaching, "no later than 9 a.m. on May 13." The instructions were clear, specifying that each household only take what was absolutely important.

As frequently displaced refugees for more than ten years, my parents had nothing really important to sort and decide, except a few new clothes kept in the bottom of a large airplane-rice sack. There was no time to sort and select anything. To my mother, the most important thing was having clothes to wear. She stuffed some more clothes on top of what was believed to be new clothes. With two shoulder straps made of long pink waist sashes, my dad carried the large sack on his back.

The rumors traveled like shockwaves across the mountain hills, reaching everyone in a matter of hours and causing panic and chaos. By 7 a.m. the school ground was jammed and packed with panicked Hmong, using their keenest hearing to listen and their eyes to look toward the horizon every minute, expecting a fleet of American helicopters to appear.

We thought we would be taken to a new land as the Americans had promised. We thought we would be in a different world, leaving behind the world in which we had lost everything and had nothing more to lose. The remote villagers, uninformed of the chaos in Long

Chieng, falsely believed the mighty United States had the power to do anything.

"America is the world superpower," Uncle Song Chai proudly said. "They have the power to take us to a place far away and safe."

Everyone waited patiently until 9 a.m. There was no sign of helicopters coming. By noon, there still were no sounds of helicopters coming.

People still had not given up hope. They opened up their lunch. The children started crying because they were hungry. While eating, some people ran down to check with local Chief Yong Zoua Vang not far down the slope, who had a Fortmai radio, and ask him to call Long Chieng to find out what caused the delay. No one answered. He called several times. Again, there was no answer. Finally, two soldiers arrived from Long Chieng.

"Don't waste your time waiting!" one of the men yelled in anger. "People in Long Chieng were in chaos, fighting to board airplanes! They were about to kill each other! Gen. Vang Pao has left. Go home and find your own way. Who told you Gen. Vang Pao would send planes to pick you up?"

"Two men came from Long Chieng yesterday and told us with specific instructions," a man said. "Why did they tell us to prepare for evacuation?"

"It was a lie!" one of the men said angrily. "It was a tactical plan to prevent people from overwhelming the air evacuation in Long Chieng."

Everyone was disappointed, angry, and scared. People started calling their children and going home in disappointment. My father carried the big sack all the way back home.

My mother opened up the sack to check what was

in the bottom. What she found were shreds of old fabric and dry corncobs that my sisters, Pai and Ker, used for making dolls. She was furious. Then she started laughing, then crying.

"Is this all we have in our life?" she cried as she asked herself. "What a crazy and funny world. What more do we have to lose?"

It was 4 p.m. The villagers were scared and became agitated. Watching from the mountain, the only zigzagging dirt road connecting Colonial Route 13 with the rest of the mountainous towns and villages on the northeast, including Ban Xorn and Long Chieng, became busy with traffic going in both directions. The residents in Phou Kho villages rushed down to the valley.

Some boarded taxis to go to Vientiane and flee the country. Others, especially the poor, traveled back to Long Chieng to pick up ammunition and escape to the mountains before the Communists arrived.

Youa, Blia, and I were among the first who arrived at the road in the bottom of the valley. The scene was in a state of chaos and resembled an evacuation to escape a coming catastrophic storm—a typhoon or hurricane. The sun was shining; the crystal clear creek was still flowing; the fish were playing as usual; the trees and vegetation were peaceful; the birds were flying; and the sky was clear. What was happening? It was a human-killing storm created by a few individuals intoxicated with power indulgence. The scene was depressing and scary.

My mind was dominated with all these thoughts as I walked back up the hill to find out why my parents had not gone down to the valley. Uncle Song Chai, too, would not let them fall behind. I walked up the hill for one hour to get them down.

When I arrived in the village, it was eerily quiet. There were three families remaining, including my parents. My mom and my dad were crying. They did not have the money to pay for the expensive taxi fare for ten people plus whatever costs that would come after that. They would rather stay and die. The kids were terrified. They were trembling and leaning against each other with their eyes flooded with tears.

"Mom and dad, let's go," I said. "Don't worry. We'll do everything we can to help. We'll go together or die together. Uncle Song Chai was waiting for you down there."

"If not for you and all the children who are still young, we would rather die here," my father said.

The kids wiped away their tears and each grabbed his or her little pack, which only contained clothes, blankets, and rice, nothing precious. It was about 7 p.m. and the sun, in the long summer days, was nearly behind the Phou Kho Mountain on the west. We walked down the familiar trail on which we had traveled nearly every day to Ban Xorn or to nearby rice fields. This time the purpose was different and the destination was unknown. The kids walked innocently with their packs bouncing on their backs, occasionally looking back at me—their big brother—as if I knew the answer, although I was just as helpless as they were. Even the king was helpless and unable to help his children in the event of war—the game of cruelty, killing talents, human viciousness, destructions, and death.

When we arrived at the road, where Youa and Blia stayed with a large crowd of people—waiting for taxis to come by, we were told—while I was gone, Uncle Song Chai's family had left, but had sent an empty taxi for my parents. Since they were not there, other people climbed on and it left. We spent the night there to catch taxis the next day.

There were jeep- and pickup-converted taxis, heavily loaded with passengers, passing by all night long. The next morning, we ate breakfast early so some of us could go to Ban Xorn to get taxis.

Some people returned and said the Hin Heub checkpoint was closed to all vehicles with Hmong passengers. So, the gate to heaven was closed, and we were stranded in hell. Everything changed. We returned home to decide what to do next.

Some people came up with a new idea. They worked with taxi drivers to drop them off before the checkpoint. They walked around the village to where they would meet the drivers downstream. The drivers would drive the empty cabs past the checkpoint and the Nam Lit River bridge to arrange boats for their passengers. This was done at a cost of a fortune to desperate Hmong families, willing to pay any price. Soon this idea was discovered and all the people, including the taxi drivers (all Laotians), were caught. The drivers were let go and they never refunded the families, claiming they were done deals. The families were forced to return to Ban Xorn.

Some people hired motorboats to take them through the giant Nam Nguem Reservoir toward the Nam Nguem Dam, where they would take taxis through the That Lat village and cross the Mekong River to Thailand by boats. After numerous cases in which some people were robbed of their belongings and their families were dumped into the water, this route ended.

Some people, like Za Houa Lee of Phou Kho, who had passed the gates and checkpoints, hoping to cross the Mekong River, were robbed of all their money and forced to surrender to the Pathet Lao. All the victims were Hmong.

The Hmong refugees, mostly women and children, who peacefully fled the country after a war and regime change, were robbed by crooks. Women and children were searched, nearly stripped naked, for money. They were killed by soldiers and crooks alike.

After returning home, disappointed, scared, and confused, I visited my grandma and Uncle Ka Thai, who lived on top of the hill, about one thousand feet from the school. Because Grandma was ninety years old and Uncle Pa Xiong was disabled, Uncle Ka Thai decided on not going anywhere.

I walked over to my house and the school, which closed without my having the chance to say good-bye to the students. The scene was sad. The school was left as if everyone would come back. The chalkboards, the teachers' desks, the books, the students' benches, and the playground were all there in silence. The students' voices and laughter still vividly echoed in my memory.

I stopped by to briefly visit my two fellow teachers—Chou Lee and Sue Yang. Chou Lee, with five young children, was not financially able to flee. Sue Yang, a newly graduated teacher—with a wife, two young children, and his seventy-year-old mother—had decided not to flee. We talked briefly and found out the woman next door, whose husband died in the war a few years earlier, had moved into our house right after we walked out and taken over our mattress, blankets, and every household item. I let her have everything.

I returned the next day to take a mother pig we had bought for 65,000 kip when it was pregnant. We sold the mother and six babies to a lowland Lao merchant down the valley for 15,000 kip. My parents and other villagers also sold all their animals for any prices they could get.

I spent the next five days looking for ways to pass or go around the checkpoint just to get my large family, especially my parents, to Vientiane. I took two men with me all the way to a fishing camp by the Nam Nguem Reservoir to look for anyone willing to take us through the giant dam reservoir with a motorboat.

"We don't have boats big enough to take your large family," the fishermen told us.

That was the answer we had found after traveling nearly ten miles on a trail covered by tall grass. They, at least, honestly expressed concern that their canoe-shaped boats would be turned over and sunk by waves caused by large boats. We appreciated their honest discussion and returned in disappointment. On the way home, we saw thousands of fish spawning in a shallow creek, but were emotionally depressed and not in the mood to catch a single fish.

As a teacher with only a wife and a child, I should have easily been able to travel to Vientiane without any problem. If an ID was required, my teacher union member card with a stamped photo should have been sufficient. Why did I have the same problem as everyone? The reason was I was a Hmong. People of ethnic lowland Lao traveled back and forth between Ban Xorn and Vientiane every day. The vast majority did not possess an identification document. Lowlanders crossed the Mekong River back and forth daily without any problem.

On May 21, word came from Ban Xorn announcing there would be a march from Ban Xorn to Vientiane. The announcement excited everyone. We reviewed the idea and found there had not been any incident, at least to our knowledge, in which the government would use deadly force against refugees who peacefully marched away from violence.

We agreed to join the march, not realizing the Pathet Lao would employ deadly force on the refugees, consisting largely women and children. My parents decided to kill all their chicken for food on the march, in hope that the march would at least take the Hmong to Vientiane, where the government leaders and the international diplomats were located. If they couldn't cross the border to Thailand, at least they would be able to express their concerns and live closer to Vientiane.

On May 22, the march from Ban Xorn was joined by the Hmong in the Pou Kho region and along the road, from Km 23 to Km 18, forming the largest exodus of refugees in Laos's modern history—totaling about nine thousand people walking on foot. All were Hmong. The road was filled with foot-walking human beings, stretching over six miles on the gravel road from Ban Xorn—all aimed at reaching Vientiane.

We walked past numerous lowland Lao villages where people stared at us from their platform houses without talking to any of us. Some talked to each other: "The war is over. All the Meo will move out of Laos. There will be no Meo left!"

They were all afraid to talk to us, especially about what happened. It was an unusual situation.

On the afternoon of May 24, most of the people had arrived at Hin Heub. We camped under thick bamboo bushes on the right-hand side of the road near a creek, about a quarter of a mile from the checkpoint. There were people setting up lean-tos closer to the checkpoint.

There were more people camping behind us, stretching about a mile back on both sides of the road and crowding in wherever they could find a space for their family. The nebulous smoke of fires blurred the view of the whole area along the road.

The plan, as it was communicated to everyone, was to continue marching past the checkpoint and across the Nam Lit Bridge toward Vientiane. We were not protesters. We were peaceful refugees with mostly women and young children, trying to peacefully move out of the country. The bloody fight was over. The Communists had won. We did not anticipate a confrontation with Pathet Lao police forces or soldiers.

The afternoon was filled with people peacefully walking and talking on the gravel road. Children innocently played with road gravel, not thinking much about where the march was heading or what the reason was. The infrequently traveled road was empty most of the time. Occasionally, one or two empty Pathet Lao cargo trucks and Ban Xorn's pickup-converted taxis, filled with non-Hmong passengers, slowly ran by, trying to avoid hitting the weary foot-travelers on the road. The drivers at least seemed to act respectfully. The land they had lived in and called home for over a century had suddenly changed.

Some people who camped close to the checkpoint had even walked to buy needed food and supplies from roadside vendors around the checkpoint. Everything was calm and strangely quiet, as if something was predetermined to happen. None of the vendors dared asking questions about the march. In a country without guiding principles for rules and laws, Pathet Lao leaders might have planned and discussed what action they would take the next day, even shooting at children.

Touby Lyfoung, a long-time Hmong leader and the only Hmong beside Gen. Vang who had attained the status of lordship bestowed by the king, and who was, up to that moment, a member of the king's council, might have discussed with the Pathet Lao what they would do if the refugees marched toward the gate. He had been in Ban Xorn three days earlier, trying to persuade the Hmong not to follow Vang Pao and, even though Vang Pao was gone, he assured that he would remain a leader of the Hmong, as he had always been. According to speculations, he might have been in the Hin Heub area, planning what to do to impress the Pathet Lao. Others said he just might be helpless as anyone else under the Pathet Lao's control, including the king himself.

The Hmong had many reasons to fear for their safety. First, the Communists violated the cease-fire that all parties had agreed to, which preceded the peace agreement, stipulating how a coalition government would be formed. Second, the Communist Pathet Lao marched to the neutral zone in Vientiane with tanks, heavy armor, and troops following the fall of Cambodia and South Vietnam in a manner of bold hostility. And third, Gen. Vang Pao and other high-ranking Lao government officials had resigned and fled the country, and Prime Minister Souvanna Phouma had conceded that the Communists had taken over the government.

In addition, the Hmong had learned much about the Communist system—a military dictatorship regime that used citizens to spy on each other, a mind-control system under the guise of bottom-up democracy, and an authoritarian system without due process.

In the early morning on May 25, words were passed

on to everyone along the road letting everyone know that the march would start at 8 a.m. But, the process of getting everyone to move was delayed. By 9 a.m., the line started. Some people had walked past us. We started moving and were a bit nervous. Some men made hand gestures at the crowd. "Keep moving. Keep moving," a man said.

The road was filled beyond capacity, and the line was moving to about two hundred feet. There were explosion and gunshots ahead of us. People in the front ran back toward us in commotion.

"*Nyablaj tua neeg pem hauvntej lawm lauj!*" a man shouted, meaning "The Vietnamese have killed people in the front up there!"

More people ran back in chaos, passing us. Communist soldiers started chasing after the refugees and firing sporadic shots into the air. Women and children cried in horror. We thought everyone was going to be killed. We ran after the crowd like a herd of goats. There were continuous gunshots behind us as we ran about five hundred feet past our camp. There were bags and flip-flops scattered on the road. The soldiers had stopped their chase and gunfire. No one knew exactly what had happened at the checkpoint and how many people had been killed or injured. No one was allowed to go back and help.

We walked for two miles to a lowland Lao village by the road and saw Touby standing in front of a school building where the weary Hmong refugees rested. He was vigorously giving the crowd a lecture about the Hmong not following the rules.

"I have told you not to flee after Vang Pao," he said. "You did not listen. I spoke to you as a Hmong. You continuously defied everything I said. You got what you deserved. There is an old saying about the Hmong I have learned: 'A hard bone needs a dog to gnaw. A stubborn Hmong needs a non-Hmong to whip.'"

To this day, I have never forgotten the two sentences Touby used in his lecture. Although there was no evidence to confirm he had planned or ordered the actions in Hin Heub, he did imply the Hmong deserved a deadly punishment, better if given by non-Hmong, even though they had done nothing wrong.

Some people immediately left the crowd in anger. I left Youa and Blia with the crowd, crossed the road, and walked back toward the direction we had just come from, looking for my parents.

There was another crowd surrounding a Westerner, who was believed to be a journalist. A Hmong man in his midthirties was talking in fluent English, explaining what had happened. The white man took notes of everything he said. Ignorant and naive of how things worked in the world, we were happy that God had heard us, simply because someone spoke in English to a foreign journalist. We were wrong.

In reality, nobody cared and nobody did anything, even something horrific in a much larger magnitude. The Americans were gone, quiet, and seemingly powerless. They were there on a mission; they had failed. They would go back home, leaving the Hmong behind, perhaps without expressions of remorse. The Communists had won. We had lost and were at their mercy like mice at the mercy of the tiger. Similar or much larger tragic events had happened in the past in many lawless parts of the world. Nothing much had been done to help them.

The Hmong love talking about myths and legends, as their ancestors possessed no written characters to record what had happened in history. When we were young, we frequently crowded on Grandmas' and Grandpas' laps, competing for spaces closer to their voices to listen to horrific stories. What they told us sounded scary, but did not seem real. Now, we witness cruelty that causes the death of women and children with our own eyes. It happens to us. This is not a myth. This is not a legend. My mind was seized by these thoughts for a few moments as I was trying to understand what had happened.

For some, the horrific event on that day might soon fade away from their memory like a storm that had passed, and they would feel relieved to be alive. And what happens to people in another part of the world on another day is just another thing that happens, and it's the problem of other people. To me, it's all connected, and it's all the same human cruelty and ferociousness. When I see humans suffering atrocities and losses of lives because of conflicts and wars, I see myself with them. They are the recurrences of what had happened to me.

After the terrifying drama on the rough road, the Pathet Lao soldiers did offer some people a ride on their cargo trucks from one village to the next on their return to Ban Xorn, relieving them from the brutal foot walk, and ostentatiously showing the Pathet Lao's good will.

My parents and three other families of Phou Kho took that offer, and they were dropped off at Ban Somsanouk, a Hmong village where missionaries cared for people suffering from leprosy. They did not know where to go and did not want to return to their empty village.

Another idea was to pretend to be the unwanted people who needed to go to Vientiane for care by the missionaries. But, later they changed their minds, fearing the idea would not work because their physical appearances were different from those of people with leprosy. They abandoned the plan and returned to Ban Xorn.

Youa, Blia, and I returned to Ban Xorn right after the Hin Heub ordeal to figure out what to do next. While in Ban Xorn, we were joined by Youa's parents, her two sisters—Nou and Vaj—and her adopted aunt, Bee. They were left behind because while they were visiting Toua in the old village of Phou Xang Noy, Ma, his wife, two brothers, Neng and Thai, and adopted uncle, Dang, were evacuated by planes to Thailand.

Scared by the Communists' cruel action in Hin Heub, the majority of the Hmong who returned took weapons, gathered the Americans' remnant ammunition, and headed toward the mountains to form resistance, fighting for their lives. They hoped their leader, Gen. Vang Pao, and their American friends would return to help them—another mistake and false assumption.

In Ban Xorn, people panicked because of rumors that hundreds of Communist soldiers would soon arrive. Local Hmong leaders, including Youa's parents and other folks, took their families to hide in wild banana-grove valleys north of Ban Xorn. We took refuge with them for two weeks. Nothing happened. We returned to Ban Xorn and were joined by my parents, who arrived from Ban Somsanouk.

Hin Heub became more open for travelers. Uncle Tou, who I thought had gone to Thailand by plane, arrived from Phak Kheh. He asked if I would go with him.

I told him my parents were too poor to go and that I decided to stay. He said good-bye and left. He left behind his parents and older brother's family in Phak Kheh. They knew it was too dangerous for him to stay.

Ban Xorn was in chaos and filled with people from everywhere—all new faces. In contrast, the lowlanders—residents, vendors, and taxi drivers alike—remained calm and found business opportunities as the Hmong swarmed the town, spending their lifetime saving, including silver coins, bars, and jewelry.

Silver trading shops were making good money. I decided to go up to the mountains to buy scrap-silver jewelry. I made several trips, making good profits, half of which I shared with my poor parents. I stopped after there were reports of incidents in which people were robbed and killed on the remote trails.

On June 24, I decided to report to the Provincial School Superintendent's Office, which was only two miles east of Ban Xorn. School Superintendent Moua Lia had fled by airplane to Thailand. His deputy, Mr. Bouth Thalangsy, an ethnic lowlander, became in charge. Because more than a half of the teachers, mostly Hmong, had left the country, he was surprised, but happy to see me. The office was fully staffed as usual, but staff composition had changed from 70 percent Hmong to nearly all Lao.

The conversation was strictly about a job. Nothing about the situation was mentioned. We were talking as if the country was perfectly fine, deeply concealing our true feelings. It confirmed how the new regime would be. We feared that doors and walls had ears.

He gave me my two-month salary plus the extra salary for the adult teaching job. All salaries were paid in cash without any control mechanism. He might have pocketed a fortune from the salaries of those who had left the country or did not report to work. He asked specifically where I lived. I honestly told him I lived in Ban Xorn at the moment.

"Very good!" he said loudly. "That's even better than you live on the mountain where it would be hard for me to look for you. Some teachers will be going to Long Chieng for a training tomorrow. We have already arranged transportation. Tell me exactly how I can find you."

"Tomorrow? That soon?" I asked.

"Yes, it was already arranged. I am glad you are here just in time."

I gave him directions on how to find me. I returned and told Youa. She was terrified.

"Why didn't you tell him that you would go next time, so you have time to talk to your families first?" she asked.

"Well, I decided to go. Our parents cannot go anywhere anyway," I said.

"No, I can't let you do that," she said angrily. "You have not talked to your parents and my parents to let them know. Let's talk to my dad right now."

We talked to my father-in-law, who was in the process of making a Hmong musical instrument. He was shocked and he nearly dropped his instrument.

"No, we cannot let you go. That's what we are afraid of, and the reason we are trying to flee the Communists. People go for training and never come back, you see."

"Dad, don't worry. I am a teacher."

"Son, you never trust the Communists," my father-in-law warned. "Look at what has happened in the government. Besides, you are a Hmong who would always be suspicious to them. Let's go and talk to your father now."

We went to my parents' house about a half mile away on the other side of the town, past the marketplace. When we got there, before I said anything, my father in-law told my father the story. My father was horrified.

"We are now looking to you for direction and everything. What are we going to do if you are gone? Son, if I should be killed today, but you could live for a day longer, I would be happy."

"But I already agreed. They will be coming tomorrow to look for me. If I run away, I will be a fugitive from now on."

"Leave it to me," Youa said. "I will take care of that."

"What do you plan to do?" I asked.

"You pretend to be sick tomorrow and I'll tell them when they come. I can say you will go next time. That way we will have some time to plan what we will do next."

"But, that's a lie!" I said, raising my voice. "You mean you will lie to them that I am sick?"

"So what! We are living in a system that is full of lies," Youa said as she became angry. "People lie to their advantages. Do you trust what they told you was not a lie?"

The next morning, two Pathet Lao soldiers and Bouth Thalansy, the new superintendent, came to take me as planned. I stayed in bed, playing sick. Youa went outside and talked to them. They left without questioning her, except encouraging that she should get me some medicines. We became even more scared. We feared they might spy on me for suspicion that I pretended to be sick to avoid going for training.

The Communists had taken swift actions to take control of everything. Using teachers to calm and control people's minds was crucial amid the heightened chaos and fears. That's why there was such an urgency to gather teachers for a series of training.

We immediately left the house and went to my parents' place. We found out Uncle Boua See had returned from Pha Khao where his second-youngest brother, Sai Xiong, a captain in the Royal Lao Army, had lived. Sai Xiong received a transfer order from Vientiane.

His family and his assistant's family were transported to Vientiane by helicopter. When they arrived in Vientiane, they immediately fled to Thailand.

Before leaving, he gave Uncle Boua See the transfer order, telling him to ask his niece's husband, Za Houa Lee, to take Uncle Boua See to Vientiane under the guise of Captain Sai Xiong.

Za Houa, a captain in the irregulars who had been mobbed at the Mekong River and forced to return to Ban Xorn, only spoke broken Laotian. I offered to be his soldier, accompanying him and Uncle Boua See—a deadly risk we had taken.

It was two o'clock on a sunny afternoon. I dressed up in a green military uniform—a bit too large for me. It was the first time in my life dressing up in a military uniform, which made me feel awkwardly strange. I practiced the military salute a few times. It got better each time, assuring I looked real.

We went to the marketplace where taxi drivers competed against each other for passengers. We found a pickup-converted taxi, large enough for all of us. There were plenty of people wanting to go to Vientiane, but not many, especially Hmong, could obtain travel documents. After assuring we had travel documents, we started taking the taxi around to load up our stuff.

My parents threw six small packages—tightly wrapped in white cotton cloths—which we later discovered were just blankets. My parents-in-law were watching with teary eyes. Choked with emotion, tears rolled down from our eyes, and unable to speak, we hugged each other. I assured them I would return with travel documents from Vientiane for them.

We stopped at the Ban Xorn checkpoint on the left-hand side of the road, across from the Ban Xorn Hospital built by Mr. Pop. I took the document to the guards in the box—two local police officers and two Pathet Lao soldiers—all ethnic lowlanders. I saluted them and presented the document. The incompetent guards, unable to read, simply looked at it, stamped it, and gave it back to me. We moved on, bouncing along the rough and pitted gravel road.

We stopped at the Km 22 village where I had taught for a year. Some people we had known were coincidently standing by the road and coming to say good-bye.

Four people—two men and two women—climbed on. Among them was Yeng Ly, who used to visit me while I was a teacher there. We used to cook fish and drink Lao rice wine together. He was a relative of LyTeck Ly Nhia Vue, who many Hmong believed ordered the massacre in Hin Heub.

LyTeck, who was an ambitious young Hmong man and was the first Hmong with a master's degree from France, worked in the Royal Lao Ministry of Justice. He had been helping the Pathet Lao in the coalition government negotiation and had been quoted by Hmong students in Vientiane who had heard his remarks about overthrowing the old government and replacing it with a new one. The transition of regime might have served his ambition well. Unfortunately, he was reported dead, not long after the regime change, in a reeducation camp among other ambitious fools.

Za Houa, who pretended to be Captain Sai, sat with his wife in the front with the driver. We all crowded in the back. We arrived at the Hin Heub checkpoint at about 5:30 p.m. I presented the document to the guards, while Yeng Ly's group presented no document. They came out of the box and counted the passengers as we sat nervously. They said nothing, gave me the document, lifted the bar, and gestured the driver to go. The taxi rolled on, and we sighed in relief.

At 8 p.m., we started entering the Phoun Hong plain, where the gravel road became flat, straight, and better as darkness took over daylight. Only the high-beam headlights guided the lonely taxi on the straight gravel road. Suddenly there was a car or truck coming behind us with high-beam lights, speeding toward us and closely following us. We sat nervously as the high-beam lights blinded us for about two miles. It turned away toward a road on the left. We sighed in relief, although unsure what was going to happen next.

We arrived at the Sykhai bus station at 9 p.m. It was dark in the open parking lot. As we unloaded our luggage, Blia started crying as if she was hurt or someone was pinching her. We had a pile of packages and our suitcases unloaded down from the roof of the taxi. A taxi cab came by, asking where we were going. None in our group spoke Lao nor had been in Vientiane; Za Houa only spoke broken Lao. The taxi driver needed money. Everything was in chaos.

By the time we settled, the other group had left. One more taxi came. I gave the cab driver former Col. Song Leng Xiong's address, provided by Captain Sai. We loaded everything and headed toward the former colonel's house. He had already left for Thailand, but his relatives still lived there.

It was dark and late when we got to the house. We woke up the people there and went inside the big two-story house. The first floor had a large open tile-floored living room and two bedrooms. The second floor had two bedrooms and a large open hardwood-floored foyer. The kitchen and bathroom were in two separate small outbuildings. The compound was fenced in on a half-acre lot well shaded by fruit trees.

Col. Song Leng Xiong was a native of Phou San and Phou Vieng who had served in the CIA-funded Special Guerrilla Unit (SGU) since the beginning of the Vietnam War, earning the rank of colonel. Thus, we were not strangers to the people staying in the house.

We unloaded and took everything upstairs. Suddenly, we discovered the suitcase was not ours. We asked Za Houa if we had switched suitcases. He checked and said they had all their belongings. We realized the other people got our suitcase. The situation caused neither panic nor worry. Somehow, they had our suitcase and we had theirs.

For our protection, we opened up the suitcase for eyewitness of what they had, and found some Hmong traditional dresses and valuable items such as a large silver necklace. We felt assured it would be resolved when daylight came.

The house was empty and the owner was gone. Soon, it would be taken over by the Communists. There was nothing to sleep on. But we had plenty of blankets, more than enough, except for a mosquito net. It was not a big deal for one night, if everything went as planned.

The next morning, we woke up to find Vientiane as if the world was perfectly peaceful. Za Houa and I took a taxi to the marketplace to see if the owner of the suitcase would go there to look for us.

The marketplace was packed and busy as usual, but no one was Hmong. It would not have been unusual if it were before the Communist takeover. I had been in Vientiane and enjoyed visiting the marketplace. I had never had such a feeling. Although there had been some ethnic discrimination, nothing had been terribly bad.

Motorcycles roared along Lane Xang Avenue. But the owners of the suitcase were nowhere to be found.

After looking and waiting for three hours, we returned to the colonel's house, fearing we would be followed by Pathet Lao soldiers. But the people there said they went shopping often and it was okay. It was an indication that the situation was calm in other parts of Laos, except where the Hmong lived. Only the Hmong who had fought with the Americans against the Communists were the targets. The Hmong who had chosen an alliance with the Communists in the 1950s, such as Youa's Granduncle Da Xeng and his entire extended family, would have been proud of the moment.

When we arrived, Youa told us the people had found us and took their suitcase. They promised they would come back later with ours. That's strange, I thought. But I still had not lost my faith.

LyTeck had lived in Vientiane long before the Sam

Thong Teacher Training Institute was moved to the Dong Dok Campus six years ago. Thus, unlike many of us who had only been to Vientiane a few times in our lives, his family had known every part of Vientiane well.

As a poor Hmong student, I couldn't afford to travel around Vientiane during my study there.

We were unable to find the people who had our suitcase. Why didn't they bring our suitcase to us after they had found us and we had given them theirs? Other than the worst-case scenario that something bad had happened to them, we couldn't find any sensible explanation. They knew everything in our lives was in it. Or could they have done it on purpose because they were relatives of LyTeck. His long-standing animosity toward Gen. Vang Pao might have rendered him a misanthropic feeling toward the fleeing Hmong to the extent that he had ordered the attack in Hin Heub, as some people had alleged.

We waited for two days. They never came. We lost all of our clothes and everything. And, we've never see them again, to this day.

While waiting for our suitcase, I went to the Ministry of Interior to try to get travel documents and a taxi for our parents to travel to Vientiane. I was told that under the new system, travel documents must be initiated by local authorities, not them. Obviously, the ministry was powerless. The next day, there was news stating the Nam Lit Bridge was bombed and destroyed, allegedly by Hmong resistance forces. Our parents were left behind, wondering if we had made it to Thailand.

After two days waiting for the suitcase, we decided to cross to Thailand on the third day. Leng Moua (a Hmong student at the Vientiane Technical College who was the second son of my father's distant cousin) was among the students who tried to earn an income from Hmong wanting to cross to Thailand. He helped arrange two taxi cabs and boats for us to cross the mighty river.

At 8 a.m., two cabs arrived. We loaded them up. Uncle and Aunt Boua See, one of Za Houa's children, Youa, Blia, and I tightly crammed ourselves in one cab. Za Houa, his wife, and five children squeezed in another. We were instructed to sit low to avoid two cabs filled with Hmong faces to be stopped by Communist Vietnamese and Pathet Lao police and soldiers. There would be nothing to fear if we were not Hmong. This reminded me of the Jewish trying to flee the Nazis during World War II.

The cabs rolled out of the driveway and rolled toward the well-paved Fa Ngum Road that ran along the Mekong River toward the boat landing station, Tha Deua. After a forty-minute ride, the cabs entered a driveway on the right into a garden overgrown with grass.

Looking straight down from the cabs, the muddy Mekong River was within two hundred feet. Some people were loading into a boat. A woman smiled and waved at us. The cabs stopped. We were told to get off and unload everything.

Instead of going straight down to the river where the boat was, we were led to the right, crossing a broken barbed wire fence into the woods. We walked clumsily, carrying and dragging everything in our hands to the base of a large tree. A policeman in uniform stood there, shouting at us.

"You are trying to sneak out to Thailand in my patrol area!" he shouted. "You are putting me in trouble."

We froze in terror. I felt a pinch in my heart.

"You are trying to sneak people out of the country illegally!" he shouted at the drivers. "Don't ever try to do this again."

The drivers begged for forgiveness, saying they would never do it again (this was either fake or real).

"They will pay you whatever they agreed to and you get out of here," he added.

We paid the drivers 65,000 kip (forty-six dollars in 1975 value) each—no argument and no question about the boats. They left.

"You need to pay 65,000 kip penalty, then I'll let you go!" he yelled.

We gathered money and paid him. He left. We were on our own without boats. Terrified by the situation and realizing we had been robbed by mobs, we started walking around the tree toward the mighty river to see if any boat would pass by. Suddenly, two soldiers in green uniforms stood before our eyes, yelling at us.

"We will take you to the authority if you don't pay us 110,000 kip!" one of the soldiers yelled.

"I beg you to have mercy on us," I begged with my knees on the ground. "We are all Lao facing this crisis. We don't have very much money left. We will pay you 110,000 kip, after you find boats for us. As soon as we load in the boats, we will give you the money," I said.

"Okay," a soldier said. "You stay here and don't make any sound or go anywhere," he said, and they left.

We stayed there under thick brushes, wondering if we all were going to be killed or turned over to the Pathet Lao. The soldiers came back to inform us they could not find any boat, but they were trying.

I tried to flatter them for their human hearts and for trying to help us. I told them I was a teacher—not a soldier—but all my families had left.

They left for two hours and came back with some food—some sticky rice and good beef salad, which they might have bought from a market somewhere nearby. They left again.

We feared they might try to poison us with the food. Everyone was hungry. I volunteered to eat first. I was okay after thirty minutes. Then everyone ate.

They came back and asked for forty thousand kip right away to bribe the Pathet Lao guards. We started crying. We had no more money.

"Don't worry," one of the soldiers assured. "We'll get you out today, we promise."

We gave them the money and they left for a long time. It was nearly 5 p.m. on Za Houa's watch. The sun was moving low toward the horizon. We discussed and feared they were going to kill us all at nightfall and throw us into the river. We decided to turn ourselves in if they didn't come back with a boat in thirty minutes. The situation reminded me of stories I had heard. "Vientiane is not a place where you would tell someone you are lost and you need help."

Suddenly the men came back and said, "Get your money and everything ready. The boats will be down there in ten minutes."

We gathered our money in a hurry. Everyone gathered and handed me what they had—mostly small bills. The big bills were gone.

"Fifty thousand kip now," I said. "We need sixty thousand more."

Everyone was scared and shaking. While rushing for some more money, the soldiers ran toward us and grabbed the big stack of money from my hand.

"Hurry! The boats are down there now," one of the soldiers said and ran away.

Za Houa and I threw everything on the mudslide down to the grassy riverbank while the women and Uncle Boua See ran down to help the boat operators throw them into the boats. We all boarded. The boats sped away. We prayed loudly, asking for God's protection, fearing Communist soldiers would fire at us.

The boats went farther and farther into the Thai side of the river. When we got to the other side, we asked the boat owners how much we owed them.

"Twenty-seven thousand kip per boat," one of the men said.

We paid them and thanked them with great relief. We walked up on the sandy shore past some vegetable gardens where an elderly couple worked frantically, weeding their green garden.

"God, please bless people who flee crisis to find peace," the old man said in Thai language as he stood up to look at us coming up the gentle slope.

"Uncle, is there a road up there?" I asked.

"Yes, son, just walk straight up there."

We walked for about ten minutes and past some tall bushes. Carrying and dragging our packages along a narrow trail, we arrived at a gravel road. While standing there in bewilderment, not knowing which way to go, an empty pickup-converted taxi appeared and slowed down to a stop.

"Go to refugee camp?" he asked in Thai language.

"Yes, sir. How much?" I asked.

He counted us. Six adults and seven children, including a baby.

"Twenty-seven thousand kip," he said, expecting

we would pay in Lao currency and not in Thai baht.

We climbed on and adjusted ourselves to fit. He took us on a partially dirt road, past well-shaded and above-ground houses on both sides, toward the town of Nong Khai where white two-story houses of prominent residents and roadside shops became dominant on both sides of paved streets. In about twenty minutes, he stopped in front of the camp where Thai vendors set up tents full of merchandise to cater the crowded refugee camp.

While counting the money to pay the taxi driver, an older Hmong man, a well-known former district chief, walked by. I asked him if 27,000 kip was right for a twenty-minute ride for thirteen people, because that was a lot of money in Laos.

"Son, this is how it is when you lost your country."

I asked no more questions, just handed the driver money as we had agreed to pay. The actual taxi cost, as we later traveled to find work along that road, was seven baht or 560 kip per adult. The cost for thirteen adults would have been 7,280 kip, instead of 27,000 kip. The influx of Hmong refugees had been a once-in-a-lifetime chance to earn a fortune for opportunists and crooks on both sides of the border.

It was late afternoon on June 27, 1975. The last buses taking the last group of Hmong refugees to Nam Phong camp were at the roadside nearby, ready to depart. We entered the camp from the front gate to join the refugees who came before us and watched more refugees arriving every day, carrying what they could bring in their hands through this same gate.

AT THE MERCY OF THE TIGER

I have a vivid memory of Ban Vinai refugee camp, the place where thousands of souls had been trapped in a life of despair and without hope for over a decade.

CHAPTER 15

SHEEP WITHOUT A FIELD

The Hmong who had managed to flee to Thailand alive felt their future was in limbo, while those who were left behind fled to the mountains, fighting for their lives for fear of persecution. Both groups felt neither the Americans nor the Pathet Lao wanted them, as if they had become sheep without a field.

The situation in Long Chieng during the air evacuation was surprisingly more than what the United States had calculated, should it lose the war. As the sequence of events unfolded, starting from the fall of Cambodia to the fall of South Vietnam, followed by a series of Communist hostile movements in Laos, the United States had known that Laos would fall any time, but had no evacuation budget planned for the Hmong.

What the United States had envisioned, at best, was a small-scale evacuation of Gen. Vang Pao's immediate family members, senior military officers, and CIA workers. That was the promise implied in the talk and agreement when Gen. Vang Pao was contacted by an honorable American, Col. Billy, in late 1960.

After Gen. Vang Pao angrily protested the plan, the number to be evacuated was increased to between 2,500 and 3,500. Even the latter was only a small fraction of the people who had earned hate and persecution threats through their years of fierce resistance against Communist expansion as a loyal American ally.

Junior officers, soldiers, and even teachers also feared their lives would be in danger in a country without civil conscience and guiding principles. The Long Chieng airfield was swarmed by thousands of people from Long Chieng alone, not including the mountains— far more than planned—fighting to board airplanes. Air America planes that had once flown in and out of Long Chieng airfield, making it look like a busy airport, were gone. Except for one C-130 American plane and mechanically poor old C-46 and C-47 planes, no Lao planes were available or deployed for the evacuation.

After the last day of chaotic fighting to get on board airplanes was over, the leaders and whoever could climb aboard were gone. There was no more air evacuation. The Americans were gone. The rest who were left behind began to find other means to flee the Communists who they had been fighting against for nearly two decades.

Within weeks, the stream of refugees fleeing on foot and by taxis overwhelmed temporary refugee camps on the Thai border along the Mekong River. No humanitarian aid was provided to the large influx of refugees. They had to find their own food for survival.

Uncle Song Chai's family was among the refugees who fled by taxi and crossed the Mekong River to Nong Khai, Thailand, on May 13, 1975, and were among the last to be shuttled to the Nam Phong camp. His son, Neng, and his brother, Captain Sai, who arrived later, were once again left behind in the Nong Khai camp without refugee aid, after they reunited briefly upon their arrival.

We crossed to Thailand a month later and were among the thousands who added more congestion to the crowded camp after the Nam Phong camp was closed to new refugees. Walking in from the front gate, we were met with unbelievable crowds of people walking on the road and in spaces between tarp-covered tents. The scene resembled a well-attended Hmong festival.

Within a few feet came people with familiar faces, approaching to hold hands and arms, talk, and ask questions about those left behind. Uncle Song Chai's brothers, cousins, nieces, and nephews were all there. There were people from everywhere—Phou Kho, Nam Veh, Phou Xang Noy, Ban Xorn, Long Chieng, and other villages.

We were led by Uncle Chai Houa, Uncle Song Chai's cousin, to a two-hundred-foot-long, newly and poorly built thatch building. He proudly shared with us a ten-by-ten space, enough for a bed to sleep head-to-head with his family. People walked along the aisle past our feet day and night. There were also people sleeping head-to-head on the other side of the aisle as well. The roof-ridge of the building was not covered. When it rained, there was water dripping on our feet. We shared a cooking fireplace with other people. There were more people who had large families and chose to build their own tents for larger personal spaces.

We made a knee-high bed with bamboos donated by nearby Thai residents. No rice or food was provided, except for drinking water brought by tanker trucks four times a day, and the refugees were responsible for having their own containers.

We felt relieved for being alive, but physically and

mentally stressed, confused, shocked, worried about food, and concerned about those left behind. We had 28,000 kip left which was exchanged for 350 Thai baht ($17.50). The crowded camp depended on the marketplace outside the front gate for food and everything, including cooking charcoal. Firewood could only be brought from ten miles away or farther by rental trucks.

Nong Khai was on a flat plain with poor water drainage and easily flooded when it rained. There were monsoon-rain-fed puddles of muddy water along the paved highway that were filled nearly up to the barbed-wire fence of the camp. Only shallow hand-dug trenches slowly drained away rain water into the puddles. When it rained, catfish swam up and were stranded inside flooded tents.

There was an abandoned toilet facility built for the border patrol police training camp. The roof was torn down. The walls were gone and the concrete floor was broken and without toilet seats. There were only holes on the concrete floors. The refugees fixed parts of the missing walls with rusted and torn-up sheets of old roof tins to block views from people standing around. There were no doors.

Adults held their breath, closed their eyes, and went inside. Children suffering from diarrhea would defecate anywhere outside, around, and along the barbed-wire fence, and in between tents. The situation was terrible.

The refugees had lost their homeland and ownership of everything. They felt every inch of the ground under their feet was the property of another country. They had no right to do anything. They were just happy to be alive.

Suffering from homelessness syndrome, the refugees did not know if they could build toilets or initiate anything. They did not know where they would live from one day to the next. They were in a state of shock. It was all up to the Americans who had left them. They did not understand what it meant when the Americans said they would help the Hmong if the Hmong helped them. And, if the Hmong should lose the war, they would find a place for the Hmong to live (Jane Hamilton-Merritt, 1999, p. 92).

They remembered those words were said. Some talked about a treaty of written words that was still kept somewhere. But, even if there were no written words, there was a nonwritten treaty of friendship marked by white string ties on their wrists in a basii ceremony held in December 1960, pledging to the spirits who dwelled on the Mountain of Padong for a blessing upon a mutual-interest endeavor, which could undoubtedly result in a life-and-death situation.

The words said in an honorable tone of sincerity, respect, humility, and honesty, far more powerful than thousands of written ones, were still vividly remembered by those who were there, witnessing the ceremony and drinking the Hmong rice wine to a forever friendship.

The Americans, who at one time were best friends of the Hmong, whom the Hmong respected, and whom Hmong children liked to follow when they walked in Hmong villages because they were tall, had not come to see them the way they used to since they left Laos. Now, they felt as if neither the Americans nor the Pathet Lao wanted the Hmong. The Thai government and Thai people, for the moment, opened their door for them. But, for how long? Some Hmong, however, believed the arrangements might have been made by the Americans—the people who some believed were from the sky and who they had been happy to have on their side.

Other than those vendors and taxi drivers who saw a little economic opportunity, no one wanted to go near the refugee camp. The place was horrible, worse than a prison.

We were told by relatives that everyone who arrived at the camp was required to register in the office, a fenced and gated compound, inside the camp. Thai officials in uniforms would write down basic information such as names, ages, and date of arrival.

I became sick and was taken to the medical house inside the camp. Dr. Khameung, who performed a surgery on Grandma's leg in Sam Thong Hospital eight years ago, was there. He was checking patients, although he, too, had become a refugee. I was too sick to be treated in the camp. He sent me to the Nong Khai hospital in downtown Nong Khai.

In the hospital, I was put in a bed next to a critically ill young Hmong girl. The girl's father, who had suffered from a stroke, could barely walk and could not talk. He tried to ask nurses for help, but could not speak; tears rolled down from his eyes.

After watching for awhile, Youa asked his name. He could not talk. He grabbed a pen and tried to write his name. His hand was shaking and could not hold a pen to write. He was frustrated and angry.

"You look like Uncle Cha Pao Thao," Youa said. "Are you?"

He nodded his head and cried loudly. Youa hugged him and told him who she was. They hugged each other in disbelief.

"You were not like this when I last saw you, Uncle."

He could not answer. He only cried. They both cried.

Uncle Cha Pao, Youa's mother's half-brother, was a well-known commander in the CIA-funded irregular forces. His twin brothers, Nyia and Sao Thao, were both T-28 pilots. They were both killed in action when their planes were shot down only seven years earlier.

Aunt Cha Pao had gone back to the camp to get help. She arrived shortly and met with Youa—her husband's niece whom she had met only once and completely did not recognize. They all cried and grieved when the girl died shortly after.

We remained in the hospital, unable to help them, except for crying and holding hands. Three days later, I was better. We left the hospital and went back to our empty bed in the camp. We were thankful that we both returned alive to the tiny spot that had been quiet during the time we were gone.

While I still struggled to recover, we had only twenty baht left—enough for food for two more days. Blia had a string decorated with beads and three silver coins around her wrist. We cut off the string, stripped off the beads, and took the coins to exchange in the marketplace. As the string was cut and the coins fell on the ground, we both cried. It was the last thing we did to keep us alive for one more day. I promised the baby that if we survived the dreadful condition to start a new life again, I would buy more coins for her.

The next day I started going door to door, asking residents around Nong Khai if I could do anything for them for any money they could give me to feed my family. The responses were unbelievably great. The poor residents who had no regular income, except for their rice paddy fields, would let me clean their yard, cut their firewood, and weed their gardens for ten or twenty baht. They would give me food to take to the camp for Youa and Blia. They did what they could to help me, although they did not have much money. They could have done all those things themselves, which they had done all their lives. But they let me work, and I gladly did. They asked me to stop and talk. They comforted me when I was choked with emotion. They called me "son." It was the beauty of a culture in which people called each other by title—brother, sister, uncle, aunt, niece, nephew, son, or daughter—as a way to show politeness, courtesy, and respect, even though they were not related.

They asked me what I did in Laos and why I spoke Lao so well. I told them I was a teacher. They talked to each other about me.

"He was a teacher in Laos," a woman said. "Now he is a refugee, looking for anything he can do to earn money to help his family."

"It's shameful," another woman said. "Good people have to suffer just because the leaders fight against each other for power."

There were bigger garden projects on the sandy bank of the Mekong River. I took Yaj, who nearly drowned on the trip he accompanied me on to borrow money from Uncle Tou, to work with me.

Looking across the mighty Mekong River, there was a clear view of Laos—the land that was our home less than a month ago. Thailand and Laos, only separated by a river, differed from each other as heaven and hell.

We found peace and relief being away from the camp. We returned to the camp at the end of the day to face the chaotic situation and health-hazardous condition, which could persist until the Americans returned to help.

A month later, Youa's parents, her sisters, Nou and Vaj, and Aunt Bee arrived. It was an emotionally happy moment. We never thought we would see each other again. We gladly gave them our bed and went out to buy some bamboos and thatched grass to build a ten-by-twelve-foot lean-to and a bed next to an open building—a thirty-by-sixty-foot thatch-roofed temporary waiting hall for new arrivals. It was also the coffin-building house where there was a pile of one-by-eight-inch wooden planks loosely stacked on the packed dirt floor. Every day, refugee men talked loudly late into the night as they built coffins for the dead.

The mortality rate had reached an unprecedented phenomenon. Three or four people died every day—mostly women and children. There were no rooms for funeral ceremonies, no more sounds of funeral drums and Hmong *qeej*, but voices of men and women wailing that came from every corner and quarter of the crowded camp.

Youa's parents, too, had lost everything. With Youa's parents taking care of Blia, we both traveled out farther to look for work to meet our increased living expenses.

An accident occurred when Bee walked alone across the busy road. She was hit by a car. The good driver did not run away. He paid nine hundred baht and took Bee to the hospital. Luckily, she was not seriously injured. She was released from the hospital after two days. The money was used for her recovery and also provided a relief for Youa's parents and the three girls.

Two months later, a control mechanism was formed, dividing the camp into group sections. I was elected assistant group leader.

To improve conditions in the camp, we built toilets, discussed a camp maintenance plan, and assigned cleanup crews. Conditions in the camp improved, thereby reducing sickness.

Humanitarian aid arrived, giving a great relief. Group leaders were responsible for weekly rice distribution and other functions. Other food aid came shortly thereafter, although the refugees remained in temporary shelters, the same lean-to tents they built when they arrived.

Across the road and about a quarter of a mile to the south, a different camp was set up for the lowland ethnic refugees. The two ethnic groups could not mingle in the same camp. While relations among the adults were somewhat respectful, there had been frequent fights among young adults. Therefore, ethnic segregation was a mutual choice to avoid conflicts.

Human needs in a modern world, even in the simplest lifestyle, were far more than just rice, other foods, and shelters. Excluding preferential and habitual stuff such as alcohol, tobacco, and cosmetics, there were countless necessities, such as personal care, medication, and clothing, for which money was needed. To meet these basic needs, we had to go out to work. Youa and I were among those who had violated the refugee rules and had traveled as far as Bueng Kan—a town located by the Mekong River—about seventy miles to the south. We took Blia with us on a journey, not in search of treasure or anything for enjoyment, but of what would sustain our lives for another day and month.

In that endeavor, we had met ordinary people with extraordinary understanding of human experience and suffering. Their expressions clearly indicated they had felt a sense of relief that what had happened to us stopped at the bank of the other side of the river. These experiences had become deeply trapped in our minds and, from time to time, they appear in our dreams during the hours of our sleep that vividly seem real.

Suddenly, Uncle Tou arrived from Ban Vinai camp—the new camp built for the Hmong refugees from Nam Phong camp, most of whom were evacuated by planes from Long Chieng. He had obtained a travel document showing three additional people traveling with him, but without a list of names—a common practice in an unsophisticated society—which was a good thing for our circumstance. He did not know Youa's parents had arrived. Even if he did, there would be too many people to put on one document, and it would look suspicious. The refugees in Ban Vinai could visit their relatives in other camps, but not vice versa.

It was a happy but difficult moment for us. On the one hand, we would be reunited with Uncle Tou and Youa's brothers in a better camp. On the other hand, we did not want to leave Youa's parents. My father in-law understood and supported Uncle Tou's idea.

"We don't want to continue staying in Nong Khai. We want to join our children in Ban Vinai as soon as possible. So this is a good plan, and you should go now so you can bring us to join you."

Youa's mother, on the other hand, insisted she would take a chance to go with us. She missed her other children so much that she couldn't wait. We decided to take a chance to let Youa's mother, Nou, Vaj, and Bee get on the taxi. The taxi, heavily loaded with passengers beyond capacity, headed toward Ban Vinai. At a checkpoint between Nong Khai and Loei provinces, we sat nervously, holding our breath in the back of the open pickup-converted taxi. There was no place to hide. The guards simply took a glance at the paper and let the taxi, crowded with mostly Thai passengers, pass. We all sighed in relief.

We left Nong Khai camp in June 1976, leaving my father in-law behind, alone. But within a week, we were able to bring him to join us. It was a happy family reunification for Youa's parents, after having been separated for over a year.

Because there was no family reunification program, the refugees reunited with their families in this way. But they suffered in Ban Vinai because their names were not officially reported for food rations. They also feared being punished for sneaking into the camp from another camp. But eventually, everyone was registered.

Entering from the front gate on the hill, where Thai vendors set up a marketplace with lean-to tents filled with merchandise of all kinds, Ban Vinai camp was seen in a spectacular view with long corrugated-tin roofed buildings—but it did not quite resemble Long Chieng. Crowds of refugees, with umbrellas to shield the hot and scorching sunrays, walked along the newly constructed gravel roads, leading toward the dusty soccer field. Their minds—as they walked along or past each other—seemed without a clear purpose and goal, and devoid of something planned for the next day. They were just hopeless living souls trapped in a place, waiting for some kind-hearted beings to let them out and set them free.

Ban Vinai was built in a more than four-hundred-acre, newly cleared jungle located about four miles northwest of Pak Choum town. It was a big camp, divided into four centers. Each center consisted of three groups and was headed by a center chief, all of whom were former Hmong colonels of the CIA-funded irregulars.

Each group consisted of twelve or more 150-foot tin-roofed, wooden-floored, and wooden-walled buildings and was headed by a group leader. Each family of four to six people would get a ten-by-twelve-foot room plus a dirt space in between the buildings on which they could build a thatch-roofed and dirt-floored kitchen. Room allotments were not determined based on former status or rank, but square footage per person. Thus, former senior leaders received room size based on family size as everyone else.

Most Hmong—up to the moment, and particularly the young—had been refugees all their lives, depending on airplane rice, which was later called *mov luam,* meaning "public rice." As refugees—frequently displaced, confined in refugee camps and small room allotments, depending on weekly food distributions, and without good education for more than fifteen years—the majority of Hmong did not have a clear image and understanding of the world.

Looking on the surface, Ban Vinai was a less-crowded refugee camp—far better than the one in which we had been in Nong Khai. However, in a deeper observation, there were two distinctive classes of refugees in Ban Vinai. The first class was the wealthy former senior and junior officers of the US irregulars, their relatives, upper echelon bureaucrats, and, especially, former American workers who were flown directly from Long Chieng to Nam Phong Camp, and were given food upon their arrival, would have their cash reserve to pay for personal and family necessities not covered by the weekly food distributions. This group was not seen carrying axes and sickles on the roads in Thai villages looking for work.

On the other hand, there was the second class: those who fled by taxis or boats, like myself, Uncle Song Chai, and others, who paid for their escapes with their entire life savings and who arrived in temporary camps without food aid, and were seen carrying tools looking for work every day to survive. Many of these were frequently subject to exploitation of not getting paid for their work. There was nothing they could do to complain about or dispute any mistreatment, labor fraud, exploitation, or even rape or sexual assault. They were refugees whose safe zone was limited to the confinement of the camp, inside barbed wire fences. Going out of the camp to find work, they had broken the rule, and they had put their safety at risk. They were the perfect victims if anyone intended to exploit them.

Like any society, the vast majority of people in Thailand were friendly and kindhearted. However, there were some crooks and criminals. Even if the vast majority were good and only a small fraction were bad, it was too many. Hence, refugee women were frequently raped outside the camps by armed criminals.

In August 1976, the issue of sexual assaults of refugee women by Thai criminals was brought up in a center-chief meeting, chaired by former Col. Ly Tou Pao, chief of Ban Vinai camp. The discussion only reiterated a warning to all refugees that their rights to be safe were limited within the barbed-wire fence around the camp.

Some refugees had used their small business experiences in Laos to open small retail shops to cater the tightly confined refugee population. While this practice was permitted inside the camp, refugee leaders established flea marketplaces from which they collected booth fees to cover administrative supply expenses.

On January 26, 1977, our second child was born—a boy. We gave him a unique name, Saleng, meaning "seven men." Actually, we named him after my great-grandfather, Song Leng. Later, other people had started naming their boys Saleng or Yeeleng, meaning "eight men."

After Saleng was born, Youa and I decided to rent a small booth for a retail shop to cater to the growing refugee population, which we did well enough to prevent us from continuing carrying tools looking for work outside the camp, like we used to. Through this endeavor, we had made many good friends of Thai merchants in Muang Loei, the provincial town, located twenty miles northwest of the refugee camp. Later, these good friends had trusted us and allowed us to have boxes of merchandise without paying for them upfront.

After we had sold the merchandise, we would turn in the money and keep the profits. Good communication, honesty, good personal ethics, and good management had been the key to success for us. This would have been a successful business venture. But the refugee camp was not a permanent settlement and a place we would settle to do business. In fact, many of the Thai friends had encouraged us to become Thai citizens and continue doing what we had been doing well.

At first, there were not very many countries willing to accept Hmong refugees for final resettlement, putting the future of refugees in limbo. Countries that had voiced interest, such as Australia, Canada, France, and, especially, the United States, had considered taking only those who could speak their languages and who would be likely to become self-sufficient as soon as possible. The vast majority had been left in limbo, for lack of literacy skills or formal education.

France began taking those who had served in the French Maquis, or whose parents had, and also considered putting a small number in French Guyana. A Catholic church organized its members, desperate to move out of the refugee camp, to resettle in Guyana, where they live to this day in a farming tradition almost similar to their way of life in Laos, but more economically sustainable.

A small number of Hmong refugees who hardly anyone noticed resettled in Canada, and the same was true in Australia. Frustrations were high, particularly among former senior and junior officers who had served in the US-funded irregulars during the war. The culture of having more than one wife became an issue. Asking Hmong men to let go of one of their wives to qualify for resettlement in the US was heatedly contended. Eventually, their families had to be divided and apply for resettlement separately. The choice of which wife and children should become without a father as head of household was a sad decision for many families.

Gradually, the United States opened its doors wider to accept more refugees from Laos, whom it classified as Categories 2, 3, and 4. These were refugees who had either sponsoring relatives or nonrelative sponsors in the United States. I petitioned to go to France, although it was not my first choice. My application was accepted for resettlement in France and I was given the flexibility to remain in the camp for as long as I liked on the condition that I served as an interpreter for the screening process for refugees who wished to go to France.

Then, the Americans came to conduct intake assessments. I took that opportunity and was accepted for resettlement in the US. The process went well to the final decision.

Uncle Tou, who had just left the camp for the United States a year earlier, was pleased to be informed of the good news. Calvary Lutheran Church in Lee County, Illinois, contacted the Lutheran Immigration Refugee Service (LIRS), indicating its interest in sponsoring a Hmong refugee family. Based on our application, in which we listed relatives in the US, Jan Wiseman and Molly Wiseman (now Molly Clemons) approached Uncle Tou about their interest in sponsoring a refugee family. They gladly accepted us—a young family of four. We were informed of the final status of our application and that we would possibly depart to the United States in early December 1978.

We were overwhelmingly happy and feeling as if our souls floated above the dusty camp waiting for the day to arrive. I took a deep breath to withdraw our resettlement in France and resign as a French interpreter.

We closed the retail shop from which we earned our daily living, gave away the shop and the remaining inventory to Ma and his wife, Keo, started visiting different parts of the camp like tourists, and proudly told people we were going to America. The people who had shops next to us or across the aisle from us, who did not do too well, were pleased their tough competitor would be gone.

"What state will you be going to?" a woman asked.

"We will go to Illinois," we would proudly tell them. Some people would ask us to say hello to their relatives, assuming everyone who went to America would live in the same camp, despite that the United States is forty-one times the size of Laos.

On November 24, 1978, my brother, Teng, and thirty other young Hmong arrived from Laos in tatters with their long hair reaching their waist. Teng was still wearing the same clothes he wore when we left him three years ago. Their purpose was to explore the escape route to Thailand.

There was an announcement on the loudspeaker:

"The following families are scheduled to depart to Phananikhom in the middle of December in preparation to go to America."

We were among those on the list. It was the moment we had been waiting for, but something had suddenly changed everything. The biggest thing on our minds was my parents, whom we had not heard from for more than three years. Suddenly we got the news, telling us they were still alive—living across the river and on the mountains in Laos. They were okay, but poor; they had no food; they had no clothes; they looked worse than Teng, who only had some tiny pieces of clothing clinging to his body. They were hungry, surviving on shoots and roots of anything edible. There was a chance that they would be coming while we would be leaving, going to America, and ignoring them. We were the souls they had thought of every moment; they had held on to their lives hoping to see us, and they were waiting for Teng to go back with good news—that we would still be in the camp, waiting for them.

I went to talk to the Americans who worked busily, interviewing people. Through an interpreter, I explained the situation and asked if I could postpone my departure for a month. The request was granted, but I was told I only had one more chance and that they would not approve a second request for postponing.

At least we had thirty days or more to do something for my parents. Using almost all the money that we had, we bought each of them a pair of clothes for Teng to take to them. There were ten of them. We asked Uncle and Aunt Tong Yia, Yaj's parents, who lived next door, to help keep our room vacant; take care of our pots and pans, including all our dishes; keep our bed and blankets intact; and keep all the tools, including two knives, two sickles, an ax, and two garden hoes for my parents if they arrived after we had left. We did everything we could to prepare everything in anticipation that my parents would arrive in the camp soon.

Two weeks later, we still had not heard anything about my parents. Teng and his crew who were supposed to return to bring their families to Thailand were still in the camp. He knew about everything we had planned.

In the United States, Jan, Molly, and members of the church were excited about our coming. They had the apartment ready and furnished, cleaned, and heated; they had put fresh food, including meat, vegetables, fruits, and milk, in the refrigerator. Jan and Molly excitedly called Uncle Tou and told them to meet them at O'Hare Airport. They waited at the gate as the plane arrived. The gate was opened and the passengers started coming out of the large aircraft until there were no more passengers. We were not on board. We had postponed our departure.

Somehow, the cancellation was not communicated to the sponsoring agency in the United States. Jan and

Molly, and Uncle Tou, were disappointed. We took it as our fault, imagining the inconvenience we had caused them. If we had known of how much trouble postponing our departure would cause, we would not have done so.

Our names were again on the list of the next group to depart to the United States in two weeks and announced on the loudspeaker. This time we knew we could not request and would not be granted another delay.

We left the Ban Vinai refugee camp on January 8, 1979, to go to Phananikhom transitional camp in Bangkok, Thailand, where we joined a large number of Hmong refugees—all coming to the United States, but different parts and places, not all of their preferred choices. Some would go to places far from their relatives and where they would find themselves lonely in remote towns, unable to find anyone who spoke their language.

After a long trip, including an overnight stay in Hong Kong, a stop in Tokyo, Japan, and a stop in Seattle, Washington, we arrived in O'Hare Airport, Chicago, Illinois, on January 17, 1979, at about 9 p.m.

At the gate of the airport, we saw Uncle and Aunt Tou, Uncle Kou—son of Granduncle Chia Koua—and other Hmong family members who had come to welcome their relatives, who arrived on the same plane. Uncle Kou, who came to the US six months earlier and who spoke some English, introduced us to two complete strangers with whom we could not communicate to express our appreciation.

Jan and Molly extended their hands to welcome us. They handed us heavy winter coats without communicating verbally, but with warm expressions on their smiling faces, telling us it was cold outside.

Confused, ignorant, and naive, we followed Jan and Molly to the parking lot while Uncle Tou and others went home in different directions. Outside, the temperature was below freezing with piles of white snow on the ground. We were glad they insisted we put on the heavy coats—on top of what we thought we had been well prepared by wearing. Jan threw me a ball of the white salt-like substance. I caught it. It was cold. I put it to my nose and smelled it and they laughed. It had no odor. They were glad I didn't taste it.

We traveled to our new home on a four-lane highway and saw plow trucks working frantically, trying to keep the roads open, making the scene look as if the roads were under construction. Jan was driving nervously as Molly watched quietly, making sure he didn't stray off the road. We sat in the backseat in bewilderment, not knowing what was going on.

It was one of the worst snowstorms in Illinois with a total of twenty-seven inches of snowfall in a couple of days. Schools and businesses were closed for days as we helplessly sat by the windows of our second-floor apartment, watching the white blanket of snow and quiet houses around us with only steam coming out of their chimneys.

The past only seemed like a dream, but the memory was real. The origin of our new home was found and the journey of our new life started to unfold with even more complex challenges.

The world without boundaries was not found in the world of men, and it will never be found, for we face boundaries at every turn of our lives. There are national, legal, social, economic, and political boundaries that will always challenge us. However, the imaginary existence of a world without boundaries is real, because the effects of catastrophes and humans extending hands to help each other have no boundaries.

EPILOGUE

Brought to a largely farming community sixty-four miles west of Chicago, Illinois, Youa, Blia, Saleng, and I were lonely like a family of straying tropical birds. We were the only Asians, not to mention Hmong, in the village of seven hundred people, which looked larger to us than it really was.

In the first few days, the brutal weather conditions in January had kept us away from having any contact with neighbors, town residents, and relatives who had come to other parts of the United States. The orange rotary phone was hung on the kitchen wall on the left-hand side of the door, but neither Youa nor I dared to put our hands on it, even when it rang, fearing someone might talk to us in English.

Within a week, the weather conditions had improved and the roads had become passable. Jan and Molly took us for a visit to Kishwaukee College, located about fourteen miles north of Shabbona, where it was surrounded by immense cornfields, extending as far as your naked eyes could see.

The community college, where Jan worked as dean of community education, also housed the refugee program which provided many services to refugees, including translation, English as a Second Language (ESL), job placement, and job-related support. In the next brown building we met with Jim Grenell, director of the refugee program—a man in his midforties in casual clothes with an unsuspicious personality. The program was closed due to bad weather. He smiled humbly as he shook our hands and introduced us to the one-room office of four staff members, the classroom, and the supply room. Not understanding a word of what he said, we simply nodded our heads, pretending we understood. For a year, communication, even with Jan and Molly, was minimal. Mostly, they talked and we nodded our heads.

A few days later, a man came to the door—an Asian man. I could undoubtedly tell he was not Hmong or Lao. He might be Chinese or Vietnamese, I thought.

"*Bonjour, Monsieur,*" he said, and continued with an introduction of himself in French.

"My name is Van Lu. I am an interpreter from the refugee program."

Jan might have informed him or Jim Grenell that I spoke French. I invited him inside and we had a nice conversation in our small, but nicely furnished living room.

The purpose of his visit was to ask for my help with an unfinished job while taking me to register at Job Service. I was needed to help translate for a Hmong family that had arrived a month earlier.

He drove me to Dekalb—where Molly taught in a high school as a journalism teacher—a large town with busy streets, three times larger than Vientiane, the capital city of Laos. He wiggled his small car through busy traffic on a three-lane street, past tall buildings of the Northern Illinois University on the left, and past many busy intersections, before turning to an old neighborhood where leafless large maple trees stood in lines among electrical posts along old streets.

In an upstairs old-wood-floored apartment lived

a young Hmong refugee family. The man and his wife had known my name from Ban Vinai refugee camp, but I didn't know them. The man took a close look at me, face to toes and toes to face.

"Are you bearded-Ge?" he asked reluctantly.

"Do you know me?" I asked.

He looked more certain as he recognized my voice.

"You have shaved your beard!" he said loudly as he looked at me front and back.

"How do I look?" I asked.

The man, who only spoke Hmong, heavily put his left hand on my right shoulder as tears flooded his eyes and his voice choked with emotion.

"I never thought you would be here," he said. "It's like a dream. I can't believe it's really you. You probably don't know me, but I saw you every day in Ban Vinai when you served as secretary for Col. Vang Yee, president of Ban Vinai camp. Everyone called you bearded-Ge because you had a long beard," he added as he laughed. "My name is Long Yang. My wife is Col. Vang Yee's niece."

Several appointments had been scheduled for them to get done on that day, while I was there to help: at the Job Service office for the old CETA program, the public aid office for the medical assistance program, and the health department for immunization. The translation process was longer and more complicated than usual. It went from Hmong to French, then to English, and then the sequence in reverse. But the job, which had not been done otherwise for a month, was accomplished.

Van Lu and I became good friends. He and I enjoyed speaking French (and that hindered my learning of English). He visited me in my apartment whenever

EPILOGUE

he could. He brought newspapers and read them to me and explained in French. He asked me to read and he would correct my pronunciations of some of the words, such as "explosion and tunnel," which were heavily interfered with my French accent. And he had taken me to visit his retired father who spoke fluent French.

The elderly man who had, no doubt, been well educated in his youth, asked me about the trip from Thailand. I told him it was long and strange.

"Yes, I know the feeling when you fly on an airplane for the first time," he said in French.

"We have a hard time adjusting our sleep," I tried to explained. "We can't sleep at night, but feel asleep during the day."

The refugee program, which once served predominantly Vietnamese refugees, became crowded with Hmong, Laotian, and Cambodian refugees. Van Lu's service was no longer needed. He left the program to start a restaurant across street from the university. To serve the needs of the new refugee population, Koua Xiong, who was fluent in Hmong, Lao, and English, was hired.

People of each ethnicity would sit close together and talk loudly in their own languages, and they would let their attention stray away from the English class. Ms. Evelina Cichi, the ESL teacher, would frequently yell at the groups.

"English! English!"

Ms. Cichi, who was from the Philippines and whose father was a well-known short story writer, would put me in the supply room, by myself. She would give me more advanced books to read, including one written by her father.

As the rest of the class, including Youa, learned to

write short sentences, I would practice short story writing. Occasionally, Ms. Cichi would come around to check how I was doing or I would go to her if I had a question or needed her to pronounce some words for me. She would sit with me for a short time, listening while I read aloud, but then had to go back to the large group.

Part of my progress was largely attributed to my job at the Shabbonat Nursing Home. It was the best job I could get in a town of seven hundred people. The job itself was not as good as the process of getting it.

One afternoon, in the middle of February, a month after our arrival, Jan and Molly told me they had a job interview for me, and I didn't know exactly what it was. They drove me to a large H-shaped building on West Commanche Street, about a quarter of a mile from my apartment.

It was an unusual job interview, making the part-time job important, because there were five people, Jan, Molly, Van Lu, the nursing home director, Mrs. Laura Larson, and I, involved in the process. We were sitting in a nice room behind Mrs. Larson's office.

Mrs. Larson explained the job function and responsibilities as a nurse's aide, and Van Lu translated in French. I nodded my head, signaling I understood. Everyone was fascinated as they watched and listened to my responses. I could see how they reacted on their faces. At the end, I was offered the job.

"Do you have any questions?" Van Lu translated Mrs. Larson's question.

"When will I start?" I asked in French.

Van Lu translated and everyone laughed. I froze, thinking I had said something wrong.

"Did I say something wrong?" I asked Van Lu in

French.

He translated and everyone laughed again.

"Please tell Ge the reason we laughed was that both questions were good," Mrs. Larson said and Van Lu translated. "We are impressed."

Unable to drive, I walked to work every day. My co-workers talked and joked with me mercilessly as if I were one of them. And I shamelessly asked them questions about what I didn't know or understand.

I knew I had many weaknesses, but did not know exactly what they were and had difficulties sorting them. That was one of the places I discovered my disadvantages. I could not speak English, at least not good enough to communicate with my patients. I felt tears in my eyes sometimes.

All the patients were nice and lovely. They said "Thank you" and "Good night" to me all the time.

"You will grow up to be a good man," a female patient said. "If I were still a girl, I would marry you when you grow up."

"He is a married man," Mary Lou, my co-worker, said. "He can't marry you."

"Oh, I thought he was still a young boy," the woman said.

Her husband, who was also a patient in the same room, was laughing. The elderly couple was wonderful and lovely. They reminded me of my great-grandmother, who still worked around the house when she was their age, even though she was blind. It's so unfortunate for millions of elders in other parts of the world who endure suffering in the late stages of their lives.

This experience had given me a small clue of what constituted the fabric of this nation of which I had just become a member. The elders for whom we provided care had done their deeds through their contributions in a variety of ways during their abled ages. We were employed to help them and care for them, and even feed them if they could not do it themselves.

My wife, our children, and I are pleased and proud to be a part of the fabric of this nation. Although we are not the builders of every monumental road, bridge, or building that makes this country the greatest in the world, we share the ownership by shouldering a small fraction of its construction and maintenance cost. We hope our children will find peace, love, equality, and justice in the racial, ethnic, and cultural diversities that constitute this great nation. And we hope we have found the place that represents the true world of humankind—a place we can help each other overcome boundaries.

ACKNOWLEDGMENTS

This book could not have been written without the support and encouragement of my family. Each has helped and supported in different ways, providing me the fuel needed for pursuing this undertaking from the beginning to the finish.

I want to thank each of my children, Blia, Kong, Saleng, Dan, Elizabeth, Chue Yee, Sandy, and Sarah, for their support and encouragement. Despite her busy life as a mother and a full-time student with a full-time job, Blia had helped with some editing of the first two and a half chapters of the manuscript. Saleng has contributed valuable insights through numerous good discussions with me. And Sandy has spent hours drawing the maps. Everyone has taken part in the debate of the book title to make it pertinent to its purpose.

The support of my youngest sister, Ker, has provided me with tremendous energy to undertake this work. She has read a great part of the draft and given me encouraging feedback as a reader. The enormous writing process of this book would not have been accomplished without my family's support. I wholeheartedly thank everyone for the fuel and energy they have provided me along the way.

My thanks also go to Peter Alan Lloyd for graciously allowing me to use the beautiful photo of Long Chieng posted on his website.

To Molly and Ron Clemons, I want to express from the bottom of my heart how grateful I am for their willingness to take hours of their busy time to read and edit the entire manuscript. Their decades of experience as journalism teachers have made an enormous contribution to the meaningfulness of this book. I cannot find words to sufficiently describe my gratitude toward their thorough review of every word, every paragraph, and every page of the manuscript with helpful annotations. The process of writing this book has not only brought me closer to them, but also has been a good learning experience for me. They both have been great teachers, and I am fortunate to have them as my best friends.

Last, but not least, I want to thank my wife, Youa, who shares a life and a dream with me, for her support throughout the writing process. She has spent hours reading the draft, refreshing my memory, and correcting countless forgotten accounts. Without her encouragement and support, this book could not have been written.

ABOUT THE AUTHOR

Ge Xiong, a former teacher and Hmong refugee from Laos, arrived in Shabbona, Illinois, on January 17, 1979, at age twenty-six without knowing a word of English. While working full-time, Xiong persistently endeavored to overcome the language barrier. He has a bachelor's degree in educational policy and community study from the University of Wisconsin-Milwaukee (UWM). Xiong's community service and involvement are widely known in the Hmong community throughout Milwaukee and Wisconsin.

In addition to being executive director of Hmong Educational Advancements, Inc., Xiong also had served on numerous organizations' boards and task force committees, including UWM Chancellor's Board of Visitors, Milwaukee School Superintendent's Cabinet Council, Milwaukee County Board's Race Relations Task Force, and Milwaukee Mayor's Commission on Crimes. Xiong had also worked for Milwaukee Public Schools as Southeast Asian community liaison, responsible for promoting Southeast Asian parent and community involvement in the schools' decision-making process and in their children's education.

INDEX

Hmong names are entered as they appear in the text.

A

adult education, 202-203, 241-246, 275
Air America, 143-144, 149, 192, 205, 232, 234, 238, 249, 274, 323
airplane rice, 52, 55-60, 67, 80, 101, 110-111, 131-132, 140, 145, 149, 155, 162, 178, 185, 194, 197-198, 202-203, 217, 222, 246, 252, 269, 272, 275, 277, 289, 292, 334
American POWs, 285-286
Americans. *See* United States
Amkha Soukhavong, 282
animism, 95, 187, 197
Argentina, 8
Australia, 8, 336-337

B

Ban Hang, 36, 39, 45-49, 53-55
Ban Somsanouk, 305-306
Ban Vinai, 321, 332-335, 341, 346
Ban Xorn, 188-201, 212, 216-217, 222, 233, 238, 295-311
Ban Yai, 100
Bao, 72, 74
Bee, 17, 46, 270, 306, 330, 332
Bee Xiong, 161-162, 174
Ber, 16-27. *See also* Cher Pao
Billy, Colonel, 322
Black, Mr., 149-150

Blia, 288, 295-296, 304, 306, 312, 316-320, 328-331, 344
Boua See (aunt), 72, 74, 76-77, 156, 316-320
Boua See (uncle), 73-74, 103, 110, 156, 310, 316-320
Bouam Loung, 47-48, 55-63, 79-80, 105, 118, 123, 134-145, 152, 177, 217, 232-239, 250-251
Bouam Mou, 69, 111, 127, 134-136, 144
Bouth Thalangsy, 307, 309
Buddhism, 197, 210
Buell, Edgar (Pop), 108, 133-134, 149, 178-179, 216-217, 234, 311
Bueng Kan, 331
bullies, 114-115
business opportunities, 195, 202

C

calendar, 40
Calvary Lutheran Church, 338
Cambodia, 186, 285, 288, 291, 302, 322
Canada, 8, 336-337
cease-fire, 203, 271-291, 302
Cha, 72, 74, 258-260, 258-270. *See also specific events*
Cha Pao, 328
Cha Pao Thao, 327-328
Cha Thao, 112
Chai Houa, 155, 324
Chanthala, 180, 209-212, 221
Chao, 74, 146, 163
Chao (cousin), 109

INDEX

Cher Pao, 16-27, 60, 75-76, 163-164, 175. *See also specific events*
Cher Pao Moua, 47-49, 55, 59-60, 66, 79, 118-119, 143, 233, 237-238
Cherpao Xiong, 142
Chia Koua, 156-160
Chia Thong, 16-19, 22
childbirth, 17
children
    mortality, 242-244, 330
    names, 28-29
    nutrition, 87-88, 108, 242-244
    played with military gear, 49-50
    role in family farming, 45
    war games, 54
China
    and negotiations with the U.S., 201
    and the origin of Hmong, 1-2
    supported Communist expansion, 284
    treatment of Hmong in, 14, 273
Chong, 46, 67, 135
Chong Leng, 144, 147, 150
Chong Moua Lee, 57, 60, 125, 135, 165
Chong Toua, 256, 269-270
Chong Toua Moua, 41
Chou Lee, 298
Chou Ly, 289
Choua Dang Moua, 19-21
Christianity, 197
Chue, 88
Chue Ker Moua, 59, 133-134, 161-162, 216-217, 222
Chue Yang, 253-254
CIA, 58, 63, 183, 199-200, 260, 272, 286, 291, 313, 322, 328, 334

Cichi, Evelina, 347-348
Clemons, Molly, 338, 340-342, 344-345, 348
Communists. *See also* Pathet Lao; Vietnamese
    captured Uncle Ka Thai, 135-137
    government, 7-8, 300, 302, 312
    persecution and retribution, 7-8
    system of governing, 302
    violated cease-fire, 302
crime, 297-298, 317-318, 320, 335
cultural practices. *See* spirituality; traditions

D

Da Xeng, 314
Da Xeng Vang, 259
Dang, 146, 173-174, 270, 306
Dang Moua, 113, 117
Daniels, Jerry, 273-274
Der, 72, 74
dialects, 3-4
discipline, 115, 236
Dong Dok Teacher Training Institute, 211-221, 315
Doua Lee, 175

E

economic issues, 195, 198-203, 241-242, 244, 275-278, 289-290, 327, 337
education
    adults, 202-203, 241-246, 275
    bullies, 114-115
    discipline, 115, 236
    girls, 89, 91, 131, 242-243, 247, 256
    influence of, 4-5

Elai, 219-220
environmental impact, 198-199, 203, 270-271
escape, 293-320
ethnicity, 196-197, 213-215, 331
evacuations
    from Keouvanh, 100-112
    from Long Chieng, 182-188, 332
    from Phou Kho, 293
    from Phoukoum, 153-155
    to Phoukoum, 97, 144-153
    from Sam Thong, 179-182, 270
    to Thailand, 291-320
    from Thamheub, 267-269
    U.S. plan, 322-323

F

family planning, 242, 244
family reunification, 333
farming, 36-40, 43-46, 52-54, 116, 143, 183, 195, 202, 218, 240, 242, 244-245, 252, 270-276, 287-288, 337
Fay Dang Lo Bliayao, 279
foreign aid, 199, 252, 276, 323, 331, 335
France, 8, 59, 81-82, 336-338, 345-349
French colonial era, 6, 8, 12, 15-16, 22, 29, 35, 40-41, 52, 82, 129, 259, 273, 276-281, 285-286
French Guyana, 8, 337
funeral ceremonies, 5-6

G

Ge, 186-189
Ge Moua, 175

Ge Xiong
    accompanied injured grandmother to hospital, 128-137
    cared for 3-month old sister, 45
    childhood, 29-34
    children, 288, 336. *See also* Blia; Saleng
    Communist reeducation, 307-310
    courtship and marriage, 247-255
    education, 40, 89-98, 112-124, 139-145, 155-162, 158, 162, 169, 174-181, 188-189, 201-202, 205-227, 236
    impersonated soldier, 310-313
    photos, 167-171
    teaching, 231-246, 288-293, 298
    in the U.S., 341-350
gender, 41, 73, 243, 245, 256
Ger, 163
Germany, 8
girls, 29, 41, 73, 87-91, 243, 245, 256
government, 22, 42, 185, 199, 208, 241, 272, 276-286, 290-291, 300, 302, 312
Grandma Moua, 132-133
Grandmother, 15-17, 30-34, 50-51, 60-64, 67-69, 74, 76, 86, 93-94, 96, 109, 112, 123-137, 161, 163, 249, 257-258, 298, 327
    graves, desecration of, 4
Great-Grandmother, 13-18, 22-23, 30-34, 156
Grenell, Jim, 344-345
Guerre du Fou, 273

INDEX

guerrilla forces, 41, 49, 58, 81-82, 260, 267, 283, 313, 337
guns, 57-59, 81-82, 116, 238, 263, 303

H

Haje, 16
Hamkheu (Humkher), 12
hand-grenade trap, 126
health concerns, 58, 88, 243-245
Heu, 16-17, 24
Hin Heub, 222, 297-315
Hmong origins, 1-5, 8
Hnia Vue, 183
Ho Chi Minh, 286
Ho Chi Minh trail system, 281
homelessness syndrome, 325-326
Houa Lee, 112
Houayhom, 59-60
Hoy Sathout, 269
human viciousness, 235
humanitarian aid, 199, 252, 276, 323, 331, 335. *See also* airplane rice
hunting, 81-85

I

impersonations, 310

K

Ka Cheng, 144, 147, 150
Ka Thai (Ga Thai), 24, 53, 57, 61, 68-69, 111, 124-127, 134-137, 298
Kai, 17
Keo, 338
Keouvanh, 76, 78-81, 102
Ker, 72, 74-75
Ker Xiong, 146, 163, 295, 351

Khammeung, Dr., 129-134, 327
Khamphay, 213-214
Khmer Rouge, 285
Khmou, 186-187
Kia, 53, 87, 146, 163
Kilometer 22, 241, 275, 311
Kishwaukee College, 344
Ko Xiong, 232-234, 239, 251
Kong Le, 80, 267, 280, 282
Kong Le Coup, 280
Kou Xiong, 163, 232, 341
Koua Xiong, 347

L

La Xiong, 135
language
    and acculturation, 4-5
    dialects, 3-4
    and education, 4-5
    origin of, 1-2
Lao, 116-117
Lao Reunification, 284-285
Laos, map, 98
Larson, Laura, 348-349
leadership, 158-160, 209, 243
Lee, 113
Lee, Gary Yia, 2
Lee Ge, 142
Lee Houa, 139-140, 142, 145, 161-162
Lee Teng, 28
Lee Tou Bee, 28
Lee Vang, 114
Leftists, 291
Leng Moua, 315-316
Lia, 144, 147, 150
living conditions, 197-198
Lo, 113
Lo Foung, 279
Long Cheng Radio, 56-57, 83-84, 116, 290
Long Chieng
    business opportunities, 202

Communist threat, 173, 201-202, 252-253, 270, 290
cultural practices and changes, 196-197
described, 139, 190-193
economic sustainability, 198-203
environmental impact, 198-199, 203
ethnicity, 196-197
evacuation from, 294-295, 322
evacuation to, 223, 237-239, 274
food service businesses, 195
living conditions, 197-198
marketplace, 193-195
painting, 164
photo, 189
visits, 156-157, 179-186, 267
Long Yang, 346
lowland Lao, 14, 32, 36, 42-44, 65-66, 104-105, 185, 196-197, 205, 219, 276-277, 292, 299-300, 307, 331
Luang Phrabang, 104, 219, 257, 274
Ly Tou Pao, 335
Ly Teck Ly Nhia Vue, 311-315

M

Ma, 256, 259-260, 266-269, 273, 306, 338
Ma Vang, 167
Mai, 17, 28
march from Ban Xorn to Vientiane, 299-304
marriage, 16, 22-27, 72, 197, 257, 258-259, 337
massacres, 291
Mee, 53, 87, 146, 254, 259-260, 262, 266
Meo mountain tribe, 283

Meo War, 273
migration, 60-77
military gear, 49, 58, 80, 117
military service, 58, 60, 66, 124, 138, 142-143, 152, 153, 185, 193, 218, 260, 272-273, 277, 283, 310, 334, 337. *See also* guerrilla forces
military training, 57-58
Mong, Hmong differentiated from, 3-4
mortality, 17, 242-244, 330
Moua Kai, 214
Moua Lia, 118, 179, 232-234, 241, 249, 307
Moua Tou Lue, 28
Moung Soui, 155, 267
Muong Phoun, 186-187

N

Na Khang, 116-117, 138, 143-144, 152, 173
Nahai Deo, 273
Nam Kout (Nam Koot), 43-55
Nam Ngua, 273
Nam Nguem Dam, 276
Nam Phong camp, 322, 323-324
Nam Sai, 62-69
Nam Veh, 217, 233-234, 239, 249, 251, 253, 272
names, clans and traditions, 260
names and naming traditions, 27-29
Namnya, 11-34
Nao Cha, 19
Nao Lao Haksat, 50-51
National Labor Week, 245
Neng, 103, 112-115, 117, 132, 138, 166, 174, 260, 306, 323
Neng Thong Thao, 282
Neutralists, 80, 267, 280, 282, 285

INDEX

New Year celebrations, 38-40, 86-88, 247-251, 287
Nhia Vue, 279
Nong Khai, 320, 323-334
Noo, 40
North Vietnamese. *See* Vietnamese
Nou, 260, 262, 306, 330, 332
nursing home job, 348-350
nutrition, 87-88, 108, 242-244
Nyia, 328
Nyia Vaj, 27

O

opium, 12, 15, 29, 31-33, 36, 39, 42, 48, 54, 276
Outhapoun, 221

P

Pa Ger, 14
Pa Kao Vang, 289
Pa Lee Yang, 241
Pa Ma Thao, 50
Pa Xiong, 60, 76, 81, 86, 101-102, 109, 111, 135, 298
Pa Xiong Vang, 60
Pachai War, 273
Pai, 146, 153-155, 163, 295
Pao, 258, 264
Pao Vang, 175-176, 213
Pathet Lao, 6, 42, 46, 49-51, 58-59, 80, 97, 100, 102, 116, 135-137, 141, 173, 182, 198, 201, 233, 237-238, 259, 267, 269, 273, 279-286, 290-291, 298, 300-302, 305, 309, 311-318, 326
persecution, 291
Phak Keh, 222
Phananikhom, 341
Phia Lee, 266

Phong Saly, 46, 259, 275, 279
Phou Dou Noy, 68, 70-71
Phou Duu, 12, 15, 40-41
Phou Kheou, 35-36, 49, 59
Phou Kho, 241, 272, 287, 289-297, 305
Phou Mee, 270
Phou Muen, 156-157
Phou Phathi, 138, 142-143
Phou San, 12, 29-39, 48-49, 57-60, 66, 74, 93
Phou So, 3, 153-154, 241
Phou Vieng, 60, 69-70, 74, 80-81, 96-97, 101-103, 105, 116, 127, 134, 138-152, 217, 240-241, 272
Phou Xang Mountain, 201-202, 218, 222, 239, 252-253
Phou Xang Noy, 216-218, 233, 238, 249-255, 270-273, 306
Phoukeu, 257, 259
Phoukoum, 3, 97, 105-107, 117-118, 123-124, 144-146, 153
Phoumi Nosavan, 282
Phrachao Xaysethatthirath, 211
polygamy, 337
Pop, Mr., 108, 133-134, 149, 178-179, 216-217, 234, 311
population in refugee areas, 270-271, 276
POWs, 285-286
prayer. *See* spirituality

Q

Qhoua Pao Lee, 287

R

radio, 56-57, 83-84
rape, 335

Red Lao, 135-137. *See also* Communists
reeducation, 8, 310, 312
refugees
    large concentrations of, 270-271
    living conditions, 108-109, 197-198, 324-327, 330-331, 333-335
    places of resettlement, 8, 336-338
    services in the U.S., 344-348
    settlement on Phou Xang Mountain, 201-202
    treatment of, 4, 7, 291, 297-298, 303, 317-318, 320, 335
    work to support family in camp, 323, 328-331, 335-336
reincarnation, 94-95
retail shops, 335-336, 338
Rightists, 282, 285, 291
royal family, 259, 274, 278-280
Royal Lao Army, 6, 216, 277
Royal Lao Government, 201, 241, 279-280, 282, 286, 311
Royalists, 201, 279-280, 282

S

Sai Xiong, 156, 310, 312-313, 323
Saleng, 166, 171, 336, 344
Sam Neua, 275, 279
Sam Thong, 127-128, 132-133, 161, 172, 175-189, 201, 270
Sam Thong Teacher Training Institute, 179, 188, 221, 231
Sam Xan, 173-174, 180, 186
Samneua, 46, 259
San Luang, 272

Sao Thao, 328
school. *See* education
See, 144, 146-147
self-sufficiency, 194-195, 275-276
Seng Ber Lee, 80
sexual assault, 335
shamanism, 18, 27-28, 80, 112, 265-266
smoking, 63-64
solar eclipse, 263
Somphou Oudomvilay, 220
Song Chai Xiong, 56, 60, 76, 79-86, 100-101, 112, 127, 145-147, 146, 152, 155, 168, 175, 216, 221, 252, 294-296, 335
Song Leng Xiong, 14, 156, 313
Souphanouvong, 259, 278-280
Souvanna Phouma, 279-281, 284-285, 291, 302
Soviet Union, 201, 281, 284-285
Special Guerrilla Units (SGUs), 58, 81, 260, 267, 313
spirituality, 25, 41, 62, 94-95, 110, 160, 185, 187, 197, 210, 245, 260, 263, 319, 326
Sue Yang, 298
suitcase switch, 313-315

T

teacher training, 310
Teacher Training Institute Entrance Exam (TTIEE), 162, 174
teachers' salaries, 289-290
teachers' strike, 286-290
teaching, 231-246, 288-293, 298
Teng, 29, 123, 146, 166, 173, 218, 272, 339-340
Thai, 260, 306
Thailand
    destruction of graves, 4
    evacuation to, 287, 291, 293-320, 322-341

INDEX

Thamheub, 247, 259-260, 267-269, 272
Thath Luang Temple, 210-211
Tong Ger, 17, 75-76
Tong Pao, 72, 74, 76, 144, 147, 150-152
Tong Yia, 340
Tou, 28, 144, 147, 150
Tou Lee, 287
Tou Xiong, 180-186, 181-185, 222-224, 223-224, 248, 306-307, 329, 332, 338, 340-342, 341
Tou Yia Lee, 206-210, 207, 210, 290
Toua, 256, 259-260, 270, 272-273
Touby Lyfoung, 279, 302-304
traditions, 29, 55, 73, 87-88, 89-98, 131-132, 196-197, 209-210, 245-246, 256-257, 337. *See also* marriage

U

United States. *See also* Air America; airplane rice; CIA; foreign aid
  and Communism, 124, 281, 285
  evacuation plan, 322-323
  flew Grandmother to hospital, 128
  Hmong as allies, 6-8, 73, 138, 153, 273, 275, 279, 281, 283-284, 314, 323, 326-327
  Long Chieng compound, 191-192, 196-199
  population of Hmong in, 8
  resettlement in, 8, 336-342, 344-350
  secret military operation in Laos, 6-7, 41, 50-52, 117, 124, 142, 197-200, 204, 274, 285-288
  soldier saved by Hmong, 41
  weapons supplied by, 81-82, 116
  withdrawal from Laos, 7, 201, 203, 273-275, 277, 285-286, 292-294, 304, 306, 334-337
  as world power, 104, 192, 294
USAID, 111, 162, 189, 216, 232, 242, 272, 276, 289

V

Vaj, 266, 306, 330, 332
Van Lu, 345-349
Vang Foung, 201
Vang Neng, 69
Vang Pao. *See also* guerrilla forces
  alliance with the U.S., 6
  cease-fire and negotiations, 273-279, 290-294
  commanding operations, 48, 117, 119, 173, 177, 179, 185, 198-203, 282-283
  economic development program, 241-242
  fled to Thailand, 7, 291, 302-303, 306, 315, 322
  not renamed, 28
  recruiting, 66
  transferred to Vientiane, 290
Vang Vieng, 179, 241
Vapao, 40-41, 45, 49-50, 54-57, 60, 125, 135, 165
Vientiane, 46, 83-84, 179-181, 185, 201, 205, 212, 218, 222-223, 226-227, 248-249, 252, 272-286, 290, 295, 299-304, 310-318

Vientiane Radio, 288-291
Viet Minh, 46, 52, 259, 273, 278-281, 286
Vietnam War, 6-7, 42, 46, 48, 58-60, 63, 79-81, 97, 100, 116, 137, 141, 150-151, 173, 179, 190, 197-201, 233-235, 237-238, 259, 267, 269, 273-274, 281-285, 288, 292, 302-303, 316
Vietnamese, 6, 42, 48, 60, 80-81, 84, 97, 100, 116, 137, 150, 173, 179, 195, 197-198, 218, 259, 267, 269, 278, 280, 281-288, 303
village life, 13-15, 29-34, 36-40

W

Wa Kai, 27
Wa Xeng, 263, 269-270
Wang Xeng, 259
War of the Insane, 6
Watou, 258-270. *See also specific events*
weapons, 57-59, 81-82, 116, 238, 263, 303
Wiseman, Jan, 338, 340-342, 344-345, 348
Wiseman, Molly, 338, 340-342, 344-345, 348
women, 29, 41, 73, 243, 245, 256. *See also* marriage

X

Xa, 17
Xai Lue, 259-260
Xai Teng, 184
Xao, 112, 142, 146-147
Xay Dang Xiong, 153

Xee, 23-27, 29, 113, 115, 163-164, 258. *See also specific events*
Xeng Lee, 270
Xia, 253
Xia Foung, 90
Xiang Det, 153, 155, 172-173
Xieng Khouang, 6, 12, 15, 42, 46, 48, 58-60, 66, 79, 83, 161, 172, 174, 196-197, 202, 212, 217-220, 233, 275-276, 280-283

Y

Yaj, 142, 168, 222-226, 255, 329
Yamee, 258, 260-261, 264-266, 269. *See also specific events*
Yang Dao, 28
Yang Sue, 289
Yang Xiong, 167
Yapao, 93-94
Yee, 270
Yeng Ly, 311
Yia, 16, 27
Yia Vang, 257-258
Ying Pao, 17, 22
Ying Yang, 117, 141-142, 156, 201
Yong Khue, 156
Yong Zoua Vang, 294
Youa Kao, 156
Youa Pao Xiong, 27, 201
Youa Xiong, 169-171, 247-272, 288, 295-296, 304-309, 314, 316-320, 327-333, 336, 344, 347, 352

Z

Za Houa Lee, 152, 297-298, 310, 312-320
Za Teng Moua, 59
Zong Koua Lor, 69